Advance Praise for
Making Innovation Work

"This is the book I wish I had read thirty years ago. *Making Innovation Work* is an important resource for leaders who are trying to improve innovation in their organizations. It's crammed with examples and practical ideas that can trigger improvements in innovation, starting tomorrow!"

—Lew Platt, Chairman of Boeing, former Chairman and CEO of HP, and former CEO of Kendall-Jackson Wine Estates

"Davila, Epstein, and Shelton remind us that even if the end product is rocket science, the process need not be. To the contrary, tried-and-true practices of management, process, metrics, and incentives are all that it takes to let innovation happen consistently."

—Andrew Beebe, President, EnergyInnovations

"*Making Innovation Work* is a fresh approach to systematically managing innovation. It integrates the innovation management literature in a way that is insightful, creative, as well as pragmatic. Davila, Epstein, and Shelton have particularly fresh insights on learning, culture, leadership, and executing change. This book will be of great help to those managers leading innovation and change."

—Michael Tushman, Paul R. Lawrence MBA Class of 1942 Professor of Business Administration, Graduate School of Business, Harvard University, and author of *Managing Strategic Innovation and Change* and *Winning through Innovation*

"This impressive book offers specific techniques for driving systematic, repeatable, and managed innovation at all levels in your company. It will help you build a balanced portfolio that integrates both incremental and radical innovations—so you can sustain growth indefinitely, instead of flaming out."

—Guerrino de Luca, President and CEO, Logitech

"*Making Innovation Work* provides an excellent roadmap to innovation: its various facets, why each facet matters, and how they can be enhanced—separately and collectively—in any organization. It also debunks a few tenacious myths, starting with the oft-heard excuse that innovation is an inherently unpredictable and uncontrollable process. Based on their vast research and consulting expertise, Davila, Epstein, and Shelton convincingly argue that innovation performance is indeed controllable and improvable, and they provide a powerful framework to do so. If you're interested in improving your organization's innovation performance and potential, this book will tell you how. If you're not, it will tell you why you should be!"

—**Jean-François Manzoni**, Professor of Leadership and Organizational Development, IMD (The International Institute for Management Development, Lausanne, Switzerland)

"*Making Innovation Work* is an informative and practical overview of the managerial side of innovation, showing that payoffs come when innovation projects are carefully conceived and measured."

—**Rosabeth Moss Kanter**, Harvard Business School, author of *Confidence*

"*Making Innovation Work* explains why companies lose their ability to innovate and how they can get it back. And though most organizations aren't 'wired' for innovation, the authors make it clear that sustained innovation is not a 'nice to have'—it's mandatory for survival. Effective execution of innovation is one of the major determinants between winners and the losers and of who survives and who disappears from the scene. This book picks up where other books on the subject fall short; it shows you how to make it happen."

—**Ladd Greeno**, President and CEO, AgION Technologies

"An excellent overview on the importance of innovation and how to manage it successfully; must-reading for executives who wish to break out of the commodity trap."

—**Robert S. Kaplan**, Marvin Bower Professor of Leadership Development at Harvard Business School and co-developer of the balanced scorecard

"*Making Innovation Work* is a must-read for would-be innovators at all levels. The seven practical Innovation Rules lay out the things you need to know and show you how to put them to use in your organization, no matter what the industry. Even self-diagnosed 'good' innovators will learn how to take their companies to the next level."

—**Howie Rosen**, VP, Commercial Strategy, Gilead Sciences, Inc., former CEO, Alza

"Any startup that cannot effectively manage what the authors describe as the natural tension between creativity and delivering value from creativity is not likely to survive. *Making Innovation Work* shows how to manage creativity and value creation together without compromising either one. It's must-reading."

—**Arthur L. Chait**, President and CEO, EoPlex Technologies

"*Making Innovation Work* will help you think about innovation in new and extremely productive ways. From the seven 'innovation rules' at the beginning of this book to the powerful execution advice for leaders at the end, this book is replete with ideas you'll actually use. If you're ready to get past the clichés and conventional wisdom about innovation, read it—the sooner, the better."

—**Alex Vieux**, CEO of Red Herring

Ideas. Action. Impact.
Wharton School Publishing

In the face of accelerating turbulence and change, business leaders and policy makers need new ways of thinking to sustain performance and growth.

Wharton School Publishing offers a trusted source for stimulating ideas from thought leaders who provide new mental models to address changes in strategy, management, and finance. We seek out authors from diverse disciplines with a profound understanding of change and its implications. We offer books and tools that help executives respond to the challenge of change.

Every book and management tool we publish meets quality standards set by The Wharton School of the University of Pennsylvania. Each title is reviewed by the Wharton School Publishing Editorial Board before being given Wharton's seal of approval. This ensures that Wharton publications are timely, relevant, important, conceptually sound or empirically based, and implementable.

To fit our readers' learning preferences, Wharton publications are available in multiple formats, including books, audio, and electronic.

To find out more about our books and management tools, visit us at whartonsp.com and Wharton's executive education site, exceed.wharton.upenn.edu.

Making Innovation Work

How to Manage It, Measure It, and Profit from It

Tony Davila
Marc J. Epstein
Robert Shelton

Ideas. Action. Impact.
Wharton School Publishing

Library of Congress Catalog Number: 2005923660

Publisher: Tim Moore
Acquisitions Editor: Paula Sinnott
Editorial Assistant: Susie Abraham
Development Editor: Russ Hall
Marketing Manager: John Pierce
International Marketing Manager: Tim Galligan
Cover Designer: Chuti Prasersith
Managing Editor: Gina Kanouse
Project Editor: Christy Hackerd
Copy Editor: Lisa Thibault
Indexer: Lisa Stumpf
Compositor: The Scan Group
Manufacturing Buyer: Dan Uhrig

Ideas. Action. Impact.
**Wharton School
Publishing**

© 2006 by Pearson Education, Inc.
Publishing as Wharton School Publishing
Upper Saddle River, New Jersey 07458

**Wharton School Publishing offers excellent discounts on this book when ordered in quantity
for bulk purchases or special sales. For more information, please contact U.S. Corporate and
Government Sales, 1-800-382-3419, corpsales@pearsontechgroup.com. For sales outside the
U.S., please contact International Sales at international@pearsoned.com.**

Printed in the United States of America
Second Printing, September 2005
ISBN 0-13-149786-3

Pearson Education LTD.
Pearson Education Australia PTY, Limited.
Pearson Education Singapore, Pte. Ltd.
Pearson Education North Asia, Ltd.
Pearson Education Canada, Ltd.
Pearson Educatión de Mexico, S.A. de C.V.
Pearson Education—Japan
Pearson Education Malaysia, Pte. Ltd.

Receive Special Benefits by Registering this Book

Register this book today and receive exclusive benefits that you can't obtain anywhere else, including

- Access to additional chapters and related articles by the authors

- A coupon to be used on your next purchase

To register this book, use the following special code when you visit your My Account page on Whartonsp.com.

Special Code: bertWork7863

Note that the benefits for registering may vary from book to book. To see the benefits associated with a particular book, you must be a member and submit the book's ISBN (the ISBN is the number on the back of this book that starts with 0-13-) on the registration page.

Ideas. Action. Impact.
**Wharton School
Publishing**

CONTENTS

INTRODUCTION

Much that is held as common wisdom regarding how successful innovation is managed is wrong. It seems that somewhere along the line, the correct set of rules of innovation have been misplaced, distorted, or simply misinterpreted. This is not to say that organizations are not innovative—obviously many are. But how and why these companies are innovative is very different than what many managers think.

This book challenges the prevalent misconceptions about innovation, and lays out the tools and processes necessary for an organization to harness and execute innovation.

The following chapters show that, contrary to popular belief:

- **Innovation does not require a revolution inside companies**. What it does require is thoughtful construction of solid management processes and an organization that can get things done.

- **Innovation is not alchemy, with mystifying transformations.** It's much more like the basic blocking and tackling of other key business functions.

- **Innovation is not primarily about creativity and having a "creative culture."** Many companies find that coming up with good-to-great ideas is the easy part; the hard stuff is selecting the right ideas and implementing them.

- **Nor is it solely about processes and stage-gate tools.** These do count, but tools and processes alone are not effective—they must be coupled with an organization, metrics, and rewards that can make things happen.

- **Innovation does not focus exclusively on cool new technology.** Developing new business models and new strategies are every bit as important—sometimes more.

- **Innovation is not something that every company needs in large quantities.** Innovation must match the opportunity and the competencies of the organization—sometimes, with good timing, a little goes a long way.

Making Innovation Work provides three new, important perspectives for senior managers:

1. **Innovation, like many business functions, is a management process that requires specific tools, rules and discipline—it is not mysterious.** Execution is simple once it is clear how the pieces fit together. Company executives typically complain that they cannot get innovation accomplished in their organizations. *Making Innovation Work* presents an integrated framework, formal processes and tools that all managers can use to create top- and bottom-line growth from innovation. The book describes how to use these standard management tools (such as strategy, organizational design and structure, management systems, performance evaluation, people, and rewards) to dramatically increase the payoffs from innovation investments.

2. **Innovation requires measurement and incentives to deliver sustained, high yields**. Remember the saying, "You can't manage what you can't measure"? That certainly holds true for innovation, but many managers have only paid lip service to this crucial aspect. Many companies measure the wrong things and provide incentives for behavior that corrodes the systems and processes that support innovation. *Making Innovation Work* shows how to use metrics and incentives to manage every facet of innovation from creating the ideas, through selecting and forming the prototype innovations, and all the way through to commercialization. The book has metrics and incentives that can be used by companies of all sizes, complexities, and in all types of industry.

3. **Companies can use innovation to redefine an industry by employing combinations of business model innovation and technology innovation**. This book shows how to integrate changes in the existing business model and technology to redefine the competitive environment of an industry— the way Apple Computers did with the sequential introduction of iPod (a technology change) and iTunes (a business model change). Most companies are significantly better at one or the other, but few have a truly integrated capability for both significant business model and technology innovation. *Making Innovation Work* presents a unique framework that allows management to harness the power of both business model innovation and technology innovation and by combining them, create competitive advantage, grow, and significantly affect the direction of the industry.

The truth is that there is not much that is truly new about innovation. The basics have not changed for centuries. However, we have become smarter about managing innovation. By analyzing what has worked really well and what has not, *Making Innovation Work* provides new insights into how to execute innovation. It breaks things into manageable pieces that can be applied in any company.

Two ideas shape the foundations of this book:

- Innovation is a necessary ingredient for sustained success—it protects your tangible and intangible assets against the erosion of the market.

- Innovation is an integral part of the business, and as such it has to be managed—it is not a "nice-to-have" element or something that occurs on its own.

Innovation is imperative to grow your top and bottom lines. Innovation produces changes that are essential to survival of the company.

Innovation is not about secret formulas; it is about good management. The book identifies the seven Innovation Rules of good innovation management:

- Strong leadership that defines the innovation strategy designs innovation portfolios, and encourages truly significant value creation.

- Innovation is an integral part of the company's business mentality.

- Innovation is matched to the company business strategy including selection of the innovation strategy (Play-to-Win or Play-Not–to-Lose).

- Balance creativity and value capture so that the company generates successful new ideas *and* gets the maximum return on its investment.

- Neutralize organizational antibodies that kill off good ideas because they are different from the norm.

- Innovation networks inside and outside the organization because networks, not individuals, are the basic building blocks of innovation.

- Correct metrics and rewards to make innovation manageable and to produce the right behavior.

We have spent our lives working on innovation. This book is the result of years of research in the field as well as through surveys grounded on a thorough analysis of the academic and practical literature and extensive experience working with companies to enhance the value they create from innovation. Specifically, we have identified what companies need to do to become more innovative and to improve performance in innovation—and we understand why some companies fail at innovation. As part of our analysis, we examined the practices of leading companies in a range of industries through extensive surveying and numerous company interactions. In addition, we have talked with and helped senior managers in the companies in a variety of contexts and deeply researched their management practices.

Corporate CEOs that we've interacted with repeatedly mention their dissatisfaction with the innovation in their organizations. In some cases, incremental innovation crowds out larger innovations, leading to an unbalanced portfolio that rewards short-term at the expense of long-term survival. Sometimes these managers blame bureaucracy; in other instances, culture is the identified culprit. However, they all perceive selected elements of their organizations as working against the kind of innovation that is necessary to compete today. Some managers have even given up on their organization; they feel that their only hope is to buy innovation outside the organization and leverage their market power to generate value. For many, that could be a fatal mistake.

There is no silver bullet for innovation, no one formula or structure for innovation that will work for every organization. However, our research has shown that there are clear ways in which companies can improve their innovation results, create value, and grow.

Because the "how" of innovation is all-important in determining results, this book does what books focused on innovation strategy cannot—*Making Innovation Work* provides the context, framework, tools, and operating guidelines to actually make innovation happen better in your organization. And it provides the approaches to tailor innovation to a company's particular situation, business strategy, culture, technological acumen, and appetite for risk.

Making Innovation Work goes beyond ideas and inspiration to offer practical, tested advice on how to create value from the innovation investment on the level of day-to-day processes, as well as at the strategic level. It describes how to maximize your company's value by integrating the different types of innovation—incremental, semi-radical, and radical—and creating a balanced portfolio of innovations. And the book covers the entire chain of innovation tools from A through Z, so it is possible to troubleshoot your company's situation and identify what needs to be improved to maximize value for your company's particular situation and need.

Objective of This Book

- Where is your company?
  - Evaluating the innovation state of your company
  - Assessing the options going forward

- How to design an innovation strategy
  - Adapting an innovation strategy that fits your company
  - Creating a balanced innovation portfolio

- How to manage innovation
  - Fighting organizational antibodies—from bureaucracy to not-invented-here syndrome
  - Leveraging technology to design the innovation processes

- How to measure and reward innovation
  - Designing measures that encourage innovation
  - Incentives and recognition for innovation success

A Word About the Book

The seven Innovation Rules are guiding principles for executing innovation in any company, business unit, non-profit organization, or government entity. You can attain the goals embodied in the Innovation Rules by using the standard management tools—strategy, structure, leadership, management systems, and people. Because organizations are complex, no single tool is sufficient to reach any one of the goals. Every one of the Innovation Rules requires several tools as shown in Figure I.1. Black indicates that the topic is analyzed to significant depth in the chapter, gray indicates that the topic addressed to some extent, and white indicates that the topic is only slightly touched upon.

Chapter / Innovation Rules	2. Innovation Model	3. Strategy	4. Organization	5. Processes	6. Metrics	7. Rewards	8. Learning	9. People and Culture
Exert Strong Leadership on Strategy and Portfolio	Black	White	White	Gray	Gray	Gray	Gray	Black
Integration into Business Mentality	Black	Black	White	Black	Gray	Gray	Gray	Gray
Align with Strategy	Gray	Black	Gray	Gray	Black	Gray	Gray	Gray
Manage Creativity and Value Capture	White	White	Black	Black	Black	Gray	Gray	Gray
Neutralize Organizational Antibodies	White	White	White	White	Black	Black	Black	Gray
Establish Networks	White	White	Black	Black	Gray	Gray	Gray	Gray
Use Metrics and Incentives	White	Gray	White	White	Black	Black	Gray	Black

FIGURE I.1   INNOVATION RULES AND MANAGEMENT TOOLS.

For example, the first goal, Exerting Strong Leadership, requires that the CEO and the management team focus primarily on defining the innovation model, selecting the innovation strategy, and enabling the correct culture. Leadership has special responsibility for managing those three tools.

Leadership needs to define the role of business model innovation and technology innovation for the company (such as by defining the Innovation Model). Both are important to successful innovation, but often a company does not have the full set of capabilities required to deliver effective combinations of both. Without a clear, accepted definition of the innovation model and an understanding of the importance of both business model innovation and technology innovation, a company will not be able to create industry changing innovations or avoid being blindsided by innovations that they cannot effectively counter. For example, overreliance on technology innovation led to HP's inability to match Dell's business model change selling PCs and servers via the Internet.

In addition, effective leadership requires a clear decision on the innovation strategy, selecting either a Play-to–Win (PTW) or a Play-Not-to-Lose (PNTL) strategy. A company can execute one strategy or the other, but it cannot do both effectively. Without a clear decision on the roles of technology change and business model change in that strategy, the execution becomes muddled and resources are not properly allocated. For example, the R&D department might decide to produce major breakthrough technologies for new products, consistent with a PTW strategy, while the business unit managers have decided that they need to provide strong support for existing products. The product managers are focusing on the ability to stay even competitively, consistent with a PNTL strategy. This conflict results in costly inefficiencies and nasty internal fights. Selecting the strategy and ensuring alignment in the organization is leadership's responsibility.

Managing the innovation model and selecting the strategy are keys to short- and medium-term success; however, preserving the

beneficial elements of the existing culture of the company and changing the deleterious elements is the key to long-term success.
Leadership needs to be involved in the cultural aspects of innovation.
A company that does not monitor its innovation culture and make
improvements to selected portions will see its competitive advantage
wither over the long haul. This is what happened to Polaroid as the
company found itself stuck with an innovation culture that was mired
in old mindsets and practices. And Polaroid is not alone in this regard;
maintaining the correct culture is a challenge for every successful
company. Success often creates cultures that are unwilling to change.
Leadership should be held accountable for the innovative culture of
the company, and the leaders should be judged on how effectively
they contribute to capabilities for long-term, sustained innovation as
well as short-term growth.

Defining the innovation model, selecting the strategy, and guiding the evolution of the culture must be the major responsibility for
the senior management team. No one else can shoulder that responsibility as effectively.

Leadership's secondary focus should be on metrics, rewards, and
organizational learning. Leadership should oversee the development
and implementation of metrics and rewards to ensure that they support the company strategy and culture. Measurement precedes management (as in 'what gets measured gets managed') and rewards
reinforce acceptable behavior. Leadership should also be held
accountable for oversight of organizational learning and change
because a company must be able to meet changing conditions and
new challenges.

Finally, attaining the leadership goal requires a lower level of
involvement (oversight and guidance) on the innovation organization and the processes. Otherwise, these elements could significantly hinder the innovation effort. However, the CEO and the
senior executives do not need to be intimately involved in designing
and operating these elements of innovation. That is primarily the

job of others, using the guidance and direction from the selected strategy and the portfolio.

This is one example. The following chapters describe how to achieve each of the seven Innovation Rules using the standard management tools.

Execution of innovation is actually not any more difficult than other management activities, such as manufacturing or financial control. However, there are many half-truths and myths surrounding innovation that have made it appear more complex than it is. *Making Innovation Work* replaces the myths and half-truths with clear direction on how to manage and execute innovation in any organization.

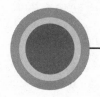

DRIVING SUCCESS: HOW YOU INNOVATE DETERMINES WHAT YOU INNOVATE

Innovation Is the Power to Redefine the Industry

For any organization, innovation represents not only the opportunity to grow and survive but also the opportunity to significantly influence the direction of the industry. Apple Computers took the industry by surprise when it launched iTunes and iPod, not so much because these were innovations that nobody had ever thought of before in the PC arena. Instead, it was the strategy of combining technology change and business model change into a one-two innovation punch. And the iTunes/iPod combination is only starting to generate new concepts; one of the latest is an iPod special edition with U2 (the famous rock band), which opens up rich partnership opportunities with content providers. Apple has put its mark again on the direction of the PC industry—a mark that will be tough to erase.

As innovation leaders like Apple, Toyota, Dell, Nucor Steel, Sony, and others have shown, making important changes to key parts of the dominant business model or the essential technology can redirect the competitive vectors of an entire industry. Innovation provides the opportunity for a company to put its mark on the evolution of business. By setting the rules of the game in their industries, these companies have taken a leadership position and play the game that favors them the most.

Innovation is not only a weapon in competitive markets; it has proven itself as an important source to redefine philanthropy and government under the umbrella of social innovation and social entrepreneurship. The idea of micro-credits, with Grameen Bank as the best-known example of these, has dramatically changed the standard of living of thousands of people who were trapped in a vicious circle where high-interest loans captured all the value from their work and kept them in poverty. Micro-credits are very small loans, as small as $30–$40, that offer individuals the chance to start or grow a business. Used to foster economic improvement for individuals, families, and regions, they are commonly made available in emerging countries and struggling economies. Micro-credit entities improve the risk profile of these loans through careful selection, social control, and diversification. Lower risk translates into better interest rates and the possibility for these people to significantly increase their standard of living.

While achieving a leadership position is not easy, maintaining it has consistently proven to be much more challenging. The ability of innovation to influence the direction of an industry does not in itself guarantee success for the innovator. Unleashing an innovation and expecting the market to reward the company with sustained growth and success is a common mistake.[1] For example, Boeing launched the highly successful 777, and established the norm for commercial airplanes in the 21st century. However, Boeing has not been able to maintain dominance of the industry, and Airbus has challenged its leadership, surpassing it in sales in 2004. All companies have seen their market advantages derived from breakthrough innovations whittled away and eventually reversed by competitors. A blockbuster innovation is not a guarantee of success, just an opportunity. It must be followed up with a successive stream of innovations, from incremental to radical. Leading companies know this and have a developed portfolio of innovations from which they can draw to sustain growth.

In the long run, the only reliable security for any company is the ability to innovate better and longer than competitors. Nokia's management has frequently said that its real business isn't phones; it's innovation. In Nokia's case, innovation is a capability fused to the core of the organization; the company calls its culture of continuous innovation "renewal."[2] The ability to innovate has taken Nokia from the equivalent of an approximately $6 billion company in 1994 to an approximately $36 billion company in 2003. But even for Nokia, innovation has not been an easy path; its financial performance faltered since early 2004, and it has been challenged as the innovation leader.

Superior innovation provides a company the opportunities to grow faster, better, and smarter than their competitors—and ultimately to influence the direction of their industry. For the CEO, this is growth on the company's own terms. The following case study shows how the role of innovation at Coca-Cola provides insight into the importance and challenges of harnessing innovation.[3,4]

Case Study: Long-Term Innovation

Company: Coca-Cola

In the 1990s, Coca-Cola appeared unstoppable with earnings growth of 15–20 percent per year. However, the Coke juggernaut sputtered, and from 1998–2000, the company turned in three straight years of falling profits. It was the worst downturn in recent memory.

There were a myriad of factors contributing to the decline, including soft demand in some regional markets and a strong dollar weakening overseas markets. But Coca-Cola's major problem was that global demand for Coke was sagging. One of the first signals was in the 1980s when Snapple took the U.S. by storm. Coke's sales volume fell 2 percent in the U.S. (the most mature market). Elsewhere in the world, growth slowed. The markets were changing with local brands springing up to fit local tastes.

The beverage industry was changing, with greater value placed on novelty. It used to be that all a beverage had to do was to refresh. New demands emerged: *keep me growing* from the kids; *keep me going* from the young adults; and *keep me interested* from the adults. To survive and grow required the ability to systematically innovate and deliver new products. For Coca-Cola, this meant moving away from a single core product and becoming a total beverage company. Coca-Cola realized that it needed new products to match new trends in beverage tastes.

This was a fundamental change in business strategy because historically its strength was having one hugely successful core product. Competitors had chipped away at that strength by introducing the new beverages. Most notably, Pepsi had beaten Coca-Cola to market with nearly every big product innovation in recent years, from diet cola in the 1980s to cola with a lemon twist in 2001 (with Cherry Coke and Vanilla Coke being the exceptions in Coca-Cola's favor).

Coca-Cola responded with a shift away from its traditional Atlanta-based operating mentality. The company's strategy under Doug Daft, CEO from 1999–2004, had been to catch up quickly by employing what we label as a Play-to-Win innovation strategy—a strategy that relies heavily on a combination of incremental and breakthrough innovation. The company began to employ innovation on both its technology and business models. Coca-Cola undertook the difficult task of creating an innovative culture across the company. To support that, the company created new organizations (referred to as *innovation centers*) and new innovation processes—

no easy task for a company that, historically, had grown through narrow focus and standardization. Now the company was operating in a decentralized environment that had been unthinkable in previous years. The new mandate changed to "Think Local, Act Local." Coke Japan had been creating products and campaigns at a blinding speed, calling on Atlanta only for final approval and funding. Likewise, operations in Mexico had developed and launched a new milk drink and managed it by themselves.

Coke has identified 32 possible beverage occasions each day. In addition, several new types of beverage types emerged: sports, water, teas, health, and the mom and kids categories. Coca-Cola's portfolio of brands has grown to include Dasani bottled waters in the U.S. (and the U.K. although with some PR problems), Qoo juice drinks in Asia, and a guarana-flavored drink in Brazil. These new products are the direct result of a shift in the basis of competition in the industry.

Coke continues to play catch-up in the market, and Daft stepped down after just five years. Performance is mixed. What will happen to Coke? Will the new approach to innovation it created be sufficient to pull itself out of its problems and into the lead? Stay tuned; a lot depends on how well Coke manages and sustains innovation.

The Innovation Imperative: Driving Long-Term Growth in Top and Bottom Lines

According to Peter Drucker, "Innovation is the effort to create purposeful focused change in an enterprise's economic or social potential."[5] That statement very accurately positions innovation as the agent for change and a crucial tool for every CEO. True enough, but it does not capture the fundamental importance of innovation to competitive survival.

More recently, James M. Kilts, then chairman and CEO of The Gillette Company (currently co-chairman of P&G after the acquisition of Gillette), summed up innovation this way: "We created a simple vision two years ago: Build total brand value by innovating to deliver consumer value and customer leadership faster, better, and more completely than our competition."

He also observed: "You need to encourage risk-taking. One of the themes in our company is to remember that the opposite of success is not failure but inertia."[6] That puts innovation in the right context; innovation is critical to growth in a competitive environment. Without innovation, you stall, your competitors take over, and you die.

Back in 1979, CompuServe began to offer online services and developed a myriad of applications including email, online banking, and online shopping. By 1990, the market amounted to about 1 million subscribers, and CompuServe was the undisputed leader. However, by the end of the decade, AOL had emerged as the dominant player in the market, buying CompuServe in 1998. CompuServe led with innovation, paused and then faltered, and eventually succumbed to a more innovative company. CompuServe is not alone in the list of dethroned leaders. Similar stories exist across every industry including airlines, investment banking, computers, and personal digital assistants (PDAs).

Innovation is the key element in providing aggressive top-line growth, and for increasing bottom-line results. Companies cannot grow through cost reduction and reengineering alone. Most of the past attempts at diversification have been largely unsuccessful in creating the required top-line growth.[7] Companies turn to innovation to produce growth when these conventional approaches fall short. For example, Figure 1.1 depicts the challenge of top-line revenue growth. The combined forces of market expansion, anticipated mergers and acquisitions, and the expected increased sales from products in the commercialization pipeline failed to produce the required revenue growth to meet targets.

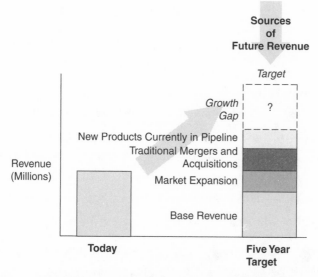

FIGURE 1.1 INNOVATION PRODUCES VALUE VIA TOP-LINE GROWTH.[8]

This real- life example is taken from a leading electronics company. The company could not achieve sufficient revenue growth through expansion of current product sales and mergers and acquisitions to satisfy its growth needs. Closing the growth gap required innovation.

Exactly what type of growth is created by innovation depends on the needs of the company and its competencies. Innovation can result in revenue growth, a stronger bottom line, improved customer relationships, more motivated employees, enhanced performance of partnerships, and increased competitive advantage.

How to Make Innovation Work: *How* You Innovate Determines *What* You Innovate

Right now, your company is perfectly designed to yield the innovation that it is currently producing. This is not a trick statement. Because every company has a unique combination of innovation strategy, organization, processes, culture, metrics and rewards, each company's innovation products will be different. What Apple develops would not come out of Dell or IBM. Likewise, what Toyota produces may be copied by General Motors or Ford, but they could not come up with Toyota's basic innovations (the specific type of lean manufacturing that swept the auto industry or the current hybrid automobile technologies). Each company creates its own type of innovation by adding its own special touches (for example, culture, specific knowledge, unique rewards)—although the basic ingredients for innovation are all the same. Less innovative firms are that way because they chose it—either consciously or by letting inertia decide for them. Changing the innovation results requires proactive management.

Research Bites: Transitioning from the First Breakthrough Innovation to an Innovative Company

A company in our field research illustrates the transition from a company built around a breakthrough innovation to a company that consistently delivers innovation. This company with more than 15,000 employees (1,000 of them in R&D) grew out of a breakthrough innovation in packaging. As the growth associated with this initial and highly successful innovation began to top off, the company started to think carefully about how to use innovation for further growth. The problem was that the approach which provided the initial innovation—unguided funding of lots of exploratory concepts—currently was not generating a portfolio of innovations that could fuel sufficient growth.

The company thus redesigned its approach to innovation. While preserving the entrepreneurial, go-for-the-breakthrough culture, the company created structures and processes to better support innovation and improve its yield. It created a chief technology officer (CTO) in charge of innovation; it installed clear metrics to better track and manage; it created portfolio management tools to balance innovation efforts; it implemented stage-gate processes to govern investments; and it established platforms where marketing and R&D work collaboratively in creating innovations. The company successfully implemented an approach that allowed the company to walk the fine line between disciplined flexibility and bureaucracy.

A fundamental tenet of innovation of which many appear to have lost sight is "*How* you innovate determines *what* you innovate." In other words, the results of innovation are not a lottery—it is not a matter of luck. Alternatively, innovation is not a commodity system that you plug into to get what you need—such as the electricity grid.

The elements of innovation—leadership, strategy, processes, resources, performance metrics, measurement, and incentive rewards—and how they are arranged—organizational structure and culture—have a huge effect on the quantity and quality of innovation that an organization achieves. The implication is that it is nonsensical to ask for more or better innovation without first looking at *how* the company innovates.

What, then, are the key drivers for innovation success? Why do some companies prosper while others languish with decreasing margins, few successful new products, and eroding market share?

The Rules of Innovation

A key to successful innovation, and something that requires the attention of the CEO, is a periodic health check to determine exactly what needs attention. Continually tinkering with all parts of innovation is unlikely to meet with success. To achieve results with limited time and resources requires the ability to focus on the parts of the innovation effort that need the most attention.

What is surprising is how few companies have effective diagnostics for their overall innovation activities. Without solid innovation diagnostics, it is hard to know where to start. Innovation processes are intertwined and without discerning diagnostics, it is hard to separate the symptoms of your problems from their causes. In addition, without periodic diagnostics, a sense of complacency builds because there is no focus on maintaining the right mix of innovation.

Table 1.1 presents the responses of two very different companies to several basic questions about innovation and illustrates the range of perspectives that we have seen. Company B suffers from not having periodic diagnostics that highlight their shortcomings. It does not even believe that innovation can be measured. However, it continues forward with its innovation program believing that it is acting correctly.

Table 1.1   Different Perspectives on How to Execute Successful Innovation

	Company A	Company B
What efforts is top management putting in place to support innovation?	Top management praises and follows carefully most innovation efforts.	Top management talks about innovation but punishes failure.
Does everybody devote part of his or her daily attention to having a better business model?	Innovation may happen anywhere within the company.	Quarterly financial targets are the main focus.
Is it clear to everybody how the company intends to innovate?	The company has a clear focus, for instance "to enhance human-machine interfaces."	The company wants to grow through innovation.
Does creativity or bureaucracy crowd out innovation?	People have the freedom and the support to research their ideas.	Every process has operating procedures that cannot be changed.
What are the reasons, if any, why innovation is not as effective as you would want it to be?	We fail to capitalize on all the ideas that are generated.	There is a lack of talent and effort from employees.
How does your company leverage its internal talent and its access to external talent?	Through interest groups and alliances with clear objectives.	Innovation is focused on the R&D department and its collaborations.
How do performance measures and rewards affect innovation?	Measures are intended to help managing projects.	We don't believe that innovation can be measured.

A list of all of the advice on innovation that has been written would stretch from the earth to the moon and back again. However, long lists are not much help for the business team with the responsibility for making things happen. Our research keeps bringing us back to a short list of the most important aspects of innovation that should therefore receive senior management attention. In companies that innovation produces best in class results, key success is tied to how well the CEO and the senior management team do the following (these are known as the *Seven Innovation Rules*):

1. **Exert strong leadership on the innovation strategy and portfolio decisions**. Clear direction from the top of the organization permeates throughout the organization to motivate, support, and reward the activities that encourage innovation as well as the innovations themselves.

2. **Integrate innovation into the company's basic business mentality**. Innovation is not a rabbit you pull from a hat on special occasions; it must be an integral part of the way a company operates every day.

3. **Align the amount and type of innovation to the company's business**. Innovation *may* or *may not* be the key to success for your overall business strategy; you have to determine the types and amounts of innovation needed to support the business strategy—and more is not necessarily better.

4. **Manage the natural tension between creativity and value capture**. A company needs strength in both. Creativity without the ability to translate it into profits (for example, execution and value capture) can be fun but it is unsustainable; profits without creativity is rewarding but only works in the short-term.

5. **Neutralize organizational antibodies**. Innovation necessitates change, and change stimulates explicit routines and cultural norms that act to block or negate change.

6. **Recognize that the basic unit (or fundamental building block) of innovation is a *network* that includes people and knowledge both inside and outside the organization**. A successful organization excels at fusing its internal resources with selected portions of the vast resources of the world's capitalist economy.

7. **Create the right metrics and rewards for innovation**.
People react to positive and negative stimuli, and your company's innovation is no exception. You will never achieve the level of innovation that you need if people do not have the proper rewards.

These innovation rules are interdependent; mastering one or two of them is a step in the right direction but won't take the organization far enough.

In the following sections, we describe the seven rules in more detail.

1. Exert Strong Leadership on Innovation Direction and Decisions

Strong leadership from senior management is essential to achieving success in innovation. Steve Jobs of Apple, Bill Gates of Microsoft, A.G. Lafley of Procter & Gamble (P&G), and Jorma Ollila of Nokia are all examples of CEOs who drive their management teams and their companies to the highest levels of innovation performance.

In a recent *Financial Times* survey, the most important factors in selecting new investments were the strength of the management team and the demonstrated strength of the business model. Technology was a close third.[9] Other data showed the following:

- 95 percent of the survey's respondents said they were looking for management strength as the most important factor in making new investments.

- 72 percent said that the prospective company should have market dominance in its industry sector (for example, demonstrated strength of business model).

- 68 percent said they were looking for technology leadership in a new portfolio company.

The CEO and senior management team must make decisions on the innovation strategy, level of risk, amount of investment, and the balance of the innovation portfolio. These decisions must be communicated throughout the organization to enable managers and members of the innovation network to execute.

It is not by chance that leadership is our first innovation rule. The most important aspect of business is people, and business is mainly about managing people. It does not matter who you ask, whether it be employees at startups or at very large firms—they all will point toward their managers as setting the innovation pace. As a startup manager in our research put it: "Most importantly, I'd say success is really a people issue; it is finding the people who can understand the high level (strategy) and the need to execute on it, and then be able to evolve as the company does."

Innovation management depends on the leadership at the top. The team at the top must want it to happen and trust its people to make it happen. It cannot be an espoused theory where top managers preach it but don't believe it. Innovation has to be a theory in action; top managers must be committed and follow their commitment with actions.[10] Then the other managers throughout the company will be motivated to follow suit.

What do we mean by leadership? It is not some grand concept of leadership—the change agent that achieves the improbable objective. Rather, we mean day-to-day leadership, a type of leadership that happens through commitment, example, and solid decisions rather than grand statements.[11]

Research Bites: The Relevance of Top Management Support

In two surveys designed to better understand the innovation process, we asked respondents to evaluate the relevance of various innovation competencies. The survey was administered in 1997 and then again in 2002 to senior technology officers in the United States, Asia, and Europe. Top management support ranked as the most important competency in both years with increasing importance within the five years.

Create a Portfolio of Technology and Business Model Innovation

Typically, when people think about innovation, they think of technological innovation. However, business model innovation is just as important and just as powerful in driving business success and revolutionizing industries. Business models describe how the company creates, sells, and delivers value to customers, and it includes in the description the supply chain, targeted customer segments, and the customers' perception of the delivered value.

A classic example of a business model change is Dell Computer, a company that radically changed the business model of the customer interface in retail personal computer sales. Dell focused its efforts on changing the business model for PCs. The company sold directly to consumers, providing new value proposition (such as customized PCs) and significantly changing the supply chain and cost structure. This was an innovation of major proportions, one that continues to influence the direction of the PC industry.

Knowing how to change business models and technology together and individually is the mark of a successful innovator. The *Innovation Matrix* shown in Figure 1.2 illustrates the interplay between technology and business model innovation. In Chapter 2, "Mapping Innovation: What Is Innovation and How Do You Leverage It?" we describe the Innovation Matrix in detail.

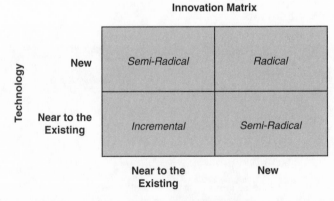

Innovation Matrix

FIGURE 1.2   THE INNOVATION MATRIX.

The Innovation Matrix highlights the fact that not all innovations are created equal. Three types of innovation exist: incremental, semi-radical, and radical. Achieving radical or semi-radical innovation requires a different mix of business model and technology change than incremental innovation. As we will discuss later, creating a portfolio of incremental, semi-radical, and radical innovation is essential to sustained innovation and growth. As with a financial investment portfolio, getting the balance out of whack decreases the return on investment and increases vulnerability. The senior management team bears the responsibility for creating a balanced portfolio of incremental, semi-radical, and radical innovations and for creating the appropriate business model and technological options.

2. Integrate Innovation into the Business Mentality

To thrive, innovation must be an integral part of the business mentality. It is not a "nice to have" element. It is essential to the continuation of the organization. 3M has said that innovation equals survival, and made it part of their culture. Recall how Gillette CEO Kilts characterized it: "Build total brand value by innovating . . . faster, better, and more completely than our competition." He has placed innovation at the heart of Gillette's business and competitive mentality. The recent merger of Gillette and P&G—two companies that appear committed to win through innovation—promises to be an interesting marriage.

Innovation encompasses two established activities. The first is traditionally thought of as technological: research and development (R&D), or new product development. The second is strategic: defining the business model. As we will describe later, focusing on only one of these will not produce successful, sustained innovation. Success depends on the integration of business model and technology change into a seamless process.

A seamless process does not imply that innovation should be contained within one organizational unit—quite the opposite. By its very nature, innovation requires resources, competencies, and experience that reside in different parts of the organization and in outside organizations. It also requires coordination and synchronized efforts across these departments to move an idea from the abstract world to a tangible product. Establishing solid internal and external collaboration is a requirement for innovation. Microsoft continues to work this critical issue as it pushes to make .NET a commercial reality. Microsoft has always relied heavily on partnerships to assist in developing products, and the new, aggressive .NET initiative will require higher levels of collaboration.

While external collaboration is essential for success, a company cannot outsource innovation completely. Some fundamental product development activities can be outsourced, as well as activities in idea generation and commercialization. But outsourcing innovation completely means relinquishing control of the technology a company uses (product, service, process, and enabling) as well as the business models that it uses to compete (such as the supply chain). Some of these elements are crucial to the survival and existence of the company. Knowing which are crucial and which can be managed with the assistance of a partner is an important part of structuring innovation within any company.

3. Match Innovation to Company Strategy

A company's business strategy is focused on winning. And innovation is a fundamental element of long-term success. However, in any given quarter or year, innovation is not necessarily a key source of competitive advantage. The importance of innovation rises and falls with time depending on the confluence of several factors including the timing of the last innovation, the nature of the competition, and the overall business strategy.

The amount and type of innovation must match the company strategy. Deciding which innovation strategy best fits the external competitive and market situation and the company's internal condition is the responsibility of the senior management team and ultimately rests upon the CEO. The experience of Durk Jager, former CEO at P&G, highlights how things can go wrong if the CEO chooses the wrong innovation strategy. It is a fundamental management decision for which top management must take responsibility— as Jager learned.[12]

There must be clarity and alignment in the organization around the selected innovation strategy; it has to fit the business situation and it has to be clear (meaning, it has to be measured and recognized with proper rewards linked to performance) throughout the organization. All too often, this fundamental first step is overlooked, and companies find themselves with poorer-than-expected results. For example, in the late 1990s, BP Exploration and Production looked long and hard at its success rate with innovation and discovered that significant effort was being placed in the wrong areas. The company was spending in strategic areas that would not and could not provide an adequate return on investment. The team shifted its emphasis to ownership and application of specific innovation platforms that would support the business strategy.

Keep in mind that more innovation is not necessarily better. Some proponents of innovation have been carried away in their apparent zeal regarding innovation; they have recommended that all businesses need significant, continual doses of innovation, especially radical, game-changing innovation. This is simply not true. Every organization that intends to survive beyond the next two product life cycles needs healthy infusions of innovation and must invest to get them. This does not mean that an organization needs constant blockbuster or breakthrough innovations. It is hard to imagine an organization that could effectively harness a constant supply of breakthrough radical innovations, each of which would cause significant change in its business and technology base. That level of change may bedevil the competition, but it would also break the back of the innovating organization, considering the huge costs of developing such a flow of innovations coupled with the huge tensions and destabilizations created in the organization by the constant, radical change.

Therefore, innovation—like most good things—is best in the right proportions. With a corollary, the right proportions are different for different companies. Thus, there is no turnkey solution, not one-size-fits-all program. Each company needs to decide how much innovation it can handle at a point in time, how much more it needs in the future, and the dynamics of how to get from the current set of possibilities to the aspired position.[13]

4. Manage the Natural Tension Between Creativity and Value Capture

Innovation is different from many other business management concerns in one important way: It includes management of large amounts of creativity. Specifically, innovation requires processes, structures, and resources to manage significant levels of creativity (developing new concepts and ways of doing things) while executing (transforming creative concepts into commercial realities).

From about 2000 up until now, Apple seems to have found the right formula for managing creativity and value capture. Its spate of new products and services—OS X, iPod, iTunes, the new iMac—demonstrated that it can come up with important new ideas and bring them to the market profitably. However, in the 1980s, Apple did not fare as well. Its innovation and new product activities in Cupertino were well financed, and many new ideas were advanced. Despite spending hundreds of millions (or quite possibly billions) of dollars, Apple came up with precious little in the way of successful commercialization during that period. The Newton (originally an operating system designed by Mac to run on its MessagePad line of PDAs) is the best remembered innovation of that era, a classic example of creative zeal crowding out commercial realities. The Newton failed not because the concept of PDAs was wrong but because the way it was executed was too little, too soon. Later PDA introductions provided much more value to the consumer and have been highly successful.

Traditional thinking is littered with misconceptions about how to manage creativity and innovation. The following example presents an alternate mental model for managing innovation.

Business Manager: Artist or Movie Director?

Many people cannot imagine how to manage the creative components of the innovation process. They wrongly assume that structure and process are the natural foes of creativity. They feel that imposing any structure on creative people will ruin the results. However, structure can, in fact, enhance creativity if built and used in the right way.

People who believe creativity cannot be managed often have a mental model of creativity requiring artistic talent—such as possessed by a painter like Rembrandt. Perhaps they envision the business manager—equipped with standard project management tools, standing at the artist's side providing advice, suggestions, and imposing a process, as he attempts to paint a masterpiece: First, don't get too caught up in the details in the beginning, just use broad brush strokes to capture the basics. Once we agree on that, you can go back and add the detail. And don't use too much of that blue you have there because the marketing folk called and said that it clashes with the intended site where they want to hang this painting. Finally, no matter what, I need a first iteration done by mid-month, and your next chunk of budget is contingent on hitting that deadline and giving me results that I like.

Clearly this intrusive approach would result in a terrible painting or, more likely, an artist who stomps out the door and refuses to paint. Trying to manage the creative aspects of innovation using the "painter in front of the canvas" mental model is unlikely to meet with success. Managing the creative process in innovation is better captured by the comparison to the balancing act of the movie director.

A movie director must manage the individual needs and temperaments of many different people from actors, camera operators, and stylists, to the movie's financial backers and the senior management of the studio. Also, the director has to anticipate the desires of the targeted market, keeping the process focused on the important factors and creating a differentiated product. The director needs to know when to stick to the script and demand perfection, and when to improvise, throwing out the script in search of something better. The director has a schedule and budget that must be met because his/her performance is being assessed, and funds are allocated on the basis of results achieved against the budget and schedule goals. However, the director has to know when to stop, suspend the plan, and spend the extra time to get a particular aspect right—even when it was not budgeted or scheduled. Then he or she has to make up the lost time and budget elsewhere. Directors face innumerable logistical and technological issues. The director needs to balance all of these—movie stars, budgets, scripts, stakeholders, schedules, and technology—staying deeply involved in all aspects and producing a blockbuster movie. The movie director's role is an apt metaphor for the job of an innovation manager.

Making Innovation Work describes how to develop an organization that combines freedom and discipline, where both creating and commercializing (value capture) innovative ideas happen at high, sustained levels. To balance and drive both these processes simultaneously is a considerable challenge and requires management of the inherent tensions between the creativity and value capture (in other words, commercialization). Many companies get one component working only to realize that their success in that area is frustrating their attempts in the other. Without management intervention— for example, providing a clear innovation strategy, well-designed processes and strong leadership—creativity crowds out commercialization, or vice versa. These two elements are the necessary ingredients for innovation but they do not coexist easily.

> **"We treat innovation as if it were magical, not subject to guidance or nurturing, much less planning. If we study history, however, we know that's simply untrue. There are times, places, and conditions under which innovation flourishes."**
>
> **—Samuel J. Palmisano, chairman, president and CEO of IBM**[14]

The inclusion of creativity into the innovation equation has kept many managers baffled and perplexed. How can you manage creativity? Won't you stifle creativity if you apply management processes? There is nothing magical about creativity. The creative aspects of innovation can be managed, measured, and directed, as shown by the creativity and innovation practices of many leading companies. The real challenge is managing creativity and value creation side-by-side without compromising either one.

There is a natural tension between being creative and delivering value from being creative. Too much emphasis on delivering value through execution can stifle the creative processes, and vice versa. Unstructured creative processes can displace effective value management, yielding a factory of great ideas but insufficient commercial successes. Innovation does not mean ignoring business imperatives, but it does mean you have to be aware of the processes within your organization that kill creativity.[15] To achieve this, managers need to be aware of which managerial practices act as a stimulus to creativity and which practices inhibit it. Commercialization processes also need to be managed to produce high-quality results fast—turning the best creative concepts into marketable products and services.

Case Study: When Creativity Displaces Commercialization

Company: Xerox PARC

A company can focus too much energy and resources on creativity. Xerox PARC (Palo Alto Research Center) is a good example of this phenomenon. In the 1970s and 80s, Xerox was a hotbed of creativity. Inside PARC, there was a very high energy level along with some brilliant minds collaborating on all kinds of groundbreaking innovations. Xerox PARC's innovation efforts produced literally thousands of ideas and hundreds of prototypes across a very broad range of computers and information services. However, something was out of balance. Although creativity flourished, PARC did not seem able to capitalize on it. Many ideas languished and never made it to commercialization. Others were developed, but their commercialization was not successful. Overall their creativity flourished but it did not produce commensurate commercial success. What happened?

It appears that Xerox paid undue attention to creativity and effectively reduced its commercialization capabilities (in other words, capturing value from the innovations). The company appeared to be so engaged with its creativity that it lost sight of the goal. With creativity crowding out concern for commercialization, Xerox found itself unable to realize the full potential value from many of its investments. Of course, Apple CEO Steve Jobs licensed a small part of what he saw when he toured PARC and turned it into a major force in the world of personal computers. And subsequently, Xerox has worked hard to restore the balance between creativity and value capture and get innovation back on track.

If the commercialization or the creative processes or mindset dominate, then the company is stuck with very poor innovation. While many companies have been frustrated in operating side-by-side creativity and commercialization, this book provides examples of how it can be done effectively.

5. *Neutralize Organizational Antibodies*

To achieve innovation success, a company must overcome the organizational "antibodies" that inevitably come out to attack and defeat innovations. Typically, the more radical the innovation and the more it challenges the status quo, the more and stronger are the antibodies. Also, the greater the past successes of a company, the greater are the organizational antibodies. When people have experienced success for a long time, there is a tendency to become complacent and resist change. In order to innovate, senior management must create a culture that has the ability and the courage to change, explore, and innovate while at the same time has the ability to be stable enough to deliver on its innovations.

Part of an innovation-friendly culture is recognizing that those things that brought success in the past will not necessarily do so in the future; core capabilities have the property of becoming core liabilities if they do not adapt and change. This requires a culture that is open to questioning assumptions and to debating alternatives to the current approach to business. Managers must also understand that only by taking risks (preferably small risks where the cost of failure is low), closely observing results, learning from them, and trying again, can innovation occur. HP used to foster risk-taking using many methods, including wakes for failed projects. At these wakes, the team mourned the failure, praised the effort, recognized the learning that came with the effort, and focused on the living—the current and next projects that needed attention. Like a real wake, the message was, "This is life, and it is the way things work. You have to keep going forward."

A culture that fosters innovation embraces communication not only within the members of the organization, but also with external constituencies. Customers have proven to be a valuable source of insight,[16] but so have suppliers, universities, competitors, or companies in other industries. The not invented here (NIH) syndrome— where a company routinely rejects external ideas because they were not created inside the company—is a sign of an arrogant culture, and where there is arrogance, strong organizational antibodies exist.

In addition, fostering a culture of risk-taking and learning requires careful attention to metrics and rewards.

6. Cultivate an Innovation Network Beyond the Organization

The primary unit of innovation is not the individual; a person is not the basic building block. Rather, it is the network that extends inside (R&D, marketing, manufacturing) and outside (including customers, suppliers, partners, and others). Innovation requires developing and maintaining this network as an open and collaborative force—no easy task considering the complexities of relationships, differing motivations, and differing objectives. Managing effective partnerships within the company and with customers, suppliers, consultants, and everyone who can help you be innovative comprise a core competency of innovation.

Many examples exist of companies that use this to their advantage. For example, 3M has always maintained a robust network of contacts in a wide range of technological areas. They regularly contact the network to get new ideas and build teams for new initiatives.

Networks are important, but without a blueprint of what kind of network is needed, an organization may end up with a set of high-maintenance, low-value networks. The concept of *innovation platforms*—successfully used in various companies—provides the required framework for the network. Integrating innovation into the business and establishing networks inside and outside of the company requires innovation platforms. The platforms focus on an area of competition (such as Nokia's Mobile Office concept) and address the range of potential incremental and breakthrough innovations. The innovation platforms cut through the normal organizational boundaries. They include networks of people inside and outside the company that have pertinent knowledge on the platform area—including customer insight, supply chain knowledge, and technical expertise. As we describe in Chapter 4, "Organizing for Innovation: How to Structure a Company for Innovation," leading companies such as Coca-Cola, Canon, DuPont, and Johnson & Johnson's have used innovation platforms to harness the right resources inside and outside of their company, make innovation an integral part of their business, and do not disrupt the overall organization.

Some companies choose to isolate innovation efforts from the organization to avoid its antibodies, through stand-alone departments or incubators. These approaches can be successful but only if they establish and maintain a rich network with the critical resources in the company and with outside partners. However, these stand-alone or incubator innovation initiatives often fail because, in an attempt to isolate the innovators from organizational antibodies, they sever critical links with key resources and ideas.

7. Create the Right Metrics and Rewards for Innovation

Corporations establish rewards to drive performance. Often these rewards focus on meeting budgets and avoiding risk. Rewards of this type cause managers to invest in safe products where there is little chance of a big loss but also little chance of a big profit; these rewards, though, totally block whatever motivation there may exist to explore riskier paths. These companies reward the speed at which low risk products are created and marketed, even if they are hoping for radical new ideas. The outcome is little appetite for risk and an overdose of incremental ideas. Interestingly, managers get frustrated with the outcome, blind to the behavior that the organization is explicitly or implicitly rewarding. A badly designed measurement or reward system will mute the rest of the rules, even if optimally designed.

The question then becomes: What should your company measure and what type of rewards would best motivate employees to get the innovation results you need? Before we answer these questions (see Chapters 6, "Illuminating the Pathway: How to Measure Innovation," and 7, "Rewarding Innovation: How to Design Incentives to Support Innovation," for detailed coverage), let us ask two more: What are most companies measuring now? And what are the results?

In some companies, the measurements are a big part of the problem. Generally, too few of the measurements used are linked to innovation strategy. Further, many companies we investigated are using metrics that are actually counterproductive. A new study has identified that U.S. firms view earnings per share (EPS) as the key metric.[17] The study identifies managers' willingness to forgo investments that would produce a positive net present value if it would interfere with meeting a company's quarterly EPS targets. In essence, managers are willing to burn economic value to meet earnings goals. For these types of companies, it is clear what metric is driving behavior—and it is not innovation-related.

One company we researched mentioned to us that it uses "Number of Products Launched" as a metric to evaluate and reward innovativeness. What behavior would you expect this metric to motivate? Product development managers at the company told us that to meet their targets and get their rewards, they focused on achieving many small product improvements. They said that more radical innovation is difficult and takes a long time. Rather than "gamble" on achieving a more radical innovation—that is, spending the considerable time and money required for semi-radical and radical innovation research and development—they focused on the less risky, shorter-term gains from incremental innovation. The product development managers' approach is understandable and justifiable, from an individual employee's point of view. In the three or more years it may take to achieve a truly radical innovation, they would have to forfeit their reward and resist considerable organizational pressure due to their perceived "non performance." Then, if they achieved a breakthrough innovation, they would be rewarded exactly the same as if they had produced an incremental improvement to an existing product, even though a radical innovation would return value to the organization magnitudes greater than an incremental innovation.

Organizational structures are often a barrier to innovation. R&D teams can develop powerful ideas, but the business units may not want to sell the product because they cannot see how it fits within their core product mix or their capabilities. Therefore, the R&D department cannot get access to the funding to develop its best breakthrough ideas to the point that the potential commercial return is clear. In other companies, product ideas are generated in the marketing departments of the business units. The department then contracts with the new product development and R&D groups to move the idea from concept to commercial reality. Within this structure, there is no reward for developing breakthrough innovations in the R&D department because employees are measured solely on how well they perform in response to each contract. Also, there is unlikely to be money available for scanning or exploring new possible radical innovations.

The clear conclusion is that organizations need systems in place that provide the proper measurement, motivation, incentives, and rewards to foster innovation that is aligned with the innovation strategy. Organizations also need to create an environment where taking risks on breakthrough innovations is recognized as valuable to the company. This recognition will help modify a unilateral short-term focus on results, to a more balanced view that encompasses a long-term perspective; in order to achieve truly valuable breakthroughs in the long term, it is necessary to accept (and learn from) failures in the short term. Such a perspective does not imply providing total freedom to product development managers. Rather, what is necessary is a carefully designed system that encourages innovation, and a structured process to guide the development of ideas.

Leadership was our first innovation rule because it is where a company needs to start. Metrics and Rewards is our seventh and last innovation rule because it closes the circle, and creates the motivational and behavioral links to all of the other innovation rules. We will discuss these further in the following chapters.

Summary: The Innovation Company

In today's economies, core competencies have short life cycles. Organizations—whether pursuing profits or investing in non-profit objectives—cannot expect to survive without innovation. Without innovation, their fate is determined; the only question is whether the end will happen suddenly because a competitor comes up with a radical innovation or if it will happen as they slowly fall behind competitors that are constantly pushing the envelope. By embracing innovation, companies can redefine their industries, create new ones, and achieve a leadership position that dictates the rules of the game in their favor.

Innovation is not reserved to a few chosen companies, nor does it depend on magic formulas available only to a few initiated. It is about good management. How your organization innovates determines what it will innovate. In the end, each company's innovation process is unique. What a company produces in the way of innovations, business growth and industry leadership will be determined by how the various pieces are arranged and how well they work together.

Mapping Innovation: What Is Innovation and How Do You Leverage It?

A New Model of Strategic Innovation

One of the most common misconceptions is that innovation is primarily, if not exclusively, about changing technology.[1] Mention innovation to many business-savvy CEOs, and they envision R&D labs where engineers and scientists are developing the next new technology. However, innovation is not just about changing technologies.

High-performing companies innovate by leveraging both new business models and improved technologies.[2] In Chapter 1, "Driving Success: How You Innovate Determines What You Innovate," we described the business model innovation of Dell and the technology and business model innovations of Apple. There are plenty of other examples. eBay developed a new online business model for auctions using readily available, albeit fairly new, Internet technology. The retail giant Wal-Mart currently dominates its retail space, and has used commercially available computer communication technologies to hyper-integrate its supply chain with suppliers, thereby creating a new business model with significant cost savings.[3]

Nick Donofrio, lead researcher at IBM, said, "We define 'innovation' as our ability to create new value at the intersection of business and technology. We have to have new insights. We have to do things differently. We cannot rely just on invention or technology for success."[4]

Even the stodgy, asset-intensive steel industry has seen innovation of this type. Nucor Steel transformed the steel industry when it developed a production technology to turn old metal into steel, and changed its business model to capture maximum value. Nucor's new business model focused on relatively small volume production of high-value products, effectively reversing the heritage industry model of large-scale production runs of commodity products. The combined effect of the technology change and the business model shift sent ripples of change throughout the industry.

Rarely does a technology change occur without also causing a change in business processes. The reverse is also true. Both innovations go together and have to be thought and implemented as a whole. For instance, a new technology may require changes in the way the manufacturing facility organizes its work, or a change in how marketing communicates with the company's customers.

One of the best-known examples of business model driven innovation is the history of the auto industry in the first half of the 20th century. Initially, all cars were manufactured in shops, and were very labor–intensive; each unit was a unique piece of artisan work. The first radical change in the business model came with Henry Ford's move toward standardization and applying the concepts of a production line to the car industry. While Ford used new technologies— mainly process technologies to increase the efficiency of its production lines and its supply chains—the radical innovation came from the business model dimension, where the whole concept of the auto industry was turned upside down: from shop work to production line, from product performance to product cost, from customization to standardization, from assembly to vertical integration, from niche market to mass market. The second transition came when General Motors again redefined the business model, this time at the expense of Ford. Alfred Sloan relied on even less technology than Ford to execute its business model transformation. His ingenuity played through the business model and management knowledge (soft technology, if you want) to overtake Ford. General Motors segmented the market, offered differentiated functionality to each segment, and introduced flexibility in the production process to offer a richer product line.

Successful organizations combine technology change and business model change to create innovation. In addition, to successfully integrate a robust model of innovation into the business mentality, the CEO and the leadership team must balance both the business and technology elements of innovation.

The six levers for change—three in business model and three in technology—are illustrated in Figure 2.1. Innovation involves changes to one or more of these six elements as we discuss later in the chapter. In this chapter, we will unpack the key characteristics of the business model and technology drivers for innovation (which we began describing in Chapter 1) and describe the six specific levers of change that are at the root of all innovations.

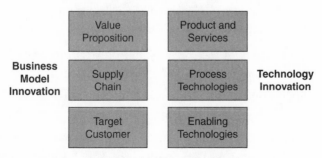

FIGURE 2.1   THE SIX LEVERS OF INNOVATION.

Business Model Change

Business models describe how a company creates, sells, and delivers value to its customers. The three areas where business model change can drive innovation are the:

- **Value proposition:** What is sold and delivered to the market.

- **Supply chain:** How it is created and delivered to the market.

- **Target customer:** To whom it is delivered.

These are the fundamental elements of every business strategy and the logical focal points for innovation.

Value Proposition

Changes in the value proposition of the product or service—essentially, what you sell and deliver to the marketplace—may be an entirely new product or service or an expanded proposition for an existing offering. For example, several brands of toothpaste have recently added whitening to their ever-growing list of delivered values such as cavity protection, breath improvement, and tartar control. Likewise, automobile manufacturers often add new features to their car and truck models, or they provide enhanced after-purchase services. In the world of computing and information management, IBM is moving away from a product-driven value proposition and tightly bundled a wide range of services with its products. In fact, services have become a major part of its business; in 2003, 48 percent of IBM's revenues came from providing services, generating 41 percent of profits. IBM's acquisition of PricewaterhouseCoopers (now IBM Global Services) and the growth of hosted applications within the OnDemand initiative are all strategic moves towards enhancing the service aspect of IBM's product offering. Amazon changed its service offering to become an online mall or retail platform selling goods from other retailers on its site, such as clothes from the Gap, Nordstrom, and Eddie Bauer and sporting goods with more than 3,000 brands.[5]

> ## Research Bite: Innovation in Product Offerings
>
> A start-up company in one of our research projects illustrates new product innovation in mature markets. The company developed products—in this case, gloves—targeted to the needs of the various crafts. An electrician requires different performance from his or her gloves compared to a construction worker, and a person working outdoors under extreme weather conditions needs different gloves from the same person working in milder climates. This required a new business model with new segmentation, new distribution channels, new advertising approaches, and a new network of suppliers to access the latest material technology to offer the highest performance designs.

Supply Chain

The second element of innovative business model change is the supply chain—*how* value is created and delivered to the market. Changes to the supply chain are usually "behind-the-scenes," changes that customers typically do not see. This type of business model change affects steps along the value chain, including the way an entity organizes, partners, and operates to produce and deliver its products and services. In the 1980s, when Sun Microsystems worked with outside organizations as strategic partners to provide value-creating activities, it created a new approach to outsourcing, and a big competitive advantage—but you could not discern it explicitly in its products. Also, supply chain changes can result from combining parts of the supply chain that typically are provided by different companies. For example, when General Electric began to couple service contracts with its manufactured electric turbines, it created new synergies and value in its part of the supply chain. Customers bought the package of hardware and service, and GE was able to secure above-average margins for the industry. This was a significant innovation with major market implications; the business model changed to include hardware and service as bundled products, requiring companies in the space to master both aspects to remain competitive.

Innovations may also come from redefining relationships with suppliers. Toyota redefined this relationship in the car industry during the 1970s. Toyota changed from the traditional confrontational relationship between suppliers and automakers to a collaborative relationship where suppliers participated in the successes and failures of the automaker. Innovations can also come from carefully managing relationships with complementary assets. The success of Microsoft's entry in the gaming market with its Xbox was dependent on the growth of game developers that would develop applications for Xbox as well as the growth of the Xbox itself.

Target Customer

Changes in *to whom* you sell—the target customer segments—usually occur when an organization identifies a segment of customers to whom it does not currently direct its marketing, sales, and distribution efforts that would consider its products and services valuable. For example, developers of the nutritional bars originally targeted athletes and extreme sports participants. Later it was realized that other customer segments—such as women—were a potentially large set of customers for the value of nutritional bars. With relatively small changes to the ingredients, packaging, and advertising, the potential market for the bars was increased several-fold.

Dockers, a brand of ready-to-wear clothing, specifically targeted the "lower-maintenance" customer group with its stain-fighting and no-iron khakis. Dockers targeted these fashion-challenged men with its signature khakis, a departure from its usual targeted segment of fashion-conscious men, and experienced renewed growth.[6]

While innovation driven by changes to the targeted customers is not as common as changes to the supply chain or value proposition, it is an important lever for innovation and should not be overlooked when companies are looking for opportunities to innovate.

These three levers—the value proposition, supply chain, and the target customer—are the basis for creating business model innovation that leading companies such as Dell, Nucor Steel, and GE have used to their advantage.

Technology Change

Sometimes new technologies are a major part of an innovation, and they stand out and garner significant attention. Other times, the new technologies are hidden out of sight and can only be seen by the technical people servicing them. Either way, technology change can fuel innovations in three distinct ways; namely in:

- Product and service offerings
- Process technologies
- Enabling technologies

Product and Service Offerings

A change to a product or service that a company offers in the marketplace—or the introduction of an entirely new product or service—is the most easily recognized type of innovation because consumers see the changes first-hand. In today's fast-changing market, consumers have come to expect significant and recurring technological innovation of this type. Consumers have been conditioned to expect product innovation to such an extent now that it is common for people to time their purchases—waiting for the release of a new model of an MP3 player with additional features and increased storage capacity.

Other examples of product-based technology innovation include the frequent new features released on mobile phones and automobiles. New "blockbuster" prescription drugs are also the result of this type of innovation. McDonald's introduction of low-fat oil enabled it to capture a new market segment—health-conscious consumers—with the same product and service offering. The new oil does not affect the taste (or perceived quality) of its offering but makes the product attractive to an entirely new segment, and possibly enhances the attractiveness to existing customers. McDonald's pioneered this approach to fast food, and it has enabled the company to maximize the value out of its existing product and service offering.

While this type of innovation is very important and can have a significant impact on company success, it is not the only form of technological innovation.

Process Technologies

When we think about technology innovation, we think about innovation that drives the performance of the products or services that the company offers. For example, when we think about memory chips we think about capacity, access speed, or even energy consumption. Product innovation comes to mind because it quickly translates into functionality that the customer can value and price. But product innovation is only one application of technology.

Changes in the technologies that are integral parts of product manufacturing and service delivery can result in better, faster, and less expensive products and services.[7] These process technology changes are usually invisible to the consumer but often vital to a product's competitive posture.[8] Examples include food processing technologies, automobile manufacturing, petroleum refining, electricity generation, and manufacturing in every industry. Process technologies also include the materials used in the manufacturing, because manufacturing and materials are intimately connected. For service providers, the process technologies are those elements that allow the service to be delivered—the equipment that sends and receives the telephone signals that make up phone service, the package sorting stations, and delivery trucks that allow packages to be delivered by express package service companies, and the airplanes and airports that provide air transport services. For products and services, process technologies are an essential part of the innovation equation.

Companies continually strive to make changes to the process technologies that could reduce cost and improve the quality of existing products or services. This is especially true in commodity products or services where it is increasingly difficult to differentiate the product or service; in commodities, cost is often the only way to compete. Certainly the electric utility industry feels this cost pressure in production, transmission, and distribution of electricity. However, the competitiveness of all products and services are benefited by improvements in process technologies.

Enabling Technologies

A third source of technology innovation resides in what we call *enabling technology*. Rather than changing the functionality of the product or the process, enabling technology enables a company to execute the strategy much faster and leverage time as a source of competitive advantage. For example, information technology facilitates the exchange of information among the various participants in the value chain. Closer communications speeds up business processes from product development to supply chain management.

Though the least visible to customers, change in enabling technologies, such as information technologies, can be very important because they help ensure better decision-making and financial management. For example, Wal-Mart has made important changes to its enabling information management technologies, with significant improvement in its ability to track and manage its partners, the supply chain, and finances.

Integrating the Innovation Model

This new model of innovation requires integrating the management of business models and technologies inside the company. But this integration does not always occur. Facing increasingly effective competition, Intel in 2004 was spending billions on developing and commercializing technology innovations but not apparently on business model innovation. The question asked in Silicon Valley was not whether Intel had the right technologies but did it have the right business model to compete in the years ahead. It appeared to many that business model and technology innovation had become separated. Traditionally, organizations create and manage the changes to business models in parts of the organization that are far removed—physically and culturally—from where the technology change is managed. Successful innovation depends on the integration of the mental models and the activities regarding business models and technology management.

CEO Considerations

- Understand your company's unique opportunities in technology and business model innovation.
- Think about technology as changes to products, to processes to deliver products, and to infrastructure that supports these products and processes.
- Think about business model as changes in the value proposition, the way products are delivered, and the targeted customers.
- Develop a plan to leverage your investments in technology with investments in business models—and vice versa—in order to hedge your bets.

Three Types of Innovation

Not all innovations are created equally. They do not entail the same risks or provide similar rewards. The generic types of innovation include the following:

- Incremental
- Semi-radical
- Radical

Incremental innovation leads to small improvements to existing products and business processes. It can be thought of as an exercise in problem-solving where the goal is clear but how to get there needs to be solved. At the opposite end, radical innovation results in new products or services delivered in entirely new ways. It can be thought of as an exercise in exploration where there might be something relevant in a particular direction but what will be found is unknown. In order to make the best strategic decisions regarding innovation, it is necessary to understand the characteristics of each type and when it is appropriate to use each. The Innovation Framework, illustrated in Figure 2.2, illustrates how the different types of innovation fit into the Innovation Matrix.[9]

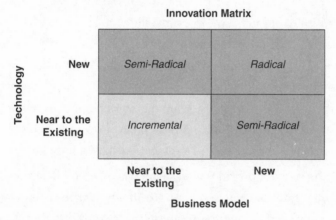

FIGURE 2.2   THE INNOVATION FRAMEWORK.[10]

For periods of time, a company can be tremendously successful with only incremental changes to its technology. A traditional model of technology change predicts relatively long periods of evolution (incremental innovation) punctuated by short periods of revolution (where incremental innovation is useless and a radical technology is required).[11]

A classic example is the refrigeration industry.[12] During the 19th century, ice was harvested from lakes, stored in caves to limit its melting, and transported as perishable goods. The technology evolved incrementally throughout several decades; the growth and harvesting processes became more efficient as new tools and techniques were applied, the storage also benefited from creativity, and the packaging to retain the cold in the ships also improved. But in the early part of the 20th century, a revolutionary technology—refrigeration—radically changed the industry. Incremental innovation in growing, harvesting, storing, and transporting ice became suddenly obsolete. Interestingly, ice companies reacted to this new technology by doing more of what they knew and doing it a lot better. The largest improvements in ice-based cooling technology happened when the technology was being phased out by this radically new approach to manufacturing cold. By the way, the reaction of the ice companies was not uncommon; they pushed the technology that they had mastered for tens of years to its limits, but they did not have the capabilities to appreciate the radical technology.[13] A similar evolution happened in shipping technology; the pace of innovation in sailing boats increased significantly when steam engine technology became a threat. And it was only a few years before the new technology displaced sailing as the means of sea transportation.[14] Thus incremental innovation may be a sustainable strategy for long periods of time, before a revolution shakes the industry.

This framework provides a powerful way to guide decisions about innovations. Because *how* you innovate affects *what* you innovate, it is vital to understand the nature of the change required so that the innovation effort can be managed, funded, and resourced appropriately.

Some people work under the misconception that innovation is always about making something new. Actually, all three types of innovation include a mixture of old and new.

Figure 2.3 depicts the six levers for innovation. Incremental innovation always firmly embraces the existing technologies and business model. Although some elements may change slightly in the incremental innovation, most stay unchanged. Semi-radical innovations include little or no changes to the levers of one of the innovation drivers—either the technology or the business model. Radical innovations include changes to levers in *both* the technology and business model but usually not to all six levers of innovation. Innovation is always about combining something old and something new from the technology and business model levers.

Levers / Types of Innovation	Business Model Levers			Technology Levers		
	Value Proposition	Value Chain	Target Customer	Product and Service	Process Technology	Enabling Technology
Incremental	*Small* change in one or more of the six levers					
Semi-Radical *Business Model Driven*	*Significant* change in one or more of the three levers			*Small* change in one or more of the three levers		
Semi-Radical *Technology Driven*	*Small* change in one or more of the three levers			*Significant* change in one or more of the three levers		
Radical	*Significant* change in one or more of the three levers			*Significant* change in one or more of the three levers		

FIGURE 2.3   THE LEVERS FOR THE THREE TYPES OF INNOVATION.

Research Bite: Incremental, Semi-Radical, and Radical Innovation Investments

Incremental, semi-radical, and radical innovations require very different types of investment. In our survey, we asked respondents to describe the budget for different types of innovation projects—changes to existing products (derivatives), new generations of existing products (new products), and radically new products (breakthroughs). Figure 2.4 describes the findings for Asia,

America, and Europe; the y-axis indicates the median size of a project in thousands of dollars.

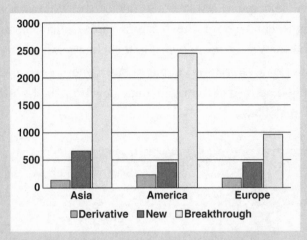

FIGURE 2.4   MEDIAN BUDGET PER TYPE OF PROJECT.

Breakthrough projects (associated with radical innovations) are much more expensive than other types of innovation projects. Notably European firms are much more conservative in funding breakthrough innovation projects than their counterparts in other world regions.

Incremental Innovation

Incremental innovation is the most prevalent form of innovation in most companies, often receiving more than 80 percent of the company's total innovation investment. Most companies' innovation portfolios are full of projects aimed at small changes to one or two of the six levers in the business model or technology.[15]

Incremental innovations are a way to wring out as much value as possible from existing products or services without making significant changes or major investments.[16] For example, car manufacturers often make slight modifications to established models every few years to create a sense that there is something fresh and to rejuvenate sales without making major changes or investments.

Incremental innovation in the business model is as important. A good part of management tools are intended to facilitate this type of innovation. Quality control techniques enable companies to constantly improve quality, financial analysis helps identify mistakes to move forward, market research provides information to better target customer needs, and supply chain management is intended to increase the efficiency of the supply chain by removing non-value added activities. In some cases, the business processes have not been tuned up for long periods of time and a more dramatic refinement is required—such as restructuring and reengineering processes.

While incremental innovation may sound like a minor piece in the equation, it is, in fact, its cornerstone. It is extremely valuable in providing protection from the competitive corrosion that eats away at market share, profitability, or both. By providing small improvements via changes in both the technology and the business model, a company can sustain its product market share and profitability for a longer time, providing better cash flow and payback on its development and commercialization investments. Gillette has done an admirable job of this with its incremental improvements to its razor technologies since 2000.

William V. Hickey, CEO and president of Sealed Air Corporation, sees incremental innovation as preventative medicine for a deadly disease: commoditization. "Our goal is to find ways to make our products non-commodities through added-value and through differentiation—through innovation."[17]

Case Study: Approaches to Incremental Innovation
Company: Magna International[18]

For automotive components and systems supplier Magna International, innovation is built into the "corporate constitution" that outlines the company's core principles—one of which is to foster innovative thinking on the part of the employees. "Incremental innovation requires the right environment. One built on fairness, security, safety, and proper communication," says Belinda Stronach, president and CEO of the $11 billion company. She adds that a comprehensive incentive program helps motivate its 72,000 employees to be creative. "We slice up the pie before it's baked." Six percent of the profits are distributed to Magna's management team—all of whom receive low base pay salaries. "Employees receive 10 percent of profits, of which a portion is in shares and a portion is in cash. We're all motivated to generate profit because we receive a percentage, and we're also required to hold shares so that we look out for the long-term interests of the company."

Magna also encourages creative thinking and idea sharing by promoting communication and a sense of security among employees. The company recently created an employee advocate position—an individual selected by employees and management who cannot be fired by management, only by employee ballot. The position is intended to foster communications between employees and management. "The mandate is to facilitate communications, keep employees happy, and bring forward new ideas," says Stronach. "We found that by making employees stakeholders and providing the right entrepreneurial environment, incremental innovation is a byproduct."

Sometimes companies do not have sufficient levels of incremental innovation in their innovation portfolio. For example, James Kilts, former chairman and CEO of Gillette, pointed out that even though Gillette had a reputation for generating new products, it had a weakness when it came to nurturing incremental innovation: "New products have traditionally been a driver to success for Gillette; in 2001, 40 percent of our sales came from products that weren't around five years ago. But when I joined Gillette a few years ago, I found that there was a lack of incremental innovation across all parts of the company."[19]

Having too little incremental innovation can be dangerous to your company's health because it allows your competitors to piggyback on your innovations and grab customers using copycat technologies and business models.

But more often, companies find themselves struggling to understand why they always seem to be stuck in the incremental innovation space. These companies invest far too much of their resources in incremental innovation and in so doing, waste time and resources that could be better used elsewhere. Alternatively, if incremental innovations are used to protect uncompetitive products or services that are past their prime and should be retired, incremental innovations divert resources away from critical efforts to create significantly new, higher-value products or services. Either way, investing in incremental innovations that do not have a sufficient return on investment robs a company of the opportunity to invest in other innovations that could provide competitive advantage.

Apparently, the natural course is for a company to gravitate over time towards increasing levels of incremental change. The problem with the center of gravity of investments being in incremental innovation is that a company cannot succeed or even survive throughout the long term without complementing its innovation portfolio with other types of innovation.

For years, companies and business units (and even government organizations) have busied themselves with exhaustive efforts to get better at what they were doing. Six Sigma, Total Quality, and other techniques have been the focus of most organizations. These provide no significant change but do provide the greatest use of the assets at hand and, as has been shown, can create real value for the business models and technologies already in place. But there is another reason why companies have been so enthralled with these efforts—it is easier. They have found it easier to work in the incremental space than to undertake semi-radical and radical changes. Basically, incremental ideas appear safer and more comfortable because they are more predictable.

The problem with incremental innovation is that it represents constrained creativity, where only small changes are permitted; it often becomes the dominant form of innovation and crowds out other potentially more valuable changes. Companies often become addicted to incremental innovation and its relative safety only to find that they cannot venture beyond even if urgently needed.

Becoming stuck in rampant incrementalism often happens to companies that have commodity products or services. Operating in the traditional commodity arena usually creates unrelenting pressure on their profit margins and a continual churn of new products. This keeps the company frantically searching for the next incremental change. Everything new that the R&D and business-planning group develops is incremental. Unfortunately, the advantage from the incremental innovations is countered almost as soon as the innovation is made and the company has to stay on the treadmill, running faster but never getting ahead. This is the dilemma that Chevron Oronite and Lubrizol faced in the lubrication additives business. The competitive environment demanded massive amounts of incremental change to hold onto market share and protect the shrinking profit margins in the industry. What each company wanted was an innovation that was big enough to create some significant competitive advantage, which could not be immediately copied. However, given the intensity of the competition, there was no time or resources to dedicate to innovations that could break the deadly spiral of rampant incrementalism.

Interestingly, many companies know that being stuck in rampant incrementalism is a trap. However, try as they might, the leadership cannot get the organization to change. Without leveraging the innovation rules, the break away from rampant incrementalism will not happen. The organization will stay stuck in incremental innovation and eventually die.

Semi-Radical Innovation

A *semi-radical innovation* can provide crucial changes to the competitive environment that an incremental innovation cannot. Semi-radical innovation involves substantial change to either the business model or technology of an organization—but not to both.[20] Often change in one dimension is linked to change in the other, although the concomitant change may not be as dramatic or disruptive. For example, semi-radical change in technology may require incremental improvement in the business model, and vice versa.

Wal-Mart, as we mentioned earlier, provides an example of semi-radical innovation of the business model. Early on, it realized that a great segment of the U.S. consumers wanted low-cost, good-quality products. To deliver effectively against that value proposition required changing the entire business model from the traditional retail outlet. The traditional business model was to locate an outlet in urban areas and to sell a limited number of goods with significant service markup. Wal-Mart's strategy was to apply the supermarket business model to retailing and couple it with a souped-up supply chain that cut costs dramatically. The company opened large store spaces, provided a wide variety of goods at discount prices (but with less service), and slashed prices. This new application of the business model has built one of the world's most successful companies.

Dow, Dupont, and Novartis have used semi-radical innovation to change the traditional agricultural chemicals market into a dynamic agro-biotech market where biotechnology and chemicals have combined to form entirely new products, such as genetically engineered plants combined with selectively acting chemicals. The competitive advantage for these innovators is tied to intellectual property in plant genetics technology that generates new value to the customer.

A more recent example occurred in the customer relationship market (CRM) of the 1990s. By the end of that decade, Siebel Systems emerged as the leading provider of systems to manage sales and marketing processes in large organizations. Siebel relied on an expensive business model, where software was installed on the customers' servers and was customized by skilled professionals. The cost of these systems ranged from hundreds of thousands to millions of dollars. But that changed when Marc Benioff founded Salesforce.com in 1999 to deliver sales, marketing, and customer service and support operations to customers via the Web. Moving away from client-server architecture, the new company relied on Internet technology so customers could readily access the software and store their data on Salesforce.com servers. Moreover, the monthly subscription—less than $100—could be paid without the need of any kind of capital expense approval. Salesforce.com buy decisions happened at lower levels in the organization and spread throughout sales and marketing groups out of the top management or the IT department's radar. Initially, the young company focused on sales force automation in small businesses. Then, over time, Salesforce.com increased its product functionality and attracted larger companies with more complex needs. At a fraction of Siebel prices, Salesforce.com offered functionality in areas where high levels of customization were unnecessary. Salesforce.com redefined the business model for a market segment that benefited from inexpensive and simple CRM.

Major changes in technology are not limited to quantum leaps in the performance of a certain component. Sometimes, the radical innovation happens at the architectural level:[21] Components are organized in a radically new way without a significant change in the technology underlying the components. Incumbents may dismiss this architectural change as being marginal because their attention is focused on the performance of the components as driving innovation rather than their interactions. Such an event happened in the photolithographic alignment equipment industry—equipment used to align the masks with the silicon wafer in chip production. While the basic technology evolved incrementally, the industry leader changed various times from Kobit to Canon to PerkinElmer to GCA to Nikon. The changes were due to new combinations of existing components that created significant shifts in product performance.

Case Studies: Semi-Radical Innovation

Companies: Southwest Airlines and Apple Computer

Southwest Airline's move away from the traditional hub and spoke business model is an excellent example of a semi-radical innovation. Southwest gained significant competitive advantage from that change and has remained profitable and growing within the past few years. Given the recent bankruptcies, near-bankruptcies, and poor performance of many players in the airline industry, Southwest's innovation appears particularly significant; it has set the new direction for the industry and established the competitive benchmark that others use to measure themselves.

Apple Computer, in a turn away from its historical focus on breakthrough technology innovation, introduced a new business model. Apple's iTunes Music Store allows consumers to purchase music from many major recording companies and electronically transfer the music to private archives. Coupled with Apple's iPod storage and listening technology and its existing PC technologies, Apple's iTunes has become a formidable new product and service introduction. This legitimate online form of music transfer steals a page from the ill-fated and illegal attempt by Napster, and offers a new business model for music purchasing and listening. Competitors are rushing to develop and introduce comparable offerings to Apple's semi-radical innovation.

Any semi-radical change in either the business model or technology always requires some degree of change in the other. However, the change in one element (in other words, either technology or business model) is much larger and more important to the success of the innovation than the other. For example, Dell's shift to a significantly new business model for PCs required some (relatively small) changes to its process and enabling technologies (such as the supply chain management and Internet technologies). However, semi-radical innovations are asymmetric because there is either a significant change to the business model levers or to the technology levers—but not to both.[22]

The two areas in the semi-radical innovation space are interrelated, and often innovations created in one area (such as technology change or business model change) create important new opportunities in the other. This two-stage innovation in the semi-radical space is a major dynamic of innovation that companies need to manage, and is an area of huge potential value creation but one that is overlooked or under-managed by many organizations.

To collaborate in two-stage semi-radical innovation, the groups need to have a map of *both* the business model and technology space in which they compete. Usually each group has a map of its own space but is not knowledgeable of the other group's space. This leads to missteps, missed opportunities, and the inability to quickly and effectively capture the two-step innovation in the semi-radical innovation space. This collaborative innovation map provides a common framework for discussion among the different groups of threats, opportunities, strengths, and weaknesses that are crucial to successful innovation.

Sensing that something is lacking in their overall innovation portfolio and feeling stuck on the treadmill of rampant incrementalism, companies often decide (or are convinced) to solve their innovation problem by launching a major innovation thrust, undertaking aggressive efforts at semi-radical or sometimes radical innovations. As a result of improper diagnosis of their problems and their capabilities, they completely overestimate their ability to use semi-radical innovation to jump-start their portfolio This rush to solve their problems with a major dose of semi-radical or radical innovation activities was a common occurrence around the time of the Internet dot-com buzz. Some of those companies that plunged into semi-radical and radical innovation endeavors have discovered that they lack the capabilities to convert their discoveries into commercial realities in a reasonable timeframe. For example, the attempt to lead the major U.S. electric utilities to innovate radically different distributed energy approaches in the grid (such as advanced distributed generation technologies and high tech demand response measures using sophisticated electronic interfaces) have been plagued by problems and moved very slowly.

Simultaneously managing both the business model and technology components of semi-radical innovation is one of the main innovation challenges for organizations. This two-stage innovation in the semi-radical space is a major dynamic of innovation that companies need to manage. Some companies are adept at managing the change in either the technology arena or the business model arena, but seldom both. This puts them at a significant disadvantage to a company that is able to manage change in both arenas.

Radical Innovation

A *radical innovation* is a significant change that simultaneously affects both the business model and the technology of a company.[23] Radical innovations usually bring fundamental changes to the competitive environment in an industry.[24] For that reason, Shell Oil's process for creating and managing radical innovations is called "Game Changers," because successful radical innovations have the potential to rewrite the rules of the game in the industry.[25]

The introduction of disposable baby diapers in the 1970s is a historical example of radical innovation. Employing radically different technologies to replace the woven cloth of traditional diapers, a company in Sweden tried a new approach. They adapted absorbent fluff pulp from wood and crafted a simple diaper that roughly matched the performance of the traditional cloth diapers. Though the diaper was bulkier than traditional cloth diapers, and looked and felt different, the new diaper was disposable and did not require laundering. Moreover, the disposables could be bought in retail stores. This new approach displaced the traditional diaper service and the diaper home-laundering business models.

The combined changes in the technological and business elements led to a fundamental change in home baby care. Because of the success of this radical innovation, companies like Procter & Gamble, Kimberly-Clark, and Johnson & Johnson (to name a few) have invested massive amounts of money and intellectual resources in the development and commercialization of advanced absorbent and containment technologies for disposable diapers.

In the past few years, there has been a new round of semi-radical innovation in the diaper arena in the form of special absorbent and containment technologies that have sparked a new generation of ultrathin diapers. Leaders such as P&G and Kimberly-Clark continue to introduce incremental improvements to the technologies. In this case, as is often true, a radical innovation has changed the industry and led to a series of cascading semi-radical and incremental innovations.

Radical innovations are all around us today. The X PRIZE is a radical innovation in the making. It is a contest designed to jump-start a private sector space race and create a space tourism industry. The contest is modeled on the Orteig Prize, the competition that led to Charles Lindbergh's transatlantic flight in 1927 in the *Spirit of St. Louis*. Competitors for the X PRIZE come from many different backgrounds and attempt to harness very different technologies to launch and return humans to and from space. The combination of the change in business models—replacing the government with private sector investors—and the change in technologies could result in a radical innovation with far-reaching consequences.

You get an idea of how risky and hard to sell radical innovation is when you listen to Peter Diamandis, chairman and founder of the X PRIZE Foundation: "I had approached well over one hundred corporate chief executive officers regarding sponsorship. Few were able to grasp the importance of this new market . . . and those who were had great difficulty accepting the risks involved."[26] This is a common litany for those embracing radical innovations.

Research Bite: Enablers and Blockers of Radical Innovation

International R&D managers in our survey of innovation practices identified the following as the main enablers and blockers of breakthrough innovation.

Forces that generate and nurture breakthrough innovation:

- Partnering with outside companies to create new ventures.
- Management commitment to supporting ideas outside the current strategy.
- Availability of resources to support breakthrough ideas.

Barriers to breakthrough innovation:

- Incentives focused (primarily) on avoiding risk.
- Breakthrough ideas are hard to implement in manufacturing and distribution.
- Perceived competition with existing businesses.

While radical innovation can create tectonic shifts in an industry and put a company in the lead, investments in radical innovation need to be approached with caution.[27] Radical innovations are by their very nature low-probability investments.[28] Investing in too much radical innovation—based on unrealistic expectations that "the next new thing" will change the fate of the company—can waste valuable resources that could be better employed on semi-radical or incremental innovations. The key is to maintain a balanced portfolio of radical innovations so that the investment matches the business needs.

Case Study: Radical Innovation

Company: Microsoft and its .NET Initiative[29]

Several years ago, John Connors, then the Microsoft chief financial officer, said what others had been thinking: "Are we nuts? Is this the mad-dog investing company?" Microsoft had embarked on heavy investments and multiple product launches. At the time, the worst recession in the history of the IT industry had forced leading companies in Silicon Valley to cut research and development. Microsoft, by contrast, launched a major new initiative, dubbed .NET (pronounced "dot-net."). Proclaimed Steve Ballmer, Microsoft chief executive, "It is the biggest thing that is going to happen in the information technology industry."

.NET is Microsoft's version of Web Services, a new breed of software that will allow computers and other devices (such as mobile phones, handheld computers, digital television sets, and radios) to communicate with each other at a deeper level than has traditionally been possible. A user will be able to access calendars, schedule an event, purchase tickets, and manage related activities in an integrated fashion.

Will the .NET Gamble Pay Off?

Developing .NET is one of the most difficult tasks that Microsoft has ever faced. The technical challenge is large in its own right. Microsoft announced in July 2002 that it was increasing research and development spending by 20 percent, from $4.3 billion to $5.2 billion that fiscal year. This includes adding 5,000 staff, approximately 10 percent of its payroll. The current spending is already more than the R&D spending of all its major rivals combined.

Further, the significant change in technology must be accompanied by an equally significant change in business models for Microsoft. In the past, Microsoft sold software packages in a set process. In the .NET model, Microsoft is wrestling with the fact that the sales appear to be transaction-based and will occur at each interaction between consumer, device, software, and supplier. This will be a major step away from the traditional business model for Microsoft. While it is possible to offer Web Service as a traditional software sale, that approach may cause the software provider to miss important opportunities for making money from the value of the service (as opposed to just the apparent value of the software). Alternately, the traditional sale of software at a price that reflects the value of the available service would turn off many consumers who would feel that they are paying for more than they will be getting. So harnessing the power of the technological innovation is tied to developing a new business model—one that fairly charges the customer for the services they use and generates equitable profits among the providers.

Ersatz Radical Innovation

Sometimes, companies like Apple combine two semi-radical innovations to create a blockbuster innovation that has a fundamental change in an industry. The effect is like a radical innovation but it is the result of two separate innovations. We call this phenomenon *ersatz radical innovation* (in other words, a substitute for radical innovation).

The development of the video rental market during the past decade is a good example of ersatz radical innovation. The video technologies that made home entertainment possible were technology-dominant semi-radical innovation. Product and equipment companies introduced new videotape technologies into the home entertainment arena through well-established sales channels and business models. The video movie rental business, a new business model, sprang from the opportunity created by the video technologies and their penetration in the home entertainment marketplace. The technology advancement was not initially coupled to a business model innovation, as it would be on a radical innovation where both would have happened simultaneously.

These two semi-radical innovations—coupled first through semi-radical technology innovation and then through semi-radical business model innovation—had a similar effect as if radical innovation had occurred and the entire industry was changed. However, as with most cases of two-stage semi-radical innovation, the risks, costs, and benefits of the two stages were borne by different groups. First, the consumer home entertainment equipment companies made the investment, bore the risk, and reaped the rewards. Subsequently, the movie companies and then the distribution/rental companies stepped into the picture.

One has to wonder what would have happened if key players from the equipment suppliers and the rental companies had collaborated. Then truly radical innovation would have occurred, and it could have been orchestrated to provide significant benefits for the collaborators.

We are seeing the home entertainment market transformed again by DVD technologies. Initially, DVD movies were handled in the same manner as videos. However, recently a new business model has emerged: Netflix and most recently Wal-Mart have changed the traditional business model.

CEO Diagnostic: Using the Innovation Framework to Understand How Your Company Plays the Innovation Game

Perform a quick diagnostic on your current innovation investment portfolio on three levels.

1. Assess the level of investment in business model change and technology change. Does the mix seem correct or is there a bias toward technology change?

2. Assess your investments as to which of the six levers of innovation change your company is using. Are there some levers unused or under-used? Are you relying on some levers too much?

3. Determine the mix of incremental, semi-radical, and radical innovation in your investment portfolio.

4. Then determine the potential source of the biases.

   • Why is technology change investment larger/smaller than business model change?

- Is incremental innovation forcing out other types of innovation that could be beneficial?

- Why are some of the six levers so heavily used?

5. Ask yourself: Are the identified biases in the three diagnostics good or bad? Which need to change?

Disruptive Technologies

Disruptive technologies are a type of semi-radical technology innovation, brought about by changing the technology basis but not the business model (upper-left quadrant).[30]

Disruptive innovation is a broader term that addresses both technology and business model changes. Disruptive innovations include technology-driven innovation (semi-radical technology innovation; upper-right quadrant). It also can mean changes to the business model in a semi-radical business model innovation (lower-right quadrant)—for example Southwest Airlines' low cost, non-hub approach. However, sometimes disruptive innovations include a combination of technology change and business model change—a radical innovation (upper-right quadrant) such as Microsoft's .NET initiative.

The term *disruptive innovation* focuses on one of the effects of innovation, namely disruption to the competitive landscape, as opposed to incremental, semi-radical, and radical innovations that describe the relative change in the technology and business model elements. As we have discussed, the disruptive innovation can be a key source of growth and is widely sought after by CEOs. However, you cannot manage toward disruption per se. For effective management of innovation, it is crucial to focus on the internal sources of change—technology and business models—and their linkages. Leveraging and linking changes in technologies and business models is how to create disruptions, as well as the spectrum of innovations, that provide growth.

Innovation Model and the Innovation Rules

The innovation model presented here forms the context for every one of the seven innovation rules. Most importantly, the model is the basis for forming the innovation strategy and the development of the port-folio aligned with the overall business strategy. The role of the CEO is to define the role and prominence of business model innovation and technology innovation in the company's overall strategy. Dell's CEO, Michael Dell, explicitly focused his company's innovation on the PC business model. That focus led to a significant change in the compet-itive dynamics of the industry and a leading position for Dell. In con-trast, Sony's former CEO Nobuyuki Idei decided to focus that company on technology innovation, specifically proprietary compo-nents to differentiate its products. As a result of that decision, during a four-year period around 2002, Sony spent 70 percent of its innova-tion investment in new chips.[31]

These CEOs made clear decisions on the relative roles of busi-ness models innovation and technology innovation for their company. They realized that direction on the innovation portfolio must come from the top.

Selecting and integrating the priorities for business model change and technology change and defining the balance between the three types of innovation in the portfolio—incremental, semi-radical, and radical innovation—are the basic responsibilities of senior manage-ment. These senior-level decisions are the basis that the organization will use to execute the strategy. They provide the context for the downstream decisions related to organizational design, the develop-ment of innovation networks, and the development and use of met-rics and incentives to drive innovation.

3

CHOOSING YOUR DESTINY: HOW TO DESIGN A WINNING INNOVATION STRATEGY

Choosing the Right Strategy

"Innovation is a survival issue."

—3M[1]

One of the first rules of innovation is that you must clearly decide how your organization is going to play the innovation game. This is senior management's responsibility. There is no menu of generic strategies from which to choose. Each company's management team has to craft its own innovation strategy, adapt to changing conditions, and choose the right time to make key moves.

The innovation strategy must support the business strategy. The amount and type of innovation (radical, semi-radical, and incremental) will vary depending on the strategy and the competitive environment. Like anything important, timing is everything.

It is crucial that the people in the organization understand the innovation strategy. Without a clear game plan, and without alignment of the key players in the organization, you cannot be very successful at innovation.

Play-to-Win or Play-Not-to-Lose Strategies

A study that scrutinized why some firms innovate significantly more than others found that in general, dominant firms are more aggressive innovators than non-dominant firms.[2] However, dominance is not a strategy—it is an outcome. You need to define more than dominance to have a viable innovation strategy.

Within the Innovation Matrix, an organization may choose to devote most of its resources to a particular part of the matrix or spread them out, creating a diverse portfolio of innovation investments across the matrix. Depending on the center of gravity and diversity of the investment within the matrix, we can talk about two classes of innovation strategies: *Playing-to-Win* (PTW) and *Playing-Not-to-Lose* (PNTL).

Play-to-Win Strategy

For an organization to launch a PTW strategy, there must be an emphatic "Yes" in response to the question, "Is the innovation investment we are making expected to create one of the key sources of our competitive advantage?" A PTW approach investment's goal is to produce significant competitive advantages that its competitors will not be able to easily or quickly match.

PTW is a market-leading strategy that relies heavily on semi-radical innovation to drive transformation in the organization and create market-changing ideas and products. In the PTW innovation mode, a company invests in changes in technology and business models with the intent of outpacing its competitors through radical innovation or, alternately, by wearing them down with repeated, frequent salvos of different types of innovation—incremental, semi-radical, and radical. Either way, investing in a PTW innovation strategy commits a company to a portfolio of investments that are fundamental for (although not the only element of) the organization's ongoing competitive success.

A PTW strategy is typical of high-technology startups. These companies are highly focused on bringing one new technology or business model to market. Frankly, one new thing is almost all they have and their future is almost entirely dependent on it. The failure rate for small companies following this strategy is large, reflecting the high risk involved with this strategy—whether it comes from the technology delivering the value promised, from the market developing fast enough to value the technology, or from the management executing on the strategy. However, the other key contributing factor in the failure rate of these high-tech startup companies is that they usually have only one or two innovation investments and do not have the strength of a strong investment portfolio. The lack of depth in their portfolios is what makes the PTW strategy extremely risky.

Research Bite: The Formation of Strategy in High-Technology Startups

In a study, we interviewed the CEOs and business development managers of 69 high-technology startup firms. We discussed the history of their firms, the challenges they faced, and the evolution of strategy. One theme that came across in almost every interview was the fluidity of their strategies. In these companies, the technologies stayed stable—only in a few cases the technology had to be replaced—but the go-to-market strategy changed in the first few years at least twice and, in some cases, three times.

Because of their limited resources, these young companies must be very focused in the beginning. Ironically, once the startups are successful, they need to shift to a more diversified innovation portfolio that puts a premium on additional incremental innovation (for example, incremental changes to protect and capture maximum value from their initial radical or semi-radical innovation). But it is not easy to do, and many companies have problems shifting from a strategy that emphasizes big radical innovation to a strategy that includes a combination of radical, semi-radical, and incremental innovation investments (such as a diversified portfolio). Along with changing the investment portfolio and modifying the strategy and the processes, it is common to see significant turnover at the top of the organization—from an entrepreneur to a seasoned manager.[3] The selection and execution of the innovation portfolio is management's responsibility. Failure to adequately change the strategy requires intervention of the board or the investors.

The early part of the dot-com phenomenon offers numerous examples of PTW strategies from startups with both success and failures as outcomes. On the failure side, Webvan received more than $700 million in funding; however, the company burned out in less than four years in an attempt to create a new business model based on a new technology. Webvan's proposition was to use the web as the supermarket storefront where customers would select the products they wanted as they would usually do in a regular supermarket, and the company would use its fleet of trucks to deliver the order to their door. The technology was the web-based software, still in a state of flux at the time but probably not at the extreme of the newness axis. The business model relied on a significant change in people's shopping habits and the assumption that avoiding costly retail space and centralizing warehousing was cheaper. The risks were high in that both technology and mostly business model were new, but the potential rewards were also significant as reflected in Webvan's market capitalization at its peak—$8.81 billion. Webvan energetically attacked the market with a clear PTW strategy. Webvan ended up closing its operation in July 2001.

In contrast, Amazon.com is a successful example of a PTW strategy. The risks were similar in that Amazon.com also relied on an evolving software technology, and a new business model that required a significant change in the purchasing habits of book customers and a significant redesign and streamlining of the book supply chain. Amazon redefined a "best-practice" by selling single books in an industry that as late as the early 1990s was accustomed to selling pallets of books (shipping a single one was considered impossible); this process innovation in order management continues to serve them well today. Amazon.com also energetically attacked the market with a PTW strategy. However, Amazon.com was able to turn the selling of books and other products over the web into a successful business model via its PTW strategy.

Managers in larger, more established firms do not need to "bet the company" as startups often do. Their broader, available resources allow them to cover a larger portfolio of investments in the Innovation Matrix, providing a hedging function and significantly lowering the risks. Many large firms have a clear PTW bent to their strategy (namely, GE, Apple, and Sony). These companies have committed to an investment portfolio that is designed to provide a formidable flow of innovations that will contribute to their dominance of their business sectors. Toyota's development of lean manufacturing and the introduction of the Prius hybrid auto are examples of a PTW innovation strategy.

For many companies, at any given moment, it is not prudent to adopt a PTW strategy. The external or internal conditions may make such a strategy choice too risky. Sometimes, it is advantageous to stay in the game, adopt a Play-Not-to-Lose (PNTL) strategy, and ultimately win through the ability to outpace competitors in pushing an innovation strategy with a significant incremental component to it or at the right opportunity.

Play-Not-to-Lose Strategy

Sometimes less-than-optimum external or internal conditions do not allow a company to adopt a PTW approach. For example, if the external competitive environment is extremely intense or uncertain (for example, there are too many strong competitors or regulatory roadblocks, or there is a high degree of uncertainty due to a shifting regulatory environment or uncertain economics), it is advisable to adopt a PNTL strategy. Likewise, if an organization has significant internal constraints (such as inadequate resources or a culture that is caught up in a non-innovative mentality), then a PTW strategy may not be a viable option. The potential costs and risks of pursuing a PTW strategy under those circumstances are likely to outweigh the benefits.

PNTL is a strategy that typically includes more incremental innovation in the portfolio than a PTW strategy, and aims to ensure the company can stay in the game by moving quickly, taking calculated risks, sometimes moving first or by matching or surpassing any moves by competitors. Johnson & Johnson apparently opted for a PNTL strategy in many of its businesses, including reliance on line extensions, cost cutting, and acquisitions. With few promising drug deliveries in the near term, Johnson & Johnson adopted a more conservative strategy to hold off the competition until more promising opportunities present themselves.[4] Hyundai's early moves reflected a PNTL strategy aimed at keeping the company in the game as the automotive giants slug it out.

Following a PNTL approach, the company would watch for improvements in the external environment, make improvements in its internal capabilities, attempt to wear down the competition, and look for opportunities to shift to a PTW strategy at the appropriate time.

Sometimes a PNTL can lead a company to the forefront of an industry without shifting to a PTW strategy. Companies with PNTL strategies are often in fragmented industries where changes to technologies and business models occur relatively infrequently. In this environment, the winners are companies that consistently beat competitors in making incremental improvements to technologies and business models. These leaders make PNTL strategies the norm for the entire industry. Such markets are for marathon runners—where the winner is the one most able to constantly deliver—rather than for sprinters.

These companies may still choose to invest in the outer quadrants, discussed in Chapter 1, "Driving Success: How You Innovate Determines What You Innovate," of the Innovation Matrix (semi-radical or radical innovation). However, these investments are not intended as much to become a PTW player as to stay connected to the activity in these quadrants, and to be able to move quickly if a radical innovation happens to shake the market.

However, we have seen that companies following this sort of PNTL model are running another significant risk. This strategy is highly vulnerable to competitors that break from the pack and shift to a PTW strategy that increasingly relies on semi-radical or radical innovations. When these shifts happen, PNTL companies can be left with insufficient capability to match semi-radical and radical innovations and little ability to compete in this new environment. Being lulled into believing your PNTL strategy is working is also a danger. Mattel learned this lesson when a competing line of dolls introduced in 2001, called Bratz (produced by MGA Entertainment), cut into Mattel's Barbie sales significantly.[5]

If you look around an industry at any given moment, you will find many companies that exhibit important aspects of the PNTL behavior, such as risk adversity and an unwillingness to attempt to first commercialize risky semi-radical or radical innovations that appears to have the ability to yield significant competitive advantage. However, this PNTL behavior may not be the result of conscious management choices. Sometimes PNTL strategies exist because the management cannot commit to a clear PTW strategy. In that case, PNTL is a compromise among parts of the organization that do not have the same view of what should be done to succeed. That sort of compromise is a very dangerous strategic choice because it blunts the effectiveness of execution. People cannot execute at maximum efficiency, speed, or effectiveness if they are getting confused signals. It is management's responsibility to clearly specify and communicate the innovation strategy throughout the company.

PNTL is sometimes mistakenly called the "fast-follower" strategy. This is the wrong mental model. A PNTL strategy is not limited to following another's move. To be successful, PNTL requires a mix of preemptive and reactive moves, all aimed at not relinquishing advantage and whenever possible, causing competitors to expend more than their fair share of resources in their actions. So playing-not-to-lose is not the same as following. An organization focused on just *following* eventually becomes limited in its competitive mindset and innovation capability, unknowingly relinquishing innovation opportunities that do not fit into the concept of following. Having said this, skilled fast-followers are often more successful than the early innovators. These fast seconds follow a PNTL strategy but deploy the capabilities to quickly copy and improve successful PTW companies to become leaders.[6] They are ready to quickly jump after a successful innovation and deploy their business processes' strengths—such as marketing, distribution, product development, or process technology—to beat the original innovator.

CEO's Responsibilities

- Choose the innovation strategy that supports the business strategy.

- Decide if the company's innovation strategy is Play-to-Win or Play-Not-to-Lose.

- Construct an investment portfolio with the right balance of incremental, semi-radical, and radical innovation to support the strategy.

- Identify the relative roles of business model change and technology change in the strategy (and the implications for the kind of collaboration and behavior you expect to see).

- Communicate the strategy to the organization many times through different channels, and emphasize that the metrics of success and the rewards are based on excellent execution of the strategy (not talking about the strategy).

- Make sure that organizational antibodies and other impediments don't limit the value of your innovation investments.

The recent competitive and regulatory environment in the U.S. electric utility industry has favored adoption of PNTL innovation strategies. While many companies attempted to be innovative in the 1990s, the swiftly changing regulatory environment and the failure of many initiatives forced many major utilities into a PNTL strategy. For the past five or more years, the major industry players have all bunched up around variations of a PNTL strategy.

However, there appears to be a turning point in the utility industry, and some utilities appear to be considering that a switch to a PTW strategy is warranted. For example, early in 2004, John Wilder, former CFO at Entergy Corporation, became president and chief executive of TXU Corporation. In his remarks to investors, Wilder made it known that TXU's back-to-basics and PNTL days were over, and that his intent was to strive for a position of industry leadership for TXU. CEOs of companies such as Constellation Energy Group, Dominion Resources, Sempra Energy, and Centrica have begun to set new business objectives and migrate to PTW strategies.

One of the major questions facing the other companies in the industry is how quickly can they shift strategies to a new PTW to address this shift by the other utilities. If those remaining companies are too slow in changing to a PNTL strategy or they lack the capabilities to shift without undue risk, then they face the prospect of being trapped in a PNTL strategy at the wrong time. Choosing a PNTL innovation strategy can be a smart management decision. However, being forced into a PNTL strategy because a company is not prepared is poor management.

In another part of the energy sector, the leading oil companies decreased their investment in finding new oil in 2003 and 2004. Lee Raymond, CEO of ExxonMobil, the world's largest energy group, said that he believed that most of the world's largest oil fields had already been found and that the next opportunities would come when investment in countries such as Russia, Iraq, and Libya become politically possible. This harsh reality of diminished exploration sent shock waves through the leaders in the oil services industry—Halliburton and

Schlumberger. They had to decide the right innovation strategy in the face of significant industry upheaval: Is it the right time to play to win?

While the two big players made decisions and second-guessed each other, the smaller players in the industry, such as Weatherford and BJ Services, had to make similar decisions: Is it the right time for the small players to play to win, and attempt to grow and take a leading position in the industry? These innovation strategy decisions made in 2005 will determine the shape of the oil services industry in the years ahead.

Utilities and oil service companies are not alone in this regard. Many other industries face similar challenges in deciding when to shift from PNTL strategies. For example, healthcare providers have been struggling for survival, and the entire industry has been locked in a PNTL innovation strategy. The major emphasis has been on cost reduction and incremental improvements to shore up revenues and profits. However, some players such as Sutter Health have shown significantly improved financial performance. With that change, some of the profitable companies may decide to shift to a PTW strategy because the timing looks good to create important competitive advantage. That shift to PTW by a few key players could change the competitive dynamics of the industry significantly.

A very interesting example of a company using a PNTL innovation strategy against a PTW strategy occurred in the so-called U.S. baby diaper wars of the 1980s and 1990s. Kimberly-Clark (KC), facing Procter & Gamble (P&G) and a host of smaller independent manufacturers, did not appear to have the positioning necessary to dominate the market, although they would have liked to. Darwin Smith, CEO of KC at that time, was an intense competitor who focused his company on creating value. However, P&G, one of the earliest participants into the diaper business arena, was fiercely defending its leading market share and profitability. P&G had dedicated significant resources and clearly signaled that it was not likely to be run out of the market. They were investing large amounts of resources on innovation.

Although it could not dominate the market with the resources at hand (it would have been very hard to outspend P&G), KC did not withdraw. KC challenged every one of P&G's innovation moves. In addition, sometimes the company took the initiative and introduced customer-preferred product features first (such as training pants). Other times it quickly and effectively countered P&G's innovations, responding with comparable or improved features and performance that mimicked the P&G innovation (such as boy and girl diapers). KC's PNTL innovation strategy combined preemptive and reactive innovations that kept P&G off-balance and unable to dominate the market. The diaper war intensity seems to have abated but it has not disappeared. Both KC and P&G are still slugging it out.

It is often the case that the external and internal forces do not dictate that a company adopts a pure PTW or PNTL strategy. They point to something in between the two extremes.

CEO Sanity Check

You need to clearly understand your current innovation strategy as it is being implemented—not as you have designed it. Here are some key questions to consider:

- Is the current innovation strategy:
  - Play-to-Win?
  - Play-Not–to-Lose?
  - A mixture?
- Is the company investing for large or small amounts of innovation? Does your company need significant amounts of innovation? Or just small amounts at the right time?
- How is the current innovation portfolio balanced? How should the innovation portfolio be balanced between incremental, semi-radical, and radical innovations?

- How well does the innovation strategy as implemented support your overall business strategy? How does it differ from the plan?

- Does the organization understand the innovation strategy? Can employees execute it faster, better, and cheaper than the competition can deliver theirs?

Case Study: Shifting from a PTW to a PNTL Strategy— and Back Again[7, 8, 9]

Company: General Electric

GE is the birthplace of many of the modern concepts of R&D, starting with Steinmetz more than 100 years ago. "Steinmetz did not want this lab to worry about next quarter's product," said Scott Donnelly, senior vice president for research. "He wanted it to work on the next big idea, even as GE's businesses were refining the last one." GE created one of the first PTW innovation strategies, with a balanced portfolio of radical, semi-radical, and incremental innovation.

Under Jack Welch, the CEO in the 80s and 90s, the labs shifted toward a PNTL mentality, serving the largely incremental needs of the business units. Welch made the business units pay for research. Welch was largely successful with a PNTL strategy in the battle to stay ahead of competitors with preferable products. GE's business strategy made that innovation strategy preferable. The current CEO, Jeffrey Immelt, faces the challenge of shifting the innovation strategy to win the value added wars.

Immelt says that he "would be surprised if a bunch of years down the road, we aren't into businesses that require new names (i.e., are significantly different from the GE heritage and brand). GE is incubating service-heavy businesses in security, water treatment, oil and gas, hydrogen fuels, and other areas that cannot be bolted onto existing GE businesses."

The R&D numbers now reflect a shift toward increased technology investment in semi-radical and radical innovations: Describing the R&D component of the PTW strategy, Immelt said, "Superior technology is the only route to consistent growth without declining margins." Of course, changing business models is also something GE does very well, so tagging technology as the *only* route seems wrong.

GE is also using major crosscutting initiatives, what we call innovation platforms (see Chapter 4, "Organizing for Innovation: How to Structure a Company for Innovation"), that will benefit several business units:

- Artificial intelligence
- Pulsed detonation
- Nanotechnology

Too Much of a Good Thing

Can you have too much innovation? We should not be misled by the frequently used expression "Innovate or Die." Those who espouse this slogan firmly believe that massive doses of radical innovation are required to survive. Is radical innovation truly necessary for survival for all organizations at all times?

A lack of innovation, especially radical innovation, can lead to failure. However, investing in radical innovation at the wrong time or in the wrong amounts can be just as fatal. In other words, it is possible to "innovate and die" by taking the wrong kinds of risk and by playing the wrong kind of strategy.

There is another risk with taking the expression "Innovate or Die" too much to heart. Too many innovative ideas out there for companies to process clouds their judgment on which ideas are truly great.[10] Clouded by the excess, the companies take on too much innovation and the wrong types of innovation, and waste their investments.

Case Study: Play-to-Win Innovation Strategy

Company: Starbucks

It is not enough to choose the right strategy once. You have to *keep* choosing the strategies to remain successful. This is the real challenge; Starbucks provides a good example.[11] Starbucks achieved a revolution in the coffee industry. Previously, the coffee brands like Folgers and Nescafe had fairly pedestrian images, and brand loyalty was not a driving force for American consumers. However by the late 1990s, if you asked an American to associate a brand with coffee, you would be highly likely to get Starbucks as the answer.

Starbucks began in 1987 and has remained successful for more than a decade. Why? Starbucks' strategy can be seen as continually changing its focus so that consumers do not grow bored. The company has also systematically built brand association with products other than coffee (for example, ice cream) to remain highly visible to consumers. Starbucks has continually adapted, experimented, and regenerated its image and its focus to maintain its edge in the industry.

Clearly Defined Innovation Strategy Drives Change

The following case study of Procter & Gamble shows that success in innovation requires a clearly defined innovation strategy that matches the current realities in the company. P&G had great difficulty transforming from its conservative and cautious organization to one that could embrace more aggressive doses of innovation. They also learned that attempting to change everything at once is not a formula for success.

Case Study: Innovation Strategy at Procter & Gamble[12]

It was no secret that by the late 20th century, P&G had lost its originality. In its heyday (roughly, the 1960s through the 1980s), P&G was a market-leading innovator in technology and new products. It had led with competitively significant improvements across its flagship categories of detergents, dentifrices, and diapers—that is, Tide, Crest, and Pampers/Luvs. However, while the company had dominated many of its market categories in the mid-1990s, by the late 1990s things had grown moribund. Senior P&G management admitted that they had not had a breakthrough innovation since 1985, and the company's continued market dominance in the years ahead was in question.

P&G was still a formidable marketing machine, but the organization had become conservative and slow moving. It was dominated by what competitors called the proctoids—bureaucrats in suits.

In 1997, realizing these problems, there was a 'think-in' among a half-dozen senior executives. Their goal was to equip P&G to dominate the consumer goods industry in the 21st century as it had in the 20th.

During that meeting, they developed a Play-to-Win strategy. This strategy aimed at boldly reclaiming their industry leadership position. They planned to create a more nimble organization and to increase the speed and quality of innovation. They also focused on improving the speed of commercialization of new products. In addition, they wanted to move the company's focus to higher growth, higher margin businesses such as health care and personal care.

Senior management knew they needed to overcome many obstacles to attain their goals. P&G's new product commercialization process was painfully slow. Fiefdoms had developed, and these had frustrated previous attempts at significant collaboration and change. Finally, the working relationship between the brand managers and the technology development managers was often strained and painful.

Despite the obstacles, senior management was determined to succeed. They had the resolve and the resources—the best in the world, they thought—to make it happen. Durk Jager was named CEO. He led the charge with a zealous pursuit of change—he changed the organization, the innovation processes, and the priority of innovation. He began to change almost every facet of doing business in P&G. In fact, Jager tried to change too much too fast. Distracted by the changes and confused by the new way of doing business, many staff at P&G had trouble performing. Growth slowed, leading to three profit warnings in three months. Several new product launches flopped, and the share price slumped along with morale. Within 18 months, Jager was forced out. The inertial forces in the organization were able to eject him mainly because he failed to produce financial returns—a sin in any company, and especially in P&G.

With Jager's departure, many felt that the drive for change would end and comfortable "business-as-usual" status would return. They were wrong. P&G appointed A.G. Lafley as the new CEO. With 25 years' experience in P&G operations, he was well respected. He worked to restore balance in the organization. However, he surprised many when he embraced the innovation thrust. He said the "broad strategic thrust was the right one."

In contrast to Jager, he paid a lot of attention to operational details, and used a collaborative approach to gain buy-in. He reduced Jager's overly ambitious approach, scaling back aggressive goals, from around 8 percent annual growth. Perhaps more importantly, he "went through the innovation garden and pulled a lot of weeds." In other words, he maintained the drive for change (innovation), but focused on priorities rather than inundating the organization. The "weeds" included some new products and some line extensions. Lafley consolidated global business units from seven to four, and fine-tuned the relationship between them and the market development organization. He followed this by devolving decision-making power to the units. He restored focus on leading brands, and reminded everyone in P&G that the measure of success was not innovation per se, but the consumers.

> ### Lessons in Innovation from Procter & Gamble
>
> - Develop a play-to-win innovation strategy that maintains profitability while rejuvenating innovation processes and creating new and improved products (unless you gain approval not to do so, and even then it is risky)
> - Have clear improvement priorities for innovation and communicate them
> - Identify what will *not* change when you improve innovation
> - Know what type of leader will work in your culture

Do You Select an Innovation Strategy?

"Over time every business model and strategy go stale in our fast forward economy, strategies reach their sell-by date faster than ever."[13]

A company's innovation strategy needs adjustment over time. A number of internal and external factors affect the selection of the best innovation strategy (see Figure 3.1). These affect the choice of the innovation strategy and the shape of the portfolio—Play-to-Win or Play-Not-to-Lose.

Internal Factors	External Factors
• Technical capabilities • Organizational capabilities • Success of the current business model • Funding • Top management vision	• Capabilities in the external network • Industry structure • Competition • Rate of technological change

FIGURE 3.1 FACTORS TO CONSIDER IN CHOOSING AN INNOVATION STRATEGY.

Internal Factors

Internal factors include the following:

- **Technical capabilities**: The amount of technology innovation depends to a large extent upon the current capabilities that the company has internally or can access through its innovation network. A company that has traditionally competed on its marketing skills and incremental technology improvements will have a tough time suddenly including a semi-radical technology dimension to its strategy.

- **Organizational capabilities**: The ability to nurture innovation also depends on whether the company has the organizational capabilities to do it. Shifting to a more radical innovation approach will not happen if the organizational and management capabilities are not present.[14]

- **Success of the current business model**: The difficulty that successful companies have in changing has been repeatedly documented. It has been described as core capabilities becoming core rigidities or the inability to grow internal ventures in successful companies. The greater the success, the greater the potential resistance to change.[15]

- **Funding**: Having the necessary economic resources is an obvious, albeit sometimes forgotten, requirement. However, too much funding may be as dangerous as too little. For example, the startups of the late 1990s and early 2000 were funded with a lot more money than they actually needed. The result was waste—a misallocation of resources chasing business models that were inadequately tested. A less generous funding environment forces innovation teams to carefully plan and test the assumptions of the model before scaling up.

- **Top management vision**: The last internal factor is top management's vision. Management has a large set of options to position the company, and management talent has a very relevant role in selecting and evolving the company's innovation strategy.

External Factors

Internal factors are not the only formative forces; external forces can also shape the innovation strategy:

- **Capabilities in the external network:** Accessing relevant capabilities is crucial. Development of new technologies or business models usually requires collaboration with other organizations that have complementary resources; for this you need a network that reaches inside and outside of your organization (Chapter 4, "Organizing for Innovation: How to Structure a Company for Innovation," deals with the critical aspect of innovation networks in more detail). The ability to create sustainable alliances with these partners becomes important in deciding the innovation strategy going forward.

- **Industry structure**: The industry itself is a factor. A careful analysis of this structure points out where the main obstacles and opportunities for innovation reside. Understanding the dominant industry value chain, who dominates and why, and the structure of the barriers to entry are important inputs to the design of an innovation strategy.

- **Competition**: The quality and speed of innovation of your competitors as well as your innovations will determine the shape of the market in the years to come. While your organization may be well positioned in the current market, competitors could change or new competitors could enter, especially if the competitive dynamics change drastically.

Useful questions include: Do strategies of your competitors open any doors for you to adopt a PTW approach? Do their actions force you to consider a PTW approach? Does their approach make a PNTL strategy relatively attractive? Without a clear innovation leader present in the arena, is an outsider likely to jump into the game and change the rules?

- **Rate of technological change**: As the world becomes more technologically advanced, the life of a product will become shorter and shorter. When new advances outdate your product, it is important to identify the change approaching before your product goes stale.[16] For example, Panasonic realized that its traditional analog products were susceptible to replacement by a whole new class of digital technologies in which they were not well versed. Panasonic set up an incubator in Silicon Valley in 2000 to move up the learning curve quickly and gain access to emerging digital technologies.

Successful long-term products can sometimes blind companies to new trends that will ultimately be picked up by their competitors—the competitor's dilemma.

Updating and improving your company's innovation strategy must address these elements. However, no formula will yield the best strategy; each company is unique even though they may share the same competitive environment. What is considered a threatening situation for one company, resulting in a PNTL strategy, could be considered an opportunity for another.

Risk Management and Innovation Strategy

When deciding what innovation strategy to pursue, risk management comes quickly to mind. Assuming that no significant disruptions occur to the competitive arena, as we move up and right on the Innovation Matrix, the level of risk that we take is higher. If a disruption has occurred, incremental activities that do not address the disruption could be the most risky path. However, assuming a disruption has not occurred recently, adding a greater component of radical innovation increases the risk. Therefore, a Play-to-Win strategy is often riskier than a Play-Not-to-Lose strategy because it relies on a larger component of semi-radical and radical innovation.

For companies intent on leading and changing the industry, the center of gravity of investment will move more towards the semi-radical and radical innovation quadrants. These companies rely on being first and creating value through larger leaps of technology or business model innovation. However, in order not to increase their risk unnecessarily, these companies invest enough in incremental innovation to be fast followers and quickly assimilate the little steps that their more conservative players take. Apple's revolutionary combination of iPod and iTunes innovations was quickly followed by incremental improvements aimed at competitors' responses to the introductions. Apple quickly followed the iPod and iTunes with the introduction of iPod mini and the sharing of the iPod technology with Hewlett-Packard, effectively blunting lower-end copycat versions of the iPod and online music offerings from Sony and Microsoft.

The center of gravity and the breadth of the innovation portfolio determine the level and type of risk that needs to be managed during execution. Risk management processes, mostly portfolio design techniques, should minimize the risk exposure of a company (see Chapter 5, "Management Systems: Designing the Process of Innovation").

Innovation Strategy: The Case of the Pharmaceutical Industry

It is useful to consider a leading industry segment and the innovation challenges it faces. Consider the pharmaceutical industry—a field with powerful, innovative players.

Every week, several articles appear describing the difficulty that leading pharmaceutical companies have maintaining their new product pipeline. Historically, the companies have successfully innovated to fuel their significant growth. For example, in 2002 some 44 million people around the world lowered their cholesterol by taking daily doses of Lipitor. In its six years on the market, Lipitor has become the largest-selling pharmaceutical in history. Within the next few years, it could very well become the world's first drug to reap in $10 billion a year.[17]

However, for many companies it is getting harder to innovate successfully, and the flow of viable new products has been difficult to maintain. In the future, Pfizer will need a strong portfolio of novel drugs to produce double-digit growth on its mammoth revenue base. For that, the company is counting on a game plan that includes examining drug targets whose role in diseases is already well established, and then choosing new targets that closely resemble these. The company is taking aim at a family of 21 enzymes the company already understands well.[18]

In 2002, the leading pharmaceutical companies spent approximately $35 billion on R&D.[19] According to a study by Tufts University, it now costs $800 million to develop each new molecule, including the cost of capital. The pharmaceutical companies are spending huge amounts on R&D and new product commercialization. Despite the enormous investment, the results have been poor, as you can see from Table 3.1.

Table 3.1   Number of New Drugs Approved by the U.S. FDA[20]

Year	Priority New Drugs Approved (NDA)	Priority New Molecular Entities (NME)
2003	14	9
2002	11	7
2001	10	7
2000	20	9
1999	28	19
1998	25	16
1997	20	9
1996	29	18

The list of companies that have been delayed or outright rejected by the U.S. FDA includes most of the industry elite: Pfizer, GlaxoSmithKline, Merck, and AstraZeneca. The problem does not appear to be related to lack of effort in R&D or poor innovation processes. Pharmaceutical companies have developed fairly sophisticated R&D processes in response to the huge risks associated with new product development in the industry. Generally, the companies consider themselves leaders in both spending and the management processes related to innovation. The root cause of the problem appears to reside in the innovation strategy.

Attempts to Solve the Innovation Problem

Leading pharmaceutical companies have tried to remedy their lack of success in innovation by improving their R&D through two methods. The first method is the use of scale. Companies have acquired other companies, thereby combining their R&D pipelines to hopefully attain economies of scale. Combining pipelines is a short-term fix that yields a temporary improvement. However, it does not solve the cause of the problem, and very quickly the company finds itself facing the same issue they sought to remedy: how to keep the product development pipeline full of winners. The hope is that economies of scale will solve that problem long-term. While economies of scale have proven valuable in some areas such as selected types of manufacturing, the jury is still out on whether that approach will solve the dry product pipeline phenomenon.

The second approach used by major pharmaceutical companies to solve their problems has been to develop closer ties to biotech and genome organizations in order to get better information on new molecules with promise for use in new drugs. This approach was intended to provide greater probability of success in identifying new molecules, prior to the ultra-expensive and lengthy clinical trials. The trials cost millions of dollars and can take three to seven years to complete. In addition to being a drain on money and time, the success rate of clinical trials is fairly low. All too often a company finds that it has invested huge amounts of its innovation money, resources, and time only to find out that the drug cannot be commercialized due to problems in the clinical test phase. On average, only one in ten are approved.

Biotech appeared to offer a more analytical and insightful method to screen potential molecules before the clinical trials. However, there has not been universal success with this approach to date. It may be that the additional insights gained via genome and biotechnology research have actually *decreased* the probability of success of developing a new drug. Previously, the researcher knew of significantly fewer options for molecular intervention. Biotechnical and genome work to date has improved the clarity surrounding molecular interactions, but it has also multiplied the number of options for developing new molecules. With time, we may overcome this and begin to capitalize on the full value of biotechnical and genome research and development. However, at the moment, the effect is to "increase costs and timelines, not reduce them," according to David Beadle, analyst at UBS Warburg.[21]

Changing the Innovation Approach

From an outsider's perspective, it appears that some of the pharmaceutical companies could benefit by changing their mental model of innovation and pursuing alternate innovation approaches. In short, they need to solve their innovation problem by being innovative— looking in areas that they have historically avoided.

Pharmaceutical companies usually invest in developing technologies that will produce major new blockbuster drugs (drugs with massive market potential). The risks of developing these new blockbusters are huge, as was described previously, and the costs and resource commitments are massive. However, the potential gains for a successful breakthrough can be tremendous—in the billions of dollars, or more, of new revenue while the patent protection is in effect.

The lure of this huge payoff keeps the pharmaceutical companies investing using the same strategy. In the future, this approach may have diminishing returns or, worse, become a major liability. It looks like the pharmaceutical companies have an unbalanced innovation portfolio and are addicted to technology.

For example, generics have threatened GlaxoSmithKline's biggest sellers, including the antidepressant Paxil. To deal with this, GSK has introduced several modified versions of older drugs, including Wellbutrin XL and Paxil CR for depression and Augmentin XR, an antibiotic. It appears the company feels the success will lie in the potential big sellers it has ready for introduction in the next two years.[22]

It would be prudent for the pharmaceutical companies to consider shifting their strategy and some of their innovation efforts away from pursuing semi-radical technology changes to pursuing breakthroughs in new business models. This would be the equivalent of becoming "the Southwest Airlines" or "the Dell" of the pharmaceutical industry—creating a new business model to challenge the traditional players in ways that they cannot easily counter. Imagine, for example, using an open source approach for drug development, similar to the growing, powerful trend in the software industry.

Consider what would happen if a major pharmaceutical company invested and operated in the second- or third-tier markets for selected types of pharmaceuticals. While considerably smaller than the blockbuster markets, these markets could be very profitable and attractive. There are examples of companies successfully competing for smaller markets. For example, before ALZA was acquired by Johnson & Johnson in 2001, it created attractive profits in markets that had sales of $100 million per year or less. ALZA's innovation process was able to effectively develop and commercialize a range of successful products in those markets. However, after the acquisition, ALZA's business model changed. Since then, the company has pursued innovations in the blockbuster arena, avoiding the business model that led them to their historic success. Likewise, Genentech launched the first highly targeted therapy five years ago and is taking the concept to the next level by demonstrating that a big-league drug maker can achieve heady growth without a heavy focus on blockbusters.[23]

Alternatively, consider a pharmaceutical company that consciously creates a more balanced portfolio, including the development of new business models. The company would invest in changes to its business model to create competitive advantage to complement its technology investments. The business model innovations would allow it to serve markets better than its traditional competitors who, bound by their historical business models, could not compete. The company would also maximize the return on its innovation investment.

Innovation options that could be considered include:

- Increased levels of service

- Change in the supply chain or a similar operational breakthrough

- Closer, better connections to the payers

These are some of the ways that a company can explore alternate innovation approaches and refresh their strategy. Of course there are others, including returning to the six key levers for innovation and assessing which of these could be best used to achieve powerful and properly tailored innovations.

CEO's Action Plan

- Identify the type of innovation strategy that fits your company best given the business strategy, competitive environment and innovation competencies:
  - Play-to-Win
  - Play-Not-to-Lose
- Define the balance of the innovation portfolio you want to see to support the strategy:
  - Mix of business model and technology change
  - Mix of incremental, semi-radical, and radical innovations

- Specify how much innovation you want in support of the business strategy.
- Define priorities and trade offs for innovation investments.
- Clearly communicate this to management team and innovation leaders.
- Repeat it until they get it—it may take several times to sink in.
- Conduct diagnostics to assess how well you are doing.
- Ensure that metrics and rewards are supporting the strategy implementation.

Strategy and the Innovation Rules

Defining the innovation strategy and the resulting portfolio characteristics (Play-to-Win or Play-Not-to-Lose and the associated mix of incremental, semi-radical, and radical innovations) are the first major responsibility of a company's leadership. Forming the strategy in the context of the Innovation Model and defining the balance of the portfolio is the responsibility of the leaders. It defines the direction and magnitude of the company's innovation efforts, it sends clear signals to the company regarding the importance of innovation, and it facilitates execution.

Steve Jobs has been the leading force in defining Apple's innovation strategy and innovation portfolio. He said, "The way we look at it is we don't want to get into something unless we can invent or control a core technology. The core technology (of consumer devices) is going to be software. We're pretty clever at hardware . . . but the competitive barrier will be software. The more consumer products evolve the more they will look like software in boxes."[24] You can argue with his logic or his conclusions regarding the competitive role of software in consumer goods, but his vision is clear and his message to his team at Apple is unambiguous: Fill the portfolio with defensible software innovations. Blend in other innovations but put your focus on innovative software.

Steve Jobs stepped up to the strategy and portfolio leadership requirements by answering three of the most important questions:

- How much innovation does my company need?

- What are the areas that I should focus the innovation?

- What portfolio of innovation types do I need? How much business model innovation? How much technology innovation? What mix of incremental, semi-radical, and radical innovations?

Senior management needs to identify its core competencies and innovate around them. Apple, Wal-Mart, P&G, Dell, GE, and Toyota have all focused their innovation of business models and technology on their core competencies. Not all companies need large amounts of innovations, but they will need them aligned with their competencies and strategy. Without a clearly defined and communicated innovation model and strategy and characterization of the type of innovation portfolio that is required, employees cannot execute well.

ORGANIZING FOR INNOVATION: HOW TO STRUCTURE A COMPANY FOR INNOVATION

4

Organizing for Innovation

Organizing for innovation continues to be a challenge for many companies. It is not enough to craft a strategy or to build innovation processes; you need to build and embed innovation into the overall organization. Successful innovation requires choosing, building, and preparing the right organization and the right people for executing and scaling the innovation.[1]

Many large firms have struggled and, by their own description, failed in the attempt to integrate innovation into their organization. They often find that the organizational components of innovation are rejected or marginalized by the mainstream organization.

Organizational antibodies are released that kill off the innovations
and often the structures, resources, and processes responsible for
the innovation. Because of this, some believe that it is not possible
or at least much harder to innovate successfully within the structure
of a large, established organization.[2]

Developing an Internal Marketplace for Innovation

One of the main approaches to ensure that innovation is successful in
your organization is to develop an internal marketplace where the
ideas and functions of innovation can flourish in a supply-and-
demand environment. In this innovation market, the true commercial
value of every idea is reflected in the management attention and
funding it receives. Truly valuable innovations are funded and
advanced to commercial realities, no matter how threatening they
may be to the existing businesses or how difficult they may appear.

For example, Bank of America, like other large U.S. banks, faced
a new challenge in the 21st century: With the opportunities for further acquisitions narrowing, it would need to find a way to grow
organically by attracting more customers and fulfilling a greater share
of their banking needs. It created the Innovation & Development
(I&D) Team, a corporate unit charged with spearheading product
and service development at the bank. The team's immediate goal was
to pioneer new services and service-delivery techniques that would
strengthen the bank's relationships with branch customers while also
achieving a high degree of efficiency in transactions. Bank of America
decided to take an unprecedented step in the conservative banking
industry: It would create an "innovation market" within the bank's
existing branches, whereby it used its locations to launch various

experiments without redesigning its branches. This approach provided a true test of the potential market value of innovations.[3]

Critical to creating such a marketplace is balancing creativity and value capture so that both thrive. Ultimately, this internal marketplace for innovation and a balance of creative and value capture may be more important than the organizational design you select. An entrepreneurial drive for innovation brought about and supported by strong internal market forces can overcome many organizational barriers.

Balancing Creativity and Value Creation

In a company where innovation thrives, you can be sure that both the creative and value capture (commercial) functions are operating at full tilt. Management—and the entire organization—recognize that successful innovation requires a *balance* of the creativity and commercialization processes (see Figure 4.1). Typically, these companies have developed their own internal marketplaces that weigh, select, and prioritize innovations for their creativity and inherent commercial value or worth to the company. CEMEX created an internal marketplace for innovation where ideas are developed, selected, and funded in an environment that honestly values the worth of an idea. The market is overseen by senior management to ensure that organizational antibodies and other forces do not skew the market's perception of potential innovations or that funding for commercialization is not out of line with the true potential of the innovation. Inside the company, innovators actually "sell" to management their creative ideas—embodied in R&D projects, product-development collaborations, new business models, and strategic alliances. The internal market works like this: If management likes what they see, they fund the projects based on their perceived commercial value to the company. Otherwise, they hold back on funding.

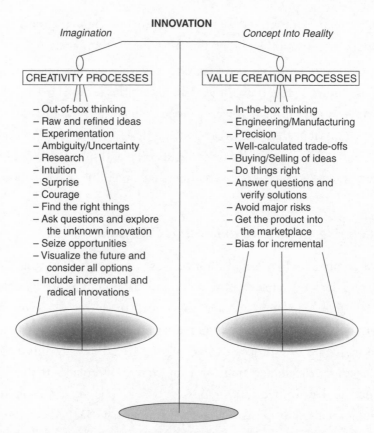

FIGURE 4.1   INNOVATION REQUIRES A BALANCE BETWEEN CREATIVITY AND COMMERCIALIZATION.[4]

Case Study: How the Marx Brothers Balanced Creativity and Value Creation[5]

Sometimes innovation comes from funny places. For insight into how to balance creativity with the practicalities of commercialization, we turn to a somewhat surprising source: the Marx Brothers, one of the world's most famous comedy teams. Each one of the Marx Brothers' acts was developed in small pieces in the creative marketplace.

"It was developed by groping, trying out, grabbing at any material that offered itself. I was just kidding around one day and started to walk funny," Groucho Marx once wrote. "The audience liked it, so I kept it in. I would try a line and leave it in too if it got a laugh. If it didn't, I'd take it out and put in another. Pretty soon I had a character."[6]

Groucho's performances—honed to perfection in rehearsal, retakes, and practice (the commercialization process)—are remarkable in that they came from years of trial and error. This was comedy shaped in both the creative and commercial marketplaces of theater and movies. Some companies say they create and experiment either to raise the right questions or to answer questions. Groucho had a different perspective. He experimented to survive, a lesson some companies may not fully appreciate.

Later in their career, when studio filmmaking threatened to deaden their experimentation and thus their survival, the Marx Brothers took the film script for *A Day at the Races* on the road. They took it to the creative marketplace in order to get it right for commercialization—otherwise the movie could flop. They knew that the studios were focused on commercialization, not creativity.

Groucho is recognized as a genius of comedy. He was also a genius because he knew when to go to the creative markets to test his ideas and when to take those ideas into commercialization. Through the course of his career, he practiced this creative/commercial balance.

The Balance Changes as the Organization Matures

In the business world, there's a natural evolution in the relationship between creativity and value capture as companies grow from emerging to mature. In the earliest stages, a company is focused on creating new, improved products or services. At that point, the attention to maximizing the value capture (such as faster, better, cheaper delivery) is relatively low. This is the problem with some startup companies. In the later stages of growth and maturity, the singular drive to be creative usually decreases and is replaced by a shift to increasing value capture—improving the process of executing, delivering, and selling its portfolio of products and services (Figure 4.2):

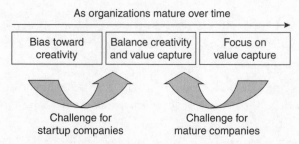

FIGURE 4.2 THE CHALLENGES OF BALANCING CREATIVITY AND VALUE CAPTURE.

- **Bias toward the creative**. Emerging companies typically place a higher premium on creativity. Their internal markets are biased toward the radical ideas and breakthroughs that can come from the creative process and then be used to leverage the young company into a competitive advantage. Many startups abound in creativity and radical new business models. For example, E*Trade was a radical new approach to the traditional financial trading business that offered a fresh new way to view how small investors can enter financial markets—with significant changes in both the traditional technology and the business model.

- **Balancing creative and value capture**. As companies grow and mature, they learn to balance their creative processes with solid commercialization skills. It's a question of survival. Radical new business approaches are not enough to make a company succeed. It also needs excellence in execution and the ability to commercialize innovations that flow from the creative processes. At first, B2C (business to consumer) Internet retail outlets, such as eToys and Amazon.com, experienced extremely high multiples because of the vitality of their breakthrough creative outputs. But Wall Street and some clicks-and-mortar competitors sent clear signals that commensurate commercial capabilities were also needed. Likewise, TiVo created a new market category with its digital video recorder but faces increasing pressure to demonstrate that it can strengthen its value capture in an increasingly competitive arena. For TiVo and many other companies that exploded onto the scene with innovative ideas, transitioning to a greater focus on value capture is not just an evolutionary next step but a matter of survival. Competitors with strong supply chains and customer connections have moved into the space created by the innovator and may take it over.

• **Focus on the value capture** As companies continue to mature, the emphasis on commercialization surpasses the attention to creative markets. The management mantra becomes "profitability, asset utilization, capital management, efficiency, benchmarking"—all of which place more value on the value capture process. Creativity, especially radical creativity, has decreasing value or even negative value as the company settles into maturity and the fight for market share. Traditional grocery companies fell in this category, and Webvan challenged their execution-oriented, value-capture mentality by introducing a radical new approach. Interestingly, Webvan failed commercially but its business model and technology innovation has been adopted by some of the traditional grocery companies such as Safeway, providing the traditional companies with an infusion of creativity that they did not receive from their internal marketplace.

Mature companies, with strong commercial yet weak creative functions, measure innovation in terms of discounted cash flow (DCF), return on investment (ROI), hurdle rates, and payback—none of which support creative activities. In many of these companies, incremental innovation is the norm. Radical and breakthrough ideas disappear and so do the people responsible for them. Having the adequate measurement systems is key to avoid this bias, a topic covered in depth in Chapter 6, "Illuminating the Pathway: How to

Measure Innovation." For example, an executive at a major auto company that was launching an innovation initiative listened carefully to the description of personality types he would need to hire to help rejuvenate the creative internal markets and offset the existing commercialization bias. His response was, "We fired all those kinds of people years ago." He was right. In the drive for excellence in value capture, his organization had removed the entire creative function.

Some potentially successful innovations in mature organizations fail because they never find a marketplace inside the company that recognizes and supports their inherent value. How many times have we heard stories about great products or business concepts that failed to get internal buy-in, only to have the innovators spin out and create a successful company? Far too often. For example, Conner Peripherals spun out of Seagate Technology and subsequently commercialized a new, smaller (3.5 inch) disc drive technology that became the major new technology in the disc drive markets. Seagate management had looked at that same technology but did not see its potential value and did not fund commercialization. Likewise, in the 1980s, Boston Consulting Group (BCG) spun out of Arthur D. Little (ADL) and brought its special brand of portfolio management to consulting. ADL did not see the value in the BCG's business model and BCG could not see letting the opportunity pass. During the next 20 years, BCG grew and eventually surpassed ADL in size. If you look for failed innovation initiatives, you will often find innovation deals that were never consummated because the internal markets were limited. The problem is rarely that a company is risk averse, blind, or resource-constrained. Instead, it usually rests in the lack of a properly functioning internal marketplace for certain types of innovation.

These symptoms illustrate a company whose internal marketplace values incremental changes to the existing products, processes, and business models—rather than radical change, breakthrough technologies, or new business approaches.

Signs That Your Creativity Is Blocked by Organizational Antibodies

Symptoms of an anemic internal market for creativity include the following:

- **The current portfolio of innovation projects consists almost entirely of incremental innovations**. This condition is called *rampant incrementalism*. One consumer-goods company was so mired in rampant incrementalism that its entire portfolio consisted of projects that would be completed in less than a year, yielding only marginal improvements in competitive advantage. That company's non-incremental improvements were only achieved through acquisitions and mergers.

- **Innovation metrics use only capital-return tools such as ROI and DCF**. Moreover, appropriate measures don't exist to evaluate creativity or potential projects in which there is uncertainty and ambiguity (see Chapter 6 for a more in-depth discussion of appropriate innovation metrics).

- **Funding for innovation is available only once a year, rather than in regular intervals or whenever great ideas present themselves**. In the world of venture capital, many sources of capital exist. And funding occurs based on merit, not on a calendar schedule. Without that availability, creativity is squashed.

- **Innovation is measured on efficiency rather than on the value of the innovation portfolio**. Making mediocre or small ideas happen faster and more efficiently is insane. The goal is value creation for the company and the performance metrics should reward that type of behavior (Chapters 6, "Illuminating the Pathway: How to Measure Innovation," and 7, "Rewarding Innovation: How to Design Incentives to Support Innovation," deal with metrics and rewards).

- **Managers respond to good new ideas with a shrug and a sense of complacency**. Meanwhile, the innovators flee the company to launch their businesses elsewhere. This story has been replayed at major companies around the world. The fact is that big companies are one of the best sources of innovative ideas— but all too often these come to fruition outside the company.

- **Managers criticize and undermine innovators rather than serve as sounding boards, role models, and sponsors.** In a major materials company, the senior manager reviewing innovation projects could not break the habit of harshly criticizing candidate projects. He single-handedly undermined the company's innovation portfolio.

The challenge for the mature company is to rejuvenate creativity without endangering its value capture capabilities. Consider the example of a premier Japanese automaker, highly focused on value capture that wanted to stimulate the internal marketplace for creativity. The company introduced a "capitalist perspective" to the product-development function in order to instill higher levels of risk-taking and creativity. Senior management created new structures and processes in the product design group to change traditional behavior and achieve a better balance between creativity and value capture.

Research Bite: Moving Beyond Incremental Innovation to a Balanced Portfolio

One of the companies in our field research was a large energy company with more than $90 million R&D budget. In the past, the company had taken an unstructured approach to radical innovation—with the assumption that freedom led to creativity and innovation. The result was the generation of lots of ideas that died for lack of acceptance inside the organization. The pursuit of radical innovations was perceived as a waste of time and money, and the backlash against this apparent waste resulted in an almost exclusive focus on incremental innovation. However, this reliance on incremental innovation did not produce a strong flow of innovations that supported the business objectives. Subsequently, the senior management team worked to achieve a more balanced innovation portfolio—containing all three types of innovation. They realized that unstructured innovation or incremental innovation could not yield the results they required. Management put in place mechanisms to achieve this balance including:

1. Grant permission to the organization to bring up ideas, with the promise that they won't be immediately killed but carefully evaluated.

2. Have a mechanism outside the current budgeting process to identify promising ideas and create the space to develop them—financial models such as discounted cash flows are biased towards incremental innovation that ends up crowding out semi-radical and radical innovation.

3. Develop new platforms as the basis to expand the company's capabilities.

4. Open up the company to external networks to leverage resources. Universities are a main target for these alliances to explore new technology platforms. But, customers also are a source of fruitful alliances.

5. Create incubators that will manage these networks, examine commercial possibilities, and link them with existing businesses or design an exit strategy.

6. Conduct careful scanning of competitive patents.

7. Conduct a periodic reassessment of budget allocation with participation at various levels of the organization.

8. Design new measurement and reward systems.

Five Steps to Balancing Creative and Commercial Markets

The best process for balancing creative and commercial processes includes five steps:

1. **Develop innovation platforms for the different types of innovation you want to pursue.** These innovation platforms act as organizing principles for innovation. (Innovation platforms are very important, and a deeper description is provided later in this chapter.) Innovation platforms cut across the business unit silos and provide an honest perspective on the value of the innovations, rather than one limited

by the perception of a single business unit. For example, Canon used innovation platforms to leverage its optics, electronics, and precision manufacturing capabilities in its existing organization to launch into business equipment. The outcome was an efficient use of resources and competencies for existing and new businesses.

2. **Create portfolios of projects in each platform.** Each project needs to be reviewed to ensure that the creative and commercialization markets are aligned and balanced. A portfolio that is overly rich in incremental projects signals an anemic market for creative ideas. A portfolio that has an overabundance of radical and breakthrough innovations signals a hyperactive creative process and an internal market that discounts commercialization.

3. **Form internal and external partnerships and networks.** Internal and external partners are essential to success. Today, leading companies such as Cisco and Millennium Pharmaceuticals work aggressively to complement their internal talent with their partners' capabilities.

4. **Ensure that markets for creativity and commercialization are open and transparent.** The last thing you want to do is create a closed internal market for either creativity or commercialization. Closed markets create an air of mistrust and can hide inefficiencies and inequities. Create semiannual, innovation events that provide visibility and total transparency. Make the events open to everybody, and make sure they're highly publicized. Send the signal that value creation via innovation is a vital part of the culture. Google has created a culture where innovation is the norm and where open, full exploration of potential innovations is valued and expected by the employees.

5. **Guard against organizational antibodies that may limit or destroy your rejuvenated creative markets and processes.** High-level senior executives should be part of an Innovation Board in charge of rejuvenating the creative market. Such visible support is necessary to offset the inherent resistance to change in the established commercialization market. Otherwise, many in the organization will view a revitalized creative market as folly or a waste of resources.

Rejuvenating the innovation process requires a significant change in mindset, requires support from top management, and a reallocation of resources. But if you approach the task with the same mindset as Groucho Marx did, you will find that innovation results from the perfect balance of the creative and value capture processes. Remember that how you innovate determines what you innovate.

Are Organizational Antibodies Blocking Innovation?

- The company suffers from the Not-Invented-Here syndrome.
- "We have always done it this way" mentality dominates decision-making.
- Failures are socially punished.
- The power structure supports status quo and fights change.
- Managers see supporting innovation as reducing efficiency and as a waste.
- Measures and rewards support a focus on short-term efficiency.
- Innovations are funded based almost entirely on financial metrics.
- There is a lack of tangible commitment to innovation from top management.
- Innovators are ignored or rewarded unfairly.
- Ideas have nowhere to go.
- Innovation is treated as discrete events rather than as a day-to-day activity.

Outsourcing Innovation

At the most basic level, the choice of structure—how to organize yourself and your people—for innovation is a choice between internal and external options.[7] Options for internal structures for innovation include funding traditional R&D departments, setting up centers of excellence, creating separate business units for innovation, and using incubators.[8] External structures for innovation are based on outsourcing to different partners—suppliers, customers and others.[9] Different structures are appropriate for different types of innovation.

Many companies are asking, "Should we outsource our innovation?" That is the wrong question. The right questions are: In which parts of our innovation should we partner? How much should we rely on partners and how much should we take on ourselves?

Innovation is too important to outsource completely. Partial outsourcing, better termed *partnering*, is a solid, proven approach to enhancing innovation (see the following section, "Making Good Use of Your Partners").

Case Study: Outsourcing at Compaq (Before It Became HP)

Compaq faced a difficult decision in the 1990s regarding chip innovation in the server arena. What chip development activities should be kept in-house, which should be co-developed with partners, and which should be outsourced? The server business had historically been a major source of profit for Compaq, and the chips were considered key to success. But the industry dynamics were changing, and profits in many product areas were thinning. Dell had started using its Internet sales tool as a new business model in the server arena, and competitors including Sun Microsystems, IBM, and Compaq were feeling the effects and market shares, and profits were shrinking.

Compaq apparently identified the chip technologies that were the key sources of competitive advantage and those that they needed but were non-core. It focused development efforts on the core technologies and relied on partners to varying degrees to support them in the non-core areas. This strategy worked for a while, but the competitive forces increased. Compaq eventually ceased chip development and relied on Intel to provide the successive generations of chips for servers. Compaq focused on the servers and customer services as a source of competitive advantage, and relied on its partnership with Intel for chip development.

Partnering is a standard and potentially valuable part of the innovation toolbox. Reaching outside for additional resources, ideas, expertise, and different perspectives can be highly valuable when combined with the internal ability to understand and use what your partners bring.

There are many examples of effective open innovation partnering structures,[10] of which the following are a few:

- Intel has opened four small labs, or "lablets," nearby university campuses in the U.S. and Great Britain to promote an exchange of ideas between the lablet and the university. Innovative ideas are expected to come out of the newly opened lablets. Eli Lilly recently launched an online knowledge broker called InnoCentive,[11] where it and other firms post R&D problems and solicit solutions from companies and individuals worldwide.

- Schlumberger sells innovative ideas in the area of oil field services to both customers and competitors. Ideas include ways to reduce drilling costs and increase data on reservoir characteristics collected during drilling. The company once sold its innovations only to customers, but selling to competitors as well now allows it to profit from its ideas in any oil well anywhere in the world.

- IBM uses excess capacity in its semiconductor fabrication facilities to manufacture chips for other companies. Recently, the company also started offering design services and now designs and manufactures some competitors' chips.

- Dreyer's Grand Ice Cream sells the use of its logistics and distribution system to competitor Ben & Jerry's. The system tracks retailers' inventory at the checkout scanner, automatically places restocking orders, and bills the retailer. Sharing its system with another supplier spreads Dryer's overhead costs across more volume and encourages additional retailers to adopt the Dryer's system because of its higher volume.

- Procter & Gamble thrived for years relying on the 7,500 employees in its R&D group to crank out new products. But as the pace of innovation elsewhere increased, P&G faltered. To fix this problem, CEO Alan Lafley has decreed that half of the company's ideas must come from outside, up from about 10 percent when he took over in 2000.[12]

There was a time when companies relied primarily on internal resources for innovation. The technology giants of the last century— DuPont, General Electric, IBM, Xerox, AT&T—relied on an innovation recipe that consisted of internal laboratories, brilliant minds, and ultimately the flow of great ideas and successful innovations. But from the 1980s onward, the companies that have flourished— including Cisco, Intel and Nokia—have not relied on the internal lab and increasingly used and acquired outside resources for their innovation. Ironically, one of the biggest companies, Microsoft, has developed an internal research lab of scale and power to rival the labs of yesteryear.[13]

No one has ever doubted the power of assembling bright people in an organization and encouraging them to do great things. However, the downside risk is that the inside organization will be too inward-looking, discount the innovations and mental models of others, and lose the cutting edge. Microsoft's innovation strategy must address this risk at some point. Even with a large, internal innovation capability, they cannot go to market and hold a dominant position without the meaningful collaboration of many other organizations.

Making Good Use of Your Partners

Developing, maintaining, and using strong relationships with partner organizations can be a key competitive advantage in innovation for your company. For example, instead of the usual R&D unit testing new products, try outsourcing innovation testing to your customers. Microsoft often avoids partnering but has relied heavily on this technique in the past,[14] using its customers to beta-test its new products.

Universities such as Stanford are potentially valuable partners because they are prolific sources of new technologies and business models with sizeable market opportunities. But, in contrast to for-profit companies, universities do not consider commercializing their ideas directly. Rather, their way to capture some of the value of these ideas is through licensing agreements in which they sell or license the technologies for other parties to bring to market. The Office of Technology Licensing at Stanford University fulfills this role. This office helps researchers find partners that are interested in transforming the ideas into value. Partners can also include venture capitalists for more radical technologies.

Open-source software development projects—Internet-based communities of software developers who voluntarily collaborate in order to develop software that they or their organizations need—have become an important economic and cultural phenomenon, and they exemplify the changing role of partnerships in innovation. SourceForge.net, a major infrastructure provider and repository for such projects, lists more than 10,000 of them and more than 30,000 registered users. The digital software products emanating from such projects are commercially attractive and widely used in business and government (by IBM, NASA, and others). Because such products are deemed a public good, the open-source movement's unique development practices are challenging the traditional views of how innovation should work.[15]

Creating and maintaining truly effective partnerships is one of the least well-understood aspects of innovation. The problem is a lack of structure in framing and selecting the type of partnership required.

The truth is that there are many types of partnerships, and a company should be very careful in selecting the one that fits the needs.

Each type of partnership requires different goals, performance metrics and incentives, conflict resolution, and governance. It also requires recognition that the partnering organizations are different (for example, culture, business objectives, performance metrics, and incentives) and that getting them to work together cohesively will take some planning and effort. Partnerships deliver in direct proportion to the adequacy of their structure and management.

Research Bite: International Attitudes Towards Partners

We explored the different attitudes vis-à-vis partners across the globe from our survey of international R&D managers. Specifically, we asked managers to rate two countervailing aspects of their partnerships: the ability to protect core competencies and IP against appropriation from partners, and the ability to learn through the partnerships. Asian managers report the highest perceived learning as well as level of protection. European firms are at the opposite end of the spectrum with low perceived ability to protect and low learning and, accordingly, lower involvement. Managers of U.S. companies showed almost as high levels of protection as the Asians but learning levels near the Europeans.

Integrating Innovation Within the Organization

Having certain innovation functions outsourced, such as ideation, may speed up the innovation process. *Ideation* is the development of good ideas that can be turned into innovations. Mattel, Wal-Mart, and other toy manufacturers and retailers use idea brokers like Big Idea Group[16] to scout on their behalf for new ideas. Big Idea Group takes submissions and refines and pitches the more promising ones. Big Idea Group has placed a number of toys with companies like Basic Fun and Gamewright.[17] The outsourced company may create ideas for innovations, but the original organization still needs committed resources within its innovation group to take the ideas to the next level.[18] One example of this is Chevron, which uses "Process Masters"—employees with specialist skills and excellent knowledge of various parts of the organization. These Process Masters meet in small groups and are responsible for identifying and transferring internal innovations around the company. They also track external capabilities and innovations that are used for internal solutions, thus utilizing the best of both worlds.

Case Study: Design of CEMEX's Innovation Structure[19, 20]

CEMEX, one of the largest cement manufacturers in the world, has developed an innovation organization and processes that provide the right atmosphere for sustained innovation. Senior management at CEMEX realized that to remain the most profitable of the global cement companies, it needed to embed innovation into its organization. But that was easier said than done. CEMEX had a deep cultural bias against anything that distracted it from operations and profitability.

CEMEX focused on developing the following:

- Core innovation organization with a staff of nine and a $3.5 million budget.

- Standing Innovation Board (comprised of seven members).

- Innovation Platform teams (five total) that explore opportunities for innovation. Teams have 10-12 members from across the company, and work together for three to four months.

- Processes include:

  - Intensive training for platform team members.

  - Identification of two or three macro opportunities, developments of hundreds of possible investments, and selection of two or three investment proposals for each macro opportunity.

  - Investment decisions made by Innovation Investment Board.

  - Return of most approved investments to operating units as projects.

  - Tracking of projects across company by Innovation Board.

The Value of Networks and Innovation Platforms

Many CEOs ponder how to organize innovation within their company. Creating and maintaining the correct structure is admittedly hard to do. Even companies that have achieved truly creative innovation centers have seen them falter and even collapse at some point; consider the ups and downs of Apple Computer and Lucent, just to name two. However, there are lessons to be learned from the companies that have been successful. The key is to throw away a major misconception and to adopt a new organizing principle. This does not preclude leaving room for individuals or teams to spend limited time in self-directed exploration like 3M or Google.

The major misconception is that innovation is present everywhere in the company, and that all employees, partners, and customers should be part of the process all of the time. Innovation does not exist evenly everywhere in the company; rather, it exists in hugely disproportionate quantities across the organization at any given time. Some individuals are very good at it, and some are not. Innovation is not a quality initiative where it is necessary to make it everyone's job all of the time in order to be successful. Those who are creative and good at innovation will become frustrated at a process that dilutes their efforts with largely untalented people. Also, innovation should happen preferentially in those areas that have been targeted in the strategy. It would be unwise and wasteful to encourage people to spend time on innovation in areas where they do not intend to follow through with investments because the strategic and financial returns would be unacceptable.

A key step to creating or maintaining innovation in an organization is to discard the idea that absolutely everyone must be involved all of the time. In some organizations, including everybody in the process may overwhelm the process and could be counter-productive. Let everyone have access to and participate in the innovation process, but make it clear that you do not expect everyone to participate equally all of the time.

That being said, it is not enough to avoid creating the "Peoples Republic of Innovation," where all are equal. In addition, it is not enough to simply hire and sponsor creative individuals. To create sustained innovation excellence in your organization, it is necessary to create innovation platforms and networks of individuals within them where the selected innovative individuals can share with each other, be managed, and grow. Overseeing the building of innovation platforms and networks to manage the resident talent and to let the best emerge and grow is the management's responsibility.

Many companies use innovation platforms, including Johnson & Johnson and Alcoa. Innovation platforms provide the organizational basis for innovation—from incremental to radical—by focusing resources on innovation and providing processes for managing innovation. *Innovation platforms* are organizational units of networks nestled within a company that direct resources *toward* specific areas of innovation. Resources dedicated to operations cannot break away from those duties to perform innovative functions. And resources dedicated to innovation—cut off from the realities of operations, markets, and finances—cannot efficiently produce valuable innovations. Platforms allow the organization to share in both operations and innovation, and networks provide the channels for communication and collaboration. Networking is widely used inside of J&J, in part because it is highly decentralized. ALZA has learned since its acquisition to act as a networker inside of J&J, leveraging its knowledge and expertise of drug delivery platforms to create innovations with low transaction costs. And because it produces more value for less cost than other approaches, Hewlett-Packard uses extensive networking across its selected innovation platforms.

Innovation platforms include:

- Broad areas of innovation (such as surface cleaning in one leading consumer goods company, improved wound treatment in a medical products company) that direct the platform's activities.
  - *Both* business model and technological change
  - A portfolio of incremental, semi-radical and radical innovations

- Networks of people inside and outside of the organization who can effectively contribute to different aspects of innovation—idea creation, selection, development, and implementation—that span the range of business and technical challenges. They also preserve the intellectual capital and knowledge in the company during downsizing.[21]

- Metrics and rewards that:
  - Focus the resources on the potentially valuable areas of innovation and consistent with the innovation strategy.
  - Capture the innovation performance of the organization and highlight the gaps and areas for improvement.
  - Encourage the desired behavior and results and mitigate organizational antibodies.

- Management systems that promote and use learning and change to improve all aspects of innovation—strategy, processes, organization, and resources.

Figure 4.3 depicts innovation platforms that span the six business units of an organization. Innovation platforms, such as surface care and cleaning, span three business units and support each. These platforms contain innovation efforts, incremental through radical, that can be applied to all three business units. This limits redundancy between the business units and also provides a portfolio of innovations that the business units can draw upon as needed to meet their business objectives. Some innovation platforms, such as odor control and disinfectancy, span more business units. These innovation platforms are common to a greater number of business units but supply the same efficiency and portfolio efficacy of the smaller platforms.

Ford Motor Co.'s iTek Center in Dearborn, Michigan, an $80 million investment, brings together teams from the business, design, and technology divisions to work on initiatives. Ford's goal is to plan, develop, and test a process or a technology application within a 90-day window.

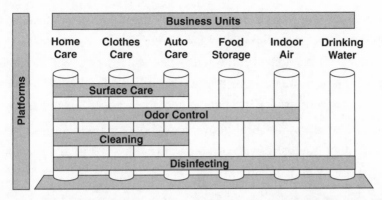

FIGURE 4.3 EXAMPLE OF INNOVATION PLATFORMS AND BUSINESS UNITS.[22]

Funding for innovation should vary based on who stands to benefit. At GE, individual businesses contract with the R&D center on enabling technology projects that let the businesses develop their next-generation products and services. That's about 60 percent of the budget. Thirty percent comes from CEO Jeffrey Immelt for longer-range technologies—projects that are five to ten years out. The final 10 percent comes from external contracts, typically with the U.S. government. For something like nanotechnology (which is a platform that has the potential to impact four or five businesses at GE but takes long-term, high-risk research to realize that potential), funding comes directly from Immelt's office rather than from the individual CEOs of each of GE's 13 business units.[23]

In addition to innovation platforms, innovation can be organized internally using alternative organizational models.

The Corporate Venture Capital Model

Corporate Venture Capital (CVC) is a model of innovation inspired by external venture capital firms. It is a useful model to consider for promoting radical innovation in your organization while not hindering incremental innovation. The basic premise of CVC is that to promote the development of commercially viable innovations (especially radical innovations) within your organization, you need to have a mechanism in place that evaluates potential innovations in the same way that an external venture capital firm would.[24] ChevronTexaco's venture capital group invests in innovations that are outside of the domain of traditional energy company R&D but has potential value to ChevronTexaco.

CVC works as a hybrid between an independent venture capital firm and an incubator within the organization (see Figure 4.4 for a description of an incubator).

Incubators have been formed by many entities to bridge the gaps between technology, business operations, and funding. Their primary purpose is to achieve "acceleration" of value creation through one or more mechanisms.

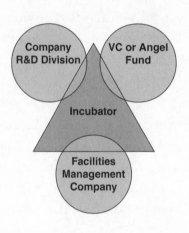

Value Creation Mechanisms

• Information and insight in leading-edge external technologies

• Acceleration to market of internal technologies

• Enhanced growth of user market

• Enhanced deal stream

• Network building

• Value Creation through equity stake

• Enhanced image with investors and employees

FIGURE 4.4   OVERVIEW OF AN INCUBATOR STRUCTURE.[25]

Typically, a venture capital team within an organization will be made up of a number of senior executives from different areas (technology, marketing, operations) and a select few external partners. The external members might be key suppliers or customers, or possibly even a venture capitalist with whom the organization has developed a relationship in order to benefit from their experience and expertise. The venture capital structure receives the radical ideas, selects those with the most potential, funds them, and then sells them. In fact, a venture capital arm within an organization acts as a radical innovation hub. An option is to have the CVC division scouting the company for ideas. This alternative requires a very well-networked division so that people with ideas feel comfortable talking to them. It is like an internal VC that funds ideas that look promising.

Case Study: Incubators in the Large Organization

A leading lubrication additives business unit of a large company developed an incubator to grow new ideas into robust opportunities. Historically, non-traditional or non-incremental ideas had a tough time getting approval and funding. Incremental improvements in the traditional business areas had fairly clear ROI and well-understood markets. In comparison, semi-radical or radical ideas were harder to measure and understand in the usual context. Therefore, these seldom competed effectively for funding and management support. Management felt that they were throwing out good ideas that might contribute to their growth and profitability, but they did not know how to remedy the situation. The solution was an incubator where the semi-radical ideas could be grown and tested in low-cost ways. Then the best of the ideas could be presented for management consideration with a much stronger story than previously. This provided management with a reasonable basis for comparison to incremental ideas.

The Ambidextrous Organization

The theory of the "Ambidextrous Organization" suggests that an organization promotes innovation and operations within its architecture through multiple groups handling different types of innovation and operations projects, thus promoting different cultures and processes for innovation needs.[26] In this way, radical innovators are kept separate from the traditionalists who run the core businesses. IBM used this approach to grow its new consulting businesses while maintaining the strength in its heritage hardware businesses. This type of separate structure is successful because different types of innovation require different types of systems, resources, and culture.[27] However, there are concerns about the Ambidextrous Organization. Is it viable? Or do organizations need that level of separation to be successful?

Some organizations have tried to insulate the innovation function by setting up a completely separate business unit. They establish different rules and culture for this business unit to foster creativity and innovation. Whether the company uses a corporate venture capital model or simply identifies a potentially successful radical innovation, moving it to a separate structure (even location) protects the project. With this structure, the project is treated as a startup even if it is part of a larger company.

Innovation teams are often allowed to operate in isolation from the company and its traditional business scrutiny. In other words, the teams must be allowed to perform, much as Lockheed's famed skunk works did when making radical advances in spy planes in the 1940s, as separate workgroups unencumbered by corporate restrictions. Today, companies such as DaimlerChrysler, BMW, Matsushita, and Microsoft have insulated their teams in Silicon Valley. Being insulated allows and encourages the team to break the rules and, most importantly, protects it from organizational antibodies.

Ideally, isolated units must have access to the brains and resources of the larger organization while still being insulated from the negatives such as organizational antibodies and distractions. However, separation sometimes results in isolation from all aspects of the organization—good and bad—rather than insulation from the bad elements, such as organizational antibodies.

A large international engineering company with a separate e-commerce unit has experienced great difficulty in selling its collaborative design and build product to clients. The main reason for their difficulties is that the company's employees are suspicious of the separate business unit and do not promote it to clients. The separate unit has processes and templates that are not fully integrated with the bricks-and-mortar processes. The idea of e-commerce is not integrated into the company culture and therefore is not utilized as a tool as it was intended.

By separating innovation into separate business units or outsourcing it, you may be significantly limiting the amount of information on innovation that is available to the organization. As illustrated by the previous example, this can have several negative consequences. If people are not aware of the range of innovation projects, the potential value of innovation, or how the general process works, several negative things can happen. There is a higher likelihood that innovation will not be an integral part of the culture and that organizational antibodies will arise to challenge the innovation once it is introduced in the marketplace.

An alternative is to integrate new business model into the existing organization. Traditional bricks-and-mortar organizations such as Charles Schwab and GE have opted to fully integrate e-commerce into their organizations with great success. This is in contrast to others, such as Barnes & Noble, that created a separate e-commerce organization which has experienced some major problems due to lack of integration.

In addition, some instances of this result in a disconnection between the innovations and management's perception of what is needed. In part, this is the problem discussed earlier of the internal market for innovation because the perceived value of the innovation may be artificially suppressed. However, it also challenges two innovation rules: neutralize the organizational antibodies and provide strong leadership of the strategy and the portfolio. If challenges to the innovation rules occur as a result of a separate organization, it could significantly diminish the return on the innovation investment and may actually threaten the viability of long-term innovation in the company.

The Leadership Role

Sometimes the CEO designates a Chief Innovation Officer to serve as manager and advisor on innovation matters. Alternately, the CEO can fulfill the role of the CIO. Either way, the leadership role includes:

- Providing a long-term view for innovation via the innovation strategy and portfolio.

- Sensitizing key leaders and managers to the dynamics of innovation.

- Nurturing key creation projects.

- Managing relationships with external partners.

- Assessing innovation implications of corporate, strategic initiatives.

- Providing an expert opinion and crucial judgment.

- Managing the balance between business and technology innovation, such as organizational dynamics, portfolio, resources and processes.

It is a fundamental truth that every innovation requires the support of a manager to survive. Initially this manager person may be a middle manager who has the decision rights, criteria, and risk behavior to support the early stages of development. Also, the manager must have sufficient resources to fund ideas that have some potential.[28] A lean organization may be good at incremental innovation but it may fail in radical innovation where it needs more experimentation and risk-taking. Finally, the manager has to be willing to run the risk associated with innovation—the risk of investing resources in a project that may have no returns or payback in the future.

Jeffrey Immelt urges investors and engineers to be patient with innovation. He has poured extra money into R&D at GE, while loosening the timelines on projects that may not pay off for ten years or more.

He says that, for established companies, investing in emerging technologies is a matter of survival. "I just see very clearly that unless you're out there pushing the envelope and driving innovation, you're not going to get the kind of margins and the kind of growth that we need for a company like GE. I really see it as an economic imperative."[29]

It is sobering to realize that the commercialization of Post-its was dependent on a mid-level manager having the good insight and gumption to fund its development. Otherwise, it never would have happened. This takes nothing away from Art Fry and his dedicated team at 3M—they created the innovation, and Art is well-known as the "Father of Post-its." But that mid-level manager was also one of the keys to success. The CEO needs to create the culture, organization, and management systems to allow that kind of mid-level support to happen.

Organization and the Innovation Rules

Partnering is a key innovation competency. Organizational issues regarding innovation always deal with the issue of what to do inside and what should be done outside.

CEO Action Plan for Improving the Innovation Organization

- Run a quick diagnostic on creativity and value capture.
  - Which one does your company do best?
  - Does your organization suffer from rampant incrementalism?
  - Does the mix of creative and value capture fit your innovation strategy?
- Develop innovation platforms for the different types of innovation you want to pursue.
- Create portfolios of the projects in each platform.

- Define the mix of internal and external resources you need and form internal and external partnerships—make partnering a core competency for innovation.

- Ensure that internal markets for creativity and commercialization are open and transparent—personally get involved to demonstrate the value of both.

- Guard against organizational antibodies that may limit or destroy your rejuvenated creative markets and processes.

- Leverage your innovation organization with the Internet (e-nnovation).

  - Identify where collaboration can be virtual and where it needs to take place physically in the same location.

  - Use the electronic collaboration tools available to create faster and better collaboration among partners and across distances.

Some innovation experts have stressed the need to outsource. This is the wrong emphasis. The correct place for management to place its attention is on partnerships and how to use them. Structuring the *internal* and *external* partnerships often receives too little attention. This includes defining the areas for partnering, defining who to partner with, and designing how to operate the partnership.

In addition to partnering, management needs to focus its organizational improvements on creating value faster, better, and cheaper than competitors. Value creation requires building networks of innovators that extend within and outside of the organization as Intel, Oracle, and P&G have done. These networks help integrate innovation into the business mentality by keeping innovation present in all the right places and for all the right decisions. Networks need to be organized around defined innovation platforms and focus the appropriate resources on a portfolio of incremental, semi-radical, and radical innovations. This keeps them operating faster, better, and cheaper. It allows active, effective management of the resources across the organization and with partners.

No single structure is appropriate for all types of innovation. The organizational structure needs to vary based on the innovation strategy and the characteristics of the portfolio. But for an organization to innovate successfully, it needs to foster a balance of creativity and value capture. Maintaining that balance requires support from metrics and rewards, and also has cultural components. However, the organization is at the core of the internal marketplace that provides for balanced creativity and value capture.

Organizational structure influences every aspect of how innovation occurs. It is a major part of the *How* variable in the equation:

How you innovate = What you innovate.

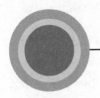

5

MANAGEMENT SYSTEMS: DESIGNING THE PROCESS OF INNOVATION

Systems and Processes Make Things Happen

Having examined strategy in innovation and the various options for structuring your organization to best enable innovation to thrive, *systems* are the next important elements to be considered.[1] The decisions you make on strategy will guide where you focus your innovation efforts. The structure you put into place will act as foundation for the innovation process. However, even with the proper strategy and structure in place, innovation could fail if your systems are inadequate. It is the management systems that are the mechanisms that to a great extent will make innovation happen.[2]

In small organizations, innovation usually happens as a natural occurrence through the insight, talent, and interaction of a small group of people. A single inventor or a group of collaborators may, for instance, launch a company with one robust idea. But as organizations expand, innovation does not happen anymore as a natural occurrence—the right people may not interact, the information may not flow to the right places, or the motivation to take risks may diminish. Organizations as large as General Electric or Procter & Gamble may develop *silos*—compartmentalized departments that barely communicate with each other, much less strive to innovate. This is why larger organizations need systems to manage innovation. Ignoring this and being anchored in the idea that innovation naturally occurs leads to frustration and failure. The argument that large companies are not able to innovate may reflect the lack of acceptance of this basic idea: Innovation has to be managed, it does not just "happen." IBM's CEO Sam Palmisano recognized this need for systemic management when he said that you have to create the right environment in the company for innovation to flourish.[3]

Innovation systems are established policies, procedures, and information mechanisms that facilitate the innovation process within and across organizations. They are the mechanisms by which innovation (and the other tasks of organizations) gets done.[4] They determine the shape of daily interactions and decisions of staff: the order in which work happens, how it is prioritized and evaluated on the daily level, and how different parts of the organization use the organizational structure to communicate. Making decisions on a product enhancement requires communications between many parts of the organization, including R&D, manufacturing, marketing and sales, and finance, as well as processes and criteria for making the decisions. Two organizations with the same structure will get very different innovation results based in part on the systems they have in place and the consistency with which they are followed.[5] For innovation to happen successfully, there needs to be an explicit process in place to manage all the steps of innovation—from design, to measurement, to reward.[6]

The Objectives of Well-Designed Innovation Systems

Many managers wrongly assume that structure and process are the natural foes of creativity. They feel that imposing any structure on creative people will have a detrimental effect on the results. What they don't realize is that structure can enhance creativity, if you build it and use it the right way.[7]

Innovation systems fulfill five important roles, as shown in Figure 5.1.[8]

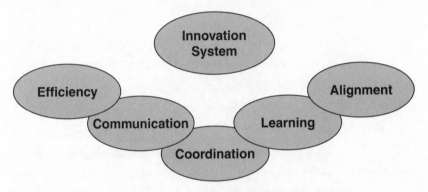

FIGURE 5.1 THE FIVE ROLES OF AN INNOVATION SYSTEM.

The first role of an innovation system is to increase the efficiency of the innovation process. The system needs to move great ideas from concept to commercialization with speed and minimum use of resources.

This role is especially relevant for incremental innovation, where following a defined set of stages and decision points accelerates time-to-market and increases the return on resources invested. For example, the product stage gate management process is used by Tetra Pak to speed effective commercialization of product improvements by moving the innovation speedily through the steps of conceptualization, initial design, prototype design, and commercialization rollout. This function is comparable to that of systems in manufacturing that codify the stages of the process (according to cost, speed, or quality) to increase efficiency. However, innovation systems are not as detailed and structured as in the systems in an assembly line where standard operating procedures dictate the actions of each person. Innovation systems—even those where efficiency is paramount— define relatively broad stages, leaving room for the team to maneuver.

The second role of innovation systems is to create the appropriate lines of communication within the company and with outside constituencies. As the innovation team demands specialized knowledge from other parts of the organization, systems facilitate timely access to it.[9] The technology development team working on a new product will need to know what the customers want and the required product features. This will direct and guide their efforts. The manufacturing team will need to inform the technology development team what is practical and cost-effective as far as manufacturing for the new product. In addition, the manufacturing team will need to know what parts of their system to change. Throughout the internal organization and with external partners involved with the innovation, information regarding the development of the innovation and its consequences needs to flow and be used.

Cross-functional teams (widely used in product development) comprised of members with different functional expertise such as R&D, manufacturing, sales, distribution, finance, and management enable communication through the different knowledge bases of team members, or through a plan that describes when certain functions will join the team. Formalized systems also facilitate communication with internal and external partners through periodic planning and review meetings, and explicit milestones. Microsoft and Compaq used these systems during software and hardware product development.

The third role of innovation systems is coordination between projects and team with the minimum effort. An example of a coordination system is a plan to allow parallel work on projects with minimal communication. For instance, offices in California, London, and

India that all use the same shared tracking system but at different hours can achieve three times the work in a day of other companies. Projects that run around the clock in different parts of the world are possible because of communication technology and the discipline that systems impose. Ensuring that resources are available on time is another coordination issue that systems facilitate. Tetra Pak was able to lower product development times by 40 percent by increasing the efficiency of its management systems, increasing the level of collaboration and involving the right people at the right time.[10]

The fourth role is learning. We dedicate an entire chapter (Chapter 8, "Learning Innovation: How Do Organizations Become Better at Innovating?") to the issue of learning because of its importance in innovation. Systems establish a discipline to manage the knowledge that is constantly created in innovation. Systems can capture the information on the innovation performance throughout the life of the initiative (idea through commercialization) and make it available to the innovation team and management. The information can be used to identify problems and potential improvements. More importantly, learning increases the understanding of the innovation process itself. Every time an innovation project is executed, something is learned about how to improve it, especially for incremental projects where similar efforts are undertaken repeatedly. Innovation systems are like software; new versions are periodically released that improve on previous versions. A system for capturing and coding learning enables that to happen. Knowledge is also generated about the business model, the technology, and opportunities that are identified but cannot be pursued within the framework of the current project. Knowledge may be relevant not only to the current project but to future projects, also. DaimlerChrysler's experience with electronic collaboration systems with its headset supplier provided important learning that can be applied on future projects regarding managing innovation within tight time constraints and working with partners spread across the globe.[11] Similarly, Audi's product development team learned that bringing the subsystem suppliers to the early stages of innovation planning was very valuable. After Continental Tire showed that it could create a smart tire capable of delivering breaking performance far ahead of what the industry had been able to do so far, Audi and other car manufacturers paid attention and built innovation systems that included the tire manufacturers.

Knowledge needs to be retained in order to benefit the organization and enhance competitive advantage. It is often said that "If our company only knew what our company knows, many problems would not exist." Knowledge management systems facilitate remembering or *knowing what you know*.

The fifth role of innovation systems is to align the objectives of the various constituencies. People throughout an organization need to understand the company strategy and its implications for operations. As a company grows larger, senior management cannot rely on informal, social interactions as the vehicle to achieve this alignment of understanding and behavior. A system is needed to ensure consistency of message and inclusiveness. Innovation systems also align organizational objectives with personal objectives. The information regarding the innovation performance needs to be communicated and compared to the innovation objectives. This allows people in the organization to assess how their actions fit the organization's innovation objectives. If the performance does not match the objectives, then time is spent analyzing the systemic cause of the discrepancy. This provides people a better understanding of the linkages between the innovation strategy and its operational context. Systems also reinforce optimal individual and group behavior to foster optimum innovation performance through well-designed incentive and reward systems.

Properly designed systems can help bring together the right people and the right knowledge to create the activities required to make innovation happen.

Choosing and Designing Innovation Systems

Innovation can be envisioned as a flow that starts with many and ends up with a few—a multitude of great ideas are created and are winnowed, selected, and refined until only the few best are brought forward to commercialization. Systems manage the flow from the many ideas to the few that reach commercialization. This process is often envisioned as a funnel—broad at the opening to accommodate the many ideas and tapering to a small diameter to allow the few to exit to commercialization. Figure 5.2 illustrates a typical funnel framework for innovation. In this depiction, innovation starts at the broad left side.

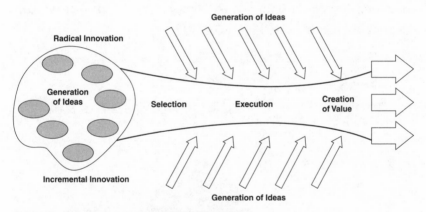

FIGURE 5.2   THE INNOVATION PROCESS.

At the beginning of the process, a lot of ideas float around; it is the *creative phase*, and more ideas are developed than can or should be used. As ideas progress through the funnel, the process rejects some ideas (they leave the funnel) and continues to evaluate others (they move forward). Ideas move through the selection process until those that are selected receive a major resource commitment and move to the *execution stage*.[12] Those ideas that become intellectual property move to the value *creation stage*.[13] At the far end, the funnel grows larger again reflecting that value creation should be maximized for the intellectual capital that has been developed (in other words, via application to more than one product or cross-licensing).[14] Consider for a moment how many ideas must have been flowing into one end of the funnel at IBM, which obtained 3,288 patents in 2001—almost twice as many as the next nearest corporation to receive patents in that year.[15]

The first stage where management systems play a role is in *ideation*: generating ideas and moving them across the organization to where funding decisions are made. The second stage is the *funding decisions* themselves, where selected innovations receive initial funding to move ahead or are discarded. The last stage is the *execution* of the innovation project (commercialization). The creation of value and commercialization of innovations follows a general path from early adoption to maturity (see Figure 5.3).

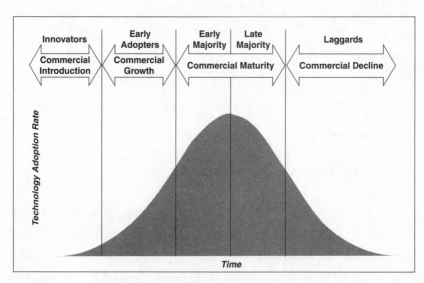

FIGURE 5.3   INNOVATION COMMERCIALIZATION PROCESS.[16]

Whichever innovations systems you choose for your organization, they must be effective in moving through all three stages from ideation to selection to execution and then onto commercialization.[17] Also, while it may appear that the stages progress in a linear fashion, they do not. Most often the stages overlap and go through several iterations. It is important to note that creativity does not stop at the ideation stage but permeates the whole process. For instance, a product improvement may be further enhanced or new innovations added to the product at any point in the innovation process right up to and including the commercialization step.

Systems for Ideation: Seeing the Gaps

The engine of innovation is ideas. Ideas begin with the recognition and understanding that somewhere a gap exists. That gap may be large or small—a new product feature, a new business model element, an improved process technology, or an entirely new business model. Apple saw gaps in the way people acquired and used music, and created the iPod and iTunes. Gillette saw gaps in shaving products and created the new MACH3 razors and blades. Southwest Airlines saw gaps in the price of service for airline travel, and designed an approach that delivered no-frills service at a significantly reduced fare. Whatever the size and type of gap, innovation depends on the realization that something is missing somewhere in the network that produces value for customers.

Because all ideas start with recognition of gaps, all processes for identifying great ideas are aimed at creating perspectives that make the gaps and holes visible. Sometimes top management sees the gap. Alternatively, a person in the ranks or a team may identify the gap. Whatever the source, these are autonomous ideas born from ingenuity or a "fortunate accident."[18, 19, 20, 21]

The management challenge is to create an environment to nurture the generation of large quantities of great ideas about gaps (without getting in the way of day-to-day business) and to move the ideas to the next stages in the innovation process. When we talk about ideas, we specifically mean ideas that address a gap and have the potential of generating economic value. By the way, experience demonstrates that it is easy to generate a lot of ideas—just reward people on the number of ideas they submit, and the suggestion box will overflow. The challenge is to nurture the generation of economically viable ideas, and to move a manageable number of ideas through the innovation process.

Structured Idea Management

Structured Idea Management (SIM) is a general ideation process that has been successfully used with many companies and industries for more than 20 years. For example, in the early 1980s, Canon used SIM to develop the concepts for new consumer cameras for the 1990-2000 timeframe. IDEO (a product design firm) uses this approach by mixing designers, social scientists, and others with valuable perspectives in a room where they intensely scrutinize a given problem and identify and explore possible solutions. It has been called managed chaos: a dozen or so very smart people examining data, throwing out ideas, writing potential solutions on big Post-its that are ripped off and stuck to a wall.[22] However, despite the appearance of chaos, at its core it is a highly structured process.

SIM is prototypical for many idea management processes. Its individual steps (illustrated in Figure 5.4) are specifically designed to maximize the achievement of three desirable end-goals:

1. Control of the working context/environment to ensure the maximum possible creativity.

2. Use of the best and most rigorous screening mechanisms to ensure the highest quality output.

3. Explicit recognition and protocols for the creative "bundling" or "clustering" of "idea fragments" to create truly breakthrough concepts.

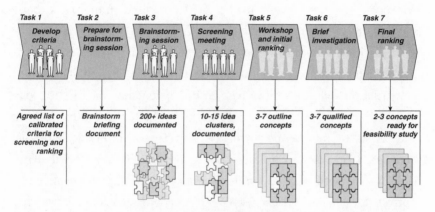

Task 1	Task 2	Task 3	Task 4	Task 5	Task 6	Task 7
Develop criteria	Prepare for brainstorming session	Brainstorming session	Screening meeting	Workshop and initial ranking	Brief investigation	Final ranking
Agreed list of calibrated criteria for screening and ranking	Brainstorm briefing document	200+ ideas documented	10-15 idea clusters, documented	3-7 outline concepts	3-7 qualified concepts	2-3 concepts ready for feasibility study

FIGURE 5.4   THE STRUCTURED IDEA MANAGEMENT PROCESS.[23]

SIM is designed to prevent the two most common mistakes made by companies undertaking the innovation process:

- **Understanding the difference between assessing incremental versus radical ideas**. Decisions about incremental and radical ideas tend to be made in the same forum, using the same criteria, although the two types of ideas need quite different approaches to development and selection. At such meetings, ideas that involve the greatest number of unanswered questions (which tend to be breakthrough ideas) are usually dropped first, leaving only the lowest-quality ideas.

- **Recognizing the value of idea fragments**. One of the most common mistakes that companies make is to use "brainstorming" meetings to generate finished concepts, rather than thinking about fragments of ideas that—if put together—could yield a major breakthrough. They lose the best "fragments," and the end results are again evolutionary developments from what has gone before.

Experimentation

Radical innovation relies to a larger extent on ongoing experiments that test, refute, modify, and validate potential radical breakthrough concepts. The participants in the X PRIZE used numerous experiments to test and refine the design of their space transportation technologies for commercial space flight. Scaled Composites has had to continually test, validate, refute, and refine the design and materials of construction of its innovative craft, SpaceShipOne. Every day included experimentation to determine if a better, faster, or cheaper way exists to hit the performance objectives—different materials, alternate fabrication techniques, new controls technologies. Likewise, experiments with business models are a key activity for innovative initiatives. One of GE CEO Jack Welch's recognized strengths was that he was always experimenting and looking for the opportunity to innovate. According to those close to him, he was always asking, "What is the business model? How can we change it to make it better?"[24]

Experiments provide a probing dynamic into new technical, business, and market spaces. Well-designed experiments provide insight and uncover hidden value. They provide learning that guides the radical innovation process by defining the right questions and suggesting the best answers.

One major study of players in the computer industry found that "using an experiential strategy of multiple design iterations, extensive testing, frequent project milestones, a powerful leader, and a multifunctional team accelerates product development."[25] A constant to remember throughout experimentation is the necessity to learn to expect the unexpected. 3M's Scotchguard was a serendipitous discovery that was the result of a trivial accident. When trying to develop a rubbery material to resist deterioration from aircraft fuels in 1953, a few drops fell on a researcher's new tennis shoe. Nothing could wipe off the substance, and the researchers had the presence of mind to realize that they had discovered something that repelled both water and oil. "The prepared mind notices when something doesn't go as expected, and curiosity is piqued by observation," said Patsy Sherman, the discoverer and developer of Scotchguard.[26]

Prototyping

In their simplest forms, *prototypes* are spreadsheets, process maps, or simulations—anything simple that enables you to visualize and understand better where your ignorance exists. The innovation team must be able to play with, change, and develop the prototype to reap valuable insight from it. Successful prototyping requires attention to three rules, described in Figure 5.5.

Rule 1 Think modularly	Do not try to solve all of the pieces. Build prototypes that provide insight into one or two key uncertainties. As goodexperimenters know, this provides valuable information into the nature of the problem as well as the potential solution.
Rule 2 Fail fast and cheaply	Define small practical tests that can be done cheaply. Build a prototype and test it quickly. It is often best to work with a partner, such as a lead customer or a supplier, to share the costs, risks, and learning. Get the results and determine what was learned and what new questions were identified. Modify the prototype.
Rule 3 Fail often in order to succeed faster	Use the "Ready, fire, aim. . . and then start over again" approach. It is crucial to overcome the old "Ready, aim, aim, aim. . ." syndrome. Remember that the plural of anecdote is data.

FIGURE 5.5   THE THREE RULES OF PROTOTYPING.[27]

Several companies have successfully used prototypes and the "probe-and-learn" approach to commercialize radical innovations. For example, using prototypes IBM developed silicon germanium devices, and Schwab created electronic trading. Howard Rosen, former president of ALZA Corp., says that undertaking anything innovative, especially in the pharmaceutical industry, requires that you fail a lot. What you want to do is fail fast and cheaply.[28] This is the role of prototypes.

Look closely at successful radical innovation, and you will find many prototype precursors. The best prototypes are those that customers and suppliers can play with so that you reduce your ignorance of what they see in the proposed concept. In early prototypes, the focus should be on extreme simplicity and learning the basics. Later, at the second and subsequent levels of prototyping, you can move to more robust, less modular representations of the innovation. More advanced prototypes should focus on the essence of the design. The best prototypes are the ones that provide designers, customers, and suppliers with the opportunity to make sequential improvements. A prototype focuses the team around a common evolving concept: It connects the team with a powerful model that clarifies both the problem and possible solutions. Also, a prototype provides powerful clues to the direction of the next steps in innovation.

Prototyping needs to be a core competency of the radical innovation team. It needs to be a primary mode of thinking and operating for the team. The competency of prototyping requires people who are capable of working with and through incompleteness. Building, testing, refining, refuting, and corroborating prototypes are essential activities because they:

- Challenge the existing mental models of the team.

- Uncover patterns of results from which the team can learn.

- Pull the team together and create a common, shared vision and language.

- Generate a level of excitement that traditional means cannot equal.

- Generate new thinking that eventually becomes the radical innovation.

Making Deals

Turning good ideas into robust innovations requires that the ideas be changed from bare bones possibilities to something in which investors can see the value. Some great ideas are overlooked because their advocates did not provide a sufficiently compelling picture of the potential attractiveness of the innovation. Instead, the advocates hoped that the value would be self-apparent (it seldom is) or they made inflated projections of the timing and size of the return on the investment, thereby alienating the investors who distrust hype. The process of idea management should include a process step that turns the idea into a sufficiently complete picture that potential investors can see the real value and risks of investing. This "deal-making" process resembles the investment process that venture capitalists require for their investments under consideration.

Deal-making positions key persons in the company as the seller and another as the buyer. The transaction is very much of seller and champion taking a deal to the buyer and getting them to "buy in." At that point, they are in the deal together. They move the deal forward by changing, accelerating, redirecting, leveraging, mortgaging, or otherwise improving the deal to meet their mutual vision. They also might divest themselves of the deal, garnering the available value and using it to make/further other deals in their portfolio.

The greater the deal flow, the greater the odds of achieving successful innovation because not every deal is destined to be a winner. Deals need other deals with which to combine and fuse. A high rate of deal flow also produces high rates of knowledge transfer among deals and potential combinations among the deals to produce better deals.

CEO Action—Let's Make a Deal

Check the deal flow to see if your company is being aggressive enough to meet the strategic innovation objectives.

Could you sell your deals to a venture capitalist (VC)? Try selling one or two to a VC; then determine what needs to be done differently:

- Do your people develop deals, or do they work on projects? Do they know the difference?

- Do the deals have the necessary business model and technology content to be saleable?

- Do the deal developers understand the concerns of a sophisticated buyer?

- Do the deals in your portfolio represent what buyers want or what the developers are comfortable selling?

Innovation That Fits

Leading companies such as Wal-Mart, GE, and P&G focus their innovation in areas that enhance their core competencies. Knowing your core competencies and innovating on and around them is a key to success. For example, easyGroup, a rapidly-growing collection of low-price companies on the Internet, follows a simple formula: Look for services with high fixed costs, price elasticity, and the ability to be ordered on the Internet, then create a frill-free offering that gives consumers few if any choices. easyJet has only one class of service; easyCar rents only one class of car and requires that it be returned, clean, to the same location. Former easyGroup CTO Phil Jones says, "We don't aspire to be all things to all people. We do one thing very well at low cost."[29]

A company sometimes unknowingly limits the innovation opportunities it considers or chooses by assuming too narrow a range of opportunities that could "fit" the company. Experience has shown that it is foolhardy and a waste of money and time (possibly even value-destroying) to go into businesses where a company has no relevant competencies or relevant experience. History is littered with the wrecks of those types of investments. Vivendi, the French water utility, moved far outside of its core when it acquired Universal Studios from the Bronfman family's Seagram Group. Eventually, Vivendi sold Universal Studios to GE's NBC unit. That entry and eventual retreat from the entertainment industry cost former chief executive Jean-Marie Messier his job and his shareholders dearly.

However, if a company too narrowly defines what *fits* and what is part of its core competencies (in other words, what business model, markets, and technologies are essential for the company to compete), it may miss important innovation opportunities. What if a company possesses four out of five key technologies required for an attractive new opportunity? Should it dismiss the opportunity because the technology is not currently in-house? Or should it gain access to the missing technology and pursue the opportunity?

The fundamental question is, how close a fit is close enough? Going too far a field is usually a disaster. However, staying too close to the existing is too limiting and loses value creation opportunities. Consider if Apple had decided that the music business did not fit its PC business; we would not have iTunes and iPod. Or if 3M had passed up Post-it Notes because it was not in the business of selling those kinds of products; they were much more comfortable with office products in the form of tapes. Or if Amazon.com had decided its business was just selling books?

Too often companies pass up really good ideas because the opportunities do not seem to be part of their business. Instead, the companies invest in less attractive opportunities that fit their concept of what business they are in. In other words, companies conform to their limited mental model of their business and core competencies instead of seeing what their real strengths are.

The key is to carefully define a company's competencies and not only focus on the obvious aspects of the business. A company has to look carefully beneath the surface to determine the real competencies and what innovations would *fit*. It has to look hard at the identified opportunities to see if the fit is good enough to warrant investment.

Consider Dell's expansion into servers, as a case in point. Dell identified its core competency as managing the Internet-based supply chain. It developed this competency in the PC arena. However, it saw an opportunity to use the same competency in a related business model providing servers. The market for servers was not exactly the same as the PC market, and it required a higher level of service than the PC market, but the business model had many similarities and used the Internet-based supply chain competency that Dell had mastered. Dell chose to enter. To date, Dell has racked up significant market share and revenue growth in the server markets. And now it is looking for other similar opportunities to leverage its competencies in new or related markets.

CEO Considerations

Make sure that you are not limiting innovation to what feels comfortable. Determine what innovation truly *fits* your company and is worthy of investment.

What are your primary core competencies?

- Business models
- Technologies

Which ones are most important to the success of your current business plan? To your innovation strategy?

Do you dominate any areas? Could you dominate some areas with the proper innovations and investments?

What other markets or businesses use your core competencies in business models and technologies?

What areas should you invest in improving or growing innovation?

Management Systems Comparison

A multitude of different types of management systems are used in innovation—stage gate project management, portfolio management, structured idea management, brainstorming, project selection processes (financial and non-financial), experimentation, prototyping, product and service rollout, and commercialization processes, just to name a few.

To highlight the different approaches and the range of options, we have identified some of the most important types of management systems and compared the different approaches required for incremental innovation and radical innovation (see Table 5.1).

Table 5.1 Comparing Innovation Systems for Incremental Versus Radical Innovation

System	Incremental innovation	Radical innovation
Rewards/recognition	Heavy use of rewards. Rewards are linked to achieving milestones and output targets. Usually cash rewards but also public recognition. Also rewards clearly defined before the start of a project.	Rewards are decided once the project is complete. Continuous support more important than working for a reward. When the project is successful, recognition but also reward that is perceived as fair.
Project planning	Lot of upfront planning, definition of milestones, clear objectives. Plan suffers small modifications.	Define broad goals, little detailed planning, but heavy reliance on experimentation. Plan constantly revisited.
Resource allocation	Based on financial metrics. Clear definition of resources committed and how they will be released.	Based on promise of technology and market. May be informal. Not clear how much will be needed.
Metrics	Clear metrics; includes input, process, outputs.	Metrics are limited to input metrics at most and experimentation-related metrics.
Monitoring	Based on whether milestones are met, by exception.	Based on subjective evaluation of whether the experiments provide learning.
Process formalization	High; based on stage gates.	Low; based on small team dynamics.

continues

Table 5.1   continued

System	Incremental innovation	Radical innovation
Market research	Traditional tools; focused groups, conjoint analysis, surveys, prototyping.	Anthropological; observation, experiential, experimentation.
Strategic boundaries	Not needed; managed through objectives/milestones.	A strategic framework may be relevant to bound the search process.
Strategic planning	Extrapolate current business model. Identify gaps.	Explore new technical approaches and business models.
Portfolio planning/ management	Straightforward, simple tradeoffs.	More complicated; risks and rewards are larger.
Culture	Focus on detail, cross-functional collaboration, experience-based.	Focus on ambition, exploration.
Learning tools	Continuous improvement tools—quality tools, cycle time, reengineering, customer feedback, optimization tools.	Experimentation tools, prototypes, learning tools.
Knowledge management	Develop systems to make knowledge accessible across the organization.	Knowledge is created and managed within the team.
Partnerships	Collaboration over various projects—long-term agreements.	Partners provide access to capabilities that the organization lacks.
External monitoring	Monitor current competitors and current eco-system.	Monitoring idea generation places—universities, labs, startups.

Management systems vary between companies. There is no set of systems that will serve all companies. The processes selected should be determined by the innovation strategy and the balance of radical, semi-radical, and incremental innovation in the portfolio.

Senior management should oversee the development and installation of the systems to ensure they match the company's needs and operating styles. Then they should monitor the systems' performance against the objectives. There is not reason to allow a management system to exist if it is not delivering the value expected of it. Management systems can and should be changed and adapted over time to match the company's changing needs.

Electronic Collaboration

People that need to work together are increasingly separated by distance—partners are in different physical locations, offices in the same business unit are often overseas, there is increased use of outsourcing, and telecommuting is becoming a common mode of work. The negative effects of the separation are often magnified due to mismatches in time zones, cultures, and communication technologies. The online revolution has made it possible for companies to virtually extend the organizational boundaries, overcome the separation, and tap into their customers, suppliers, and partners.[30] This electronic collaboration is a new, important element of innovation management.

Boeing is an excellent example of a company that has removed the distance that traditionally separates teams. The airline giant put together a computerized engineering system that wired suppliers, manufacturers, engineers, and even some customers into the development process. The result was the Boeing 777, whose CATIA and EPIC design systems (electronic design collaboration tools) have revolutionized product development. It was the first airplane designed without physical mock-ups. The design and commercialization process was faster, better, and cheaper—and it was made possible by a web-enabled collaboration that linked the different participants into a virtual design room.

In addition, open-source software development projects have become an important economic and cultural phenomenon. SourceForge.net, a major infrastructure provider and repository for such projects, lists more than 10,000 projects and more than 30,000 registered users. The digital software products emanating from such projects are commercially attractive and widely used in business and government (by IBM, NASA, and others). Because such products are deemed a public good, the open-source movement's unique development practices are challenging the traditional views of how innovation should work.[31]

Eli Lilly recently launched an online knowledge broker called InnoCentive (www.innocentive.com), where it and other firms post R&D problems and solicit solutions from companies and individuals worldwide.[32]

The packaging company Tetra Pak was having unsatisfactory results in idea generation and product development despite great effort. After examining cultural and process issues, the company instituted an Internet-based management system for product creation. The new system helped Tetra Pak reduce product development lead-time by 40 percent, and the company's yield of successful products climbed. What made that significant step change possible was the significant increase in decision-making speed. Tetra Pak not only wired the key decision makers together, ensuring that the right people were involved at the right times, but it also provided improved tools for decision-making and knowledge management that gave increased abilities to the enterprise teams. For Tetra Pak, the benefits came from a better system that resulted in faster and better decisions and implementation.

APTEC, an engineering and design company located in Florida, used electronic collaboration tools to produce a new wireless headset for DaimlerChrysler in record time without a single face-to-face meeting. The product was on budget, and schedule and met the rigorous quality requirements of the client. This was the first time that the product had been produced, and the team included partners located in the United States, South Korea, and the Philippines. They used electronic collaboration tools that allowed real-time, three-dimensional co-design. They harnessed the ability to manipulate models through iteration after iteration among the innovation partners. This resulted in significantly reduced program costs (zero travel costs, real-time and highly efficient project review meetings) and lightning-fast innovation. And all of the partners—including the customer—could review the design options and decisions.

GE Plastics developed an electronic collaboration approach to sharing product-creation knowledge across the entire organization and beyond—to employees, customers, suppliers, and so on. GE Plastics' results are stellar: The average time to close new target customers dropped from one year to 90 days. Also, more than 80,000 registered users turned to GE Plastics' new Design Solution Center in its first year, driving $1.5 billion in new revenues. New online training seminars have replaced costly in-person seminars that entailed sending managers around the country—saving more than $2.5 million in the first year.

CEO Action: Electronic Collaboration

Improved innovation via electronic collaboration can yield massive ROI because it changes the organizational and geographic boundaries that often pose barriers to meaningful collaboration. However, the investment requires some fresh thinking and altered behavior that you need to lead.

- Examine a day in the life of your product development team and determine where electronic collaboration would improve the innovation effort. Be bold and challenge the assumptions that have limited collaboration to date.

- Get rid of old mental models that block collaboration and promote new behaviors.

- Ensure a mixture of face-to-face and electronic meetings; it is healthy and forces people to reevaluate the definition of a "good meeting."

- Rev up the iterations in the design process; with electronic collaboration, it is possible to complete hundreds and even thousands of iterative designs and modifications in the time that it traditionally took to do a handful.

Electronic collaboration allows upstream and downstream players in the supply chain to work closely with manufacturers and address the whole product life cycle. They can gather information about the creation of the components through to the use and even disposal of the product, and feed this information back to create design improvements.

Management Systems and the Innovation Rules

It is not enough to have a vision, or preach about the need for innovation; companies need to use systems to achieve innovation. Management systems are the key to balancing the sometimes antagonistic aspects of innovation. Systems must be combined so that they can manage the dualities of:

- Technology and business models

- Radical and incremental innovation

- Creativity and value capture

- Networks and platforms

The unifying factor for systems is the innovation strategy and portfolio. The management systems a company chooses should flow directly from its choice of innovation strategy and balance it seeks in its portfolio. Consider how different Dell's innovation systems must be from Apple's—one focused almost exclusively on business model innovation and the other delivering a combination of technology and business model innovations. For Apple, one of the keys is to keep the technology and business model innovations in coordination. For Dell, improving the business model is the primary role of the systems, and managing technology is secondary.

The management systems should also provide for parallel creativity and value capture in the organization. In particular, the systems should allow a seamless blend of idea generation, selection, and execution by the network of innovators inside and outside of the company. Properly functioning systems provide active creation of innovations—through ideation, selection, development of ideas, and efficient execution and commercialization—through careful development of innovation prototypes and development of commercially viable changes to the business model or technology.

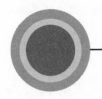

6

ILLUMINATING THE PATHWAY: HOW TO MEASURE INNOVATION

To Measure or Not to Measure?

I agree that innovation is a tricky thing to bring about. Companies want it but focus on the wrong things.

—Art Fry, developer of Post-It Notes[1]

From the amount of time and pages that have been devoted to the topic of performance measurement in the last decade, you might imagine that we know all we need to know. Frankly, many companies do not have this issue adequately covered.

Measurement is both fundamental and critical to success with innovation. However, you would not know it by the amount of thoughtful text or time given to discussing innovation metrics.

It is not enough to simply pick several areas, use whatever you happen to measure, and expect that to give you the information you need to manage innovation. With so many metrics in existence, some managers skirt the problem by measuring most of everything they can think of, and hoping that some of them prove to provide useful information. They employ dozens of measures with different criteria.[2] As well as being excessively time-consuming and a drain on productivity, this can lead to incoherent analysis and improper action. A fundamental rule of innovation is that linking strategy to innovation measurement with a few sharp metrics provides a clear picture of performance.

Creating a few sharp metrics is not to be confused with fitting them all on one page. We visited one company that literally had one page of innovation metrics. We estimate that there were approximately 60 metrics crammed onto the page. The font was so small that it was barely readable, and the four margins were the smallest possible. This one-page measurement system is useless and probably harmful.

CEO's Measurement Rules

- What gets measured gets done—so be careful what you measure.
- Understand the strategy and business model of innovation for your company, and build a measurement system for innovation that is tied to both.
- Know what you want to achieve with each measurement system at each level of the organization. There are three options: communicate the strategy and the underlying mental models, monitor performance, and learn.
- Tailor the innovation measurement system to match the mix of incremental, semi-radical, and radical innovation strategies.
- Change your measurements as your strategy and organization change.
- Build your innovation measurement system to avoid the seven barriers to its success (described later in this chapter).

What Gets Measured Gets Done

The adage "What gets measured gets done" is frequently used to argue for the need for measurement systems. While this is true, a carelessly designed innovation measurement system may do more harm than good.[3] In a recent survey, more than 60 percent of respondents indicated that innovation was a key feature in their companies' mission statement, yet more than half rated their performance measurement system for innovation as poor or less than adequate.[4]

Many large organizations throughout the world measure results using money-based metrics.[5] However, most managers in those organizations feel that non-financial measures should be used to track the execution of an innovation effort and project its future value. Managers rely on non-financial measures much more than they do on financial ones because these measures give a better real-time, granular evaluation of progress and likelihood of success.[6]

Mobil's retail division provides a vivid example of the dramatic effects of a well-designed measurement system. When a new management team came on board the $15 billion-per-year division, it was unprofitable and one of the laggards in the industry. The new management team defined a clear strategy that emphasized efficiency and focused on specific market segments that valued service and premium products. The management team translated the new strategy into a measurement system with metrics that included ROCE (Return on Capital Employed), market share in the targeted segments, and the success of specific innovation measures such as new product acceptance rate and new product ROI. The measurement system was used in all levels of the organization. This allowed all employees in the organization to have clear milestones in order to gauge their work and understand how they helped the organization succeed. The result was profound: a return to profitability and ascension to the number one company in the industry in a little more than a year.[7]

Measurement is one of the most critical elements of success in innovation. When measurement systems are not aligned with the strategy and not tailored to the portfolio's mix of incremental, semi-radical, and radical innovation, managers lose a key source of information. That translates into lower performance and decreased payoffs from innovation investments.

The Three Roles of a Measurement System

Measurement systems are managerial facilitators; they are not solutions. They fill three roles, as follows:

- **Plan: define and communicate strategy**. Make assumptions about the sources of value explicit and clear, select the intended strategy, and clarify expectations about strategy throughout the organization

- **Monitor**. Track the execution of innovation efforts to assess changes in the environment, intervene only if necessary, and evaluate performance.

- **Learn: identify new opportunities**. Learn about new solutions to achieve performance goals, new business, or technology opportunities.

Plan: Define and Communicate Strategy

A measurement system that captures the logic behind an innovation strategy facilitates agreement in terms of what is important, how day-to-day activities add value, and how each person contributes to the mission. Making the strategy explicit through a measurement system has three advantages:

- Allows a discussion about the underlying assumptions and mental models, and provides agreement in the organization about the strategy.

- Encourages the communication of the strategy and its execution throughout the organization. Communication clarifies expectations and it becomes clear to organizational members why certain actions add value while others do not.

- Tracks the evolution of the organization and the strategy. Innovation efforts frequently span long periods of time; a measurement system identifies if the organization is on the right track to achieve its innovation objectives and whether the innovation strategy is working.

An executive of a successful technology startup described the importance of planning: "I think that operating without a (strategic) plan and without a cash flow projection is like trying to walk with no eyes, it's a challenge."[8]

Monitor

The second use, and probably the most commonly thought-about function of measurement systems, is monitoring progress.[9] For example, within product development processes, the reference point for measuring progress is typically the planned performance that describes product introduction date, development budget, technical and quality specifications, and customer satisfaction targets.

When used to monitor implementation, the measurement system can identify deviations from the plan that require managerial action. In this context, a measurement system is used by exception (thus liberating managers' attention from constantly supervising the process) rather than to stimulate discussion or to make a business model explicit.

Learn: Identify New Opportunities

Innovation is heavily dependent on communication and exchange of ideas; people exchange points of view, discuss their different perspectives, and find new solutions not contemplated before.[10] This is the third role of measurement systems: to facilitate the ongoing discussion within an organization that will lead to better innovation and execution. One of the tools that *USA Today*, the leading newspaper in sales in the U.S., relied on to continually innovate its product was a detailed weekly circulation and advertising report. These reports were carefully analyzed and discussed to understand the effectiveness of new ideas, pitch new ones, and uncover new trends. Pepsi used similar weekly market share reports, with share numbers in specific counties and even cities, in its effort to beat Coke.[11] At Siemens' medical products division, project schedules stimulate innovation because the pressure to meet milestones and deadlines galvanizes discussion and creativity, and creates a bias for action. Figure 6.1 summarizes these three roles.

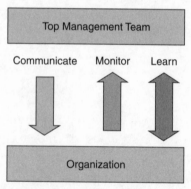

FIGURE 6.1   THE THREE ROLES OF MEASUREMENT SYSTEMS.

A Balanced Scorecard for Measuring Innovation

Designing a measurement system for innovation relies on a clear model of how innovation is managed and how ideas are created, evaluated and selected, and transformed into value. A clear model describes the inputs, processes, outcomes, and outputs from idea generation to execution and value capture. This model of innovation management can transform into a measurement system to manage innovation. Figure 6.2 illustrates these stages.

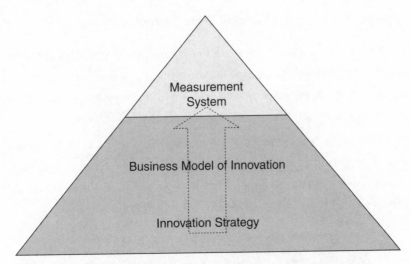

FIGURE 6.2 BUSINESS MODEL AND MEASUREMENT SYSTEM.

The Business Model for Innovation

The *Balanced Scorecard* is one of the most powerful concepts in measurement systems. While the original Balanced Scorecard focused on business strategy, its main idea is applicable to any business process including innovation management.[12]

A basic tenet of the Balanced Scorecard is that the measurement system is only as good as the underlying business model. The business model describes how the company will be innovative and how it will generate value from innovation.

This is the key to the power of Balanced Scorecards: The richer our understanding of the innovation processes, the better our business model will be and the derived measurement system will provide a more informed management of innovation. By making the business case for innovation investments, managers can integrate innovation impacts into their business strategies. This integrated perspective is directly linked to the third Innovation Rule: Integrate innovation into the company's basic business mentality.

Inputs, Processes, Outputs, and Outcomes

Putting together a business model of innovation is probably the most challenging part of designing a measurement system.[13] It forces managers to make their assumptions explicit about how to get innovation and to agree on an innovation model.

The following framework (illustrated in Figure 6.3) presents a useful approach to describe the causal relationships behind an innovation model. It can be applied not only to describe innovation at the business unit level but at any level within the organization.[14]

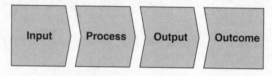

Input   Process   Output   Outcome

FIGURE 6.3   A BUSINESS MODEL OF INNOVATION.

Inputs are the resources devoted to the innovation effort. Possible inputs include tangible elements such as people, money, equipment, office space, and time, but also intangibles such as motivation and company culture. Inputs are leading measures of success. The Sears, Roebuck and Company turnaround relied to a large extent on carefully measuring the quantity and quality of the workforce as a key input to success. A significant part of Sears' measurement system was devoted to monitoring the investment on recruiting the right talent and training it, but also to monitoring the workforce commitment to change and the generation of ideas from them.[15]

The different types of inputs that might be considered in examining this part of the business model include the following:

- **Tangible resources** include capital, time, software, and physical infrastructure.

- **Intangible resources** include talent, motivation, culture, knowledge, and brands.

- **Innovation structure** includes interest groups and corporate venture capital.

- **Innovation strategy** includes innovation platforms and positioning in Innovation Matrix.

- **External network** includes partners, lead customers, and key suppliers.

- **Innovation systems** include systems for recruiting, training, continuous learning, execution, and value creation.

Processes combine the inputs and transform them. They are "real time" measures (meaning, they measure current activities) and track the progress towards the creation of outputs. Process measures are critical during execution because they can signal the need to change course or alter the execution.

- **Creative process** tracks the quality of ideas, the ability to explore them, and the conversion rate into projects and value.

- **Project execution** tracks the evolution of projects currently under way in dimensions such as time, cost, technology performance, and estimated value generated.

- **Integrated execution** tracks the aggregate performance of all projects.

- **Balanced innovation portfolio** tracks the mix of projects within the Innovation Matrix and its alignment with the strategy.

Outputs are the results of innovation effort. Output measures describe what the innovation efforts have delivered. These measures are lagging measures because they inform after the fact, once the effort is done. Output measures describe key characteristics such as whether the company has superior R&D performance, more effective customer acquisition, or better customer loyalty.

- **Technology leadership** is evaluated through number of patents, cites, seminars, technology licenses, and technology adoption in the business model.

- **Project completion** is evaluated through execution metrics vis-à-vis expectations or competitors.

- **New product introduction** is evaluated through the number of successful products, their acceptance compared to competitors, market share, and sales.

- **Business processes improvement** is evaluated through improvement in process metrics.

- **Market leadership** includes customer acquisition, customer share, and customer loyalty.

Outputs describe quality, quantity and timeliness, whereas *outcomes* describe value creation. Outcome measures capture how the innovation effort translated the outputs into value for the company and the net amount of the value contribution. If the output of a particular innovation project is successful in the market and profitable for the company, then the outcome is strongly positive. However, a similar project could produce the same quality and quantity of innovation outputs, but not lead to value creation. It may have missed the market window of opportunity or the innovation characterisitcs delivered may not have been as powerful attracting consumers as had been anticipated. In this case, the outcome would be negative at least in the sense of commercial viability; there may have been valuable learning outcomes from the project that made it worthwhile despite the cost.

Accurately measuring value is controversial. Changes in valuation of share prices should reflect the creation of value under the assumption of efficient markets. But this measure is limited to public companies and to the ups and downs of the stock market. For private companies, divisions, departments, and even specific products, a new breed of measures was developed. Broadly called *residual income*, these measures relate profitability and cash flows to investment in dollar terms (rather than as a ratio estimated by traditional measures such as ROI). Coca-Cola, AT&T, FMC, PespsiCo, and Boeing are among the numerous companies that have adopted these new measures of value creation.

Residual income = profits – capital employed × cost of capital

- **Project profitability** estimates the value generated during its life cycle compared to expectations and comparable projects.

- **Customers and products profitability** estimates the overall value of innovation from a market and product perspective.

- **Return on investment** estimates the current profitability of the organization.

- **Long-term value captured** estimates the value captured through the life of the product or product family.

From the Business Model to the Measurement System

The business model of innovation varies for different types of innovation and business processes. For example, developing a measurement system for incremental innovation[16] within the manufacturing processes requires a business model that explicitly describes:

- What resources are required from employees, external consultants, or contact with other organizations facing similar challenges.

- How these resources are combined to create innovation such as through workgroups, and development of analyses and action plans.

- How the specific innovation translates into business value via increased quality, decreased cycle time, or decreased inventories.

Figure 6.4 illustrates the innovation model at the business unit level. Inputs track the management infrastructure—strategy, structure and systems, employee commitment, and new talent. Measures include a questionnaire for employees and partners to track their understanding of the strategic direction, an audit of structure and systems, the number of ideas that are funded, and the background and diversity of the new recruits. Process objectives track the innovation portfolio, an aggregate view of effective project execution, the health of the innovation pipeline, and an evaluation of partners' added value. Outcomes track product and process performance (against competitors' products), whether existing customers commit more of their needs to the company, market share through new customers, and the quality of the technology developed. Finally, outputs track sales and profit growth as short-term measures of financial performance and share price relative to the industry as the ability to generate value for the company.

Following development of the innovation business model, the next step is identifying the measures that will describe this business model. Measures are organized into perspectives, usually between four and seven, such as inputs, processes, outputs, and outcomes. The rule of thumb is to have at most five to seven measures per perspective; that way, you avoid becoming overwhelmed because too many measures are reported, with a total that should not exceed 15 to 20 measures. Each organizational level has its own set of measures that cascade down from the model and measures defined at the business unit level. Distilling measures at each level is important to provide the adequate tools throughout the organization. Good measures at the top of the organization are a small part of a good measurement system.

In some cases, objective measures will be readily apparent, but in other cases they will be less obvious. When objective measures are not obvious, then subjective assessments are better than no measures at all. Siebel Systems, the company that developed the Customer Relationship Management (CRM) market and grew to $1 billion annual sales faster than either Microsoft or Oracle, relied on subjective measures to understand and manage the important intangibles of its standard services and innovations. Every quarter, the company administered an employee survey to measure various dimensions of employee satisfaction. Siebel Systems also complemented its daily interactions with customers—carefully recorded in its CRM system—with customer satisfaction surveys administered by a third party. These provided important understandings of how well things were working from the perspective of the customers and the employees.

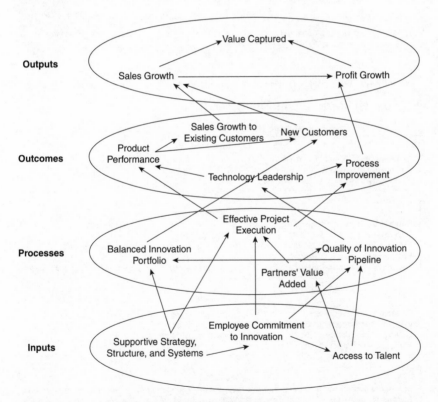

FIGURE 6.4 EXAMPLE OF A BUSINESS MODEL FOR INNOVATION UNDERLYING THE MEASUREMENT SYSTEM.

Research Bite: Subjective Measures for Selection Decisions

A medical products company that we interviewed had a systematic approach to selecting new research opportunities based on measures. The management team met twice a month to evaluate the progress of the current projects and to assess potential new products. Prior to each meeting, new opportunities were evaluated in several dimensions. The analysis included financial measures such as net present value (NPV) or return on investment (ROI); traditional assessments of the fit of the opportunity with strategy, technology, and market risks. But in addition, each manager in R&D, marketing, and business development filled out a questionnaire regarding various other aspects of the project—a subjective assessment—and ranked the project against existing ones and other project opportunities. The objective of this was to capture what objective measures cannot and provide a balanced perspective.

Figure 6.5 reflects the set of measures associated with the business model illustrated in Figure 6.4.

Value Added

Value added: Residual income for the division
Sales growth: Change in sales over same quarter last year
Profit growth: Change in profit over same quarter last year

Performance

Sales growth to existing customers: Change in sales over same quarter last year
New customers: Number of new customers for the quarter
Process improvement: On-time delivery and cost reduction over same quarter last year
Product performance: Product ratings versus competitors
Technology leadership: Percentage of products protected by patents granted over the last 3 years

---

Execution

Balanced innovation portfolio: Actual versus budgeted investments in mix of innovations
Effective project execution: Progress against expectations
Quality of innovation pipeline: Projected impact of ideas under study
Partners' value added: Percentage of investment by partner and teams' satisfaction with partner

---

Resources

Employee commitment to innovation: Employee innovation feedback
Access to talent: Quality of new recruits and quality of partnerships
Supportive infrastructure: Knowledge management system quality and employee awareness

---

FIGURE 6.5   MEASURES FOR THE BUSINESS MODEL PRESENTED IN FIGURE 6.4.

Designing and Implementing Innovation Measurement Systems

The measures for gauging innovation vary depending on how far you drill down in the organization: The measurements at the project level are very different from the measures at the strategic level.

Figure 6.6 reflects the idea that measurement systems cascade from the business unit level down to each innovation effort and extends throughout the value chain (internal as well as external). The x-axis captures the business model and value chain perspectives, and the y-axis captures the organizational dimension. Measurement systems are nested from particular projects up to the business level. At each stage, measures are aggregated and new ones are added.

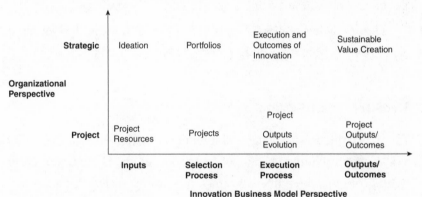

FIGURE 6.6   FRAMEWORK FOR INNOVATION MEASUREMENT.

At the venture capital division of a large technology firm, ideation is measured via the quality and quantity of the deal flow. The quality of the portfolio selection is measured by comparing the fit between the companies in which the division has invested and the markets identified by the corporation as strategic for its future. The execution measures include the number of transitions for portfolio firms through new funding rounds, sales growth, and the quality of the intellectual capital developed. Sustainable value creation at the division level includes measuring the ROI, the number of acquisitions of firms in the portfolio, and the new business brought to existing divisions.

The measurement system for an individual firm in the portfolio of the division is very different from the divisional measurement system. Project resource measures include the actual dollar investment in the startup firm, the number and types of contacts between the startup management team, and people at various divisions in the corporation who can help the startup. Project execution measures track the startup firm's development compared to its business plan, changes to its strategy, and financial indicators. Project outcomes and outputs are evaluated at the exit event, and include ROI and intellectual capital as well as new business generated for the corporation.

The following sections describe in more detail the development of measurement systems at the strategic organizational level.

Measures for Ideation

The flow of ideas with which to fuel innovation depends on the ability to leverage the human capital of the organization. The measurement system for innovation needs to track the various pieces of the human capital equation:

- Culture

- Exposure to innovation stimuli

- Understanding of innovation strategy

- Management infrastructure for ideation

There is a significant amount of qualitative information generated through the regular human resource mechanisms including performance evaluations, exit interviews, and external audits that can be used to diagnose the state of the innovation culture. In addition, employee surveys can enrich the understanding of innovation culture. In combination, these can give a quite accurate picture of the state of the innovation culture and climate in the organization.[17]

There are also objective measures like employee turnover, applicants per position, or employee involvement in innovation initiatives. But even objective measures need to be carefully applied. *Red Herring*, a leading magazine in the technology industry space, went through three editors-in-chief before it found the right person for the culture of the company and the requirements of the job. It expected the need to experiment to find the right match. Turnover in this case was a good thing rather than a negative.

The second aspect of a healthy idea flow is the exposure that the organization has to innovation stimuli. Similar to the sales process where lead quality and volume depends on the depth and breath of the marketing process, the quality and quantity of ideas depend on the exposure of the organization to internal and external innovation forces.[18] The effectiveness of internal innovation efforts—quality circles, brainstorming groups, training sessions—can be measured to give the organization a sense of whether it is devoting sufficient resources to these efforts and if they are successful. A company can quantify the number of efforts as well as its effectiveness as measured by satisfaction and effectiveness surveys. British Petroleum (BP) encouraged and tracked internal efforts including:

- **Peer assists**, where managers from other divisions would assist a particular division to solve a unique problem.

- **Peer groups**, in which managers from different divisions met periodically to support each other and transfer knowledge.

- **Federal groups**, made up of formal projects to solve a problem cutting across various divisions.

Measurement of external stimuli—from suppliers, customers, partners, infrastructure providers, and experts—is also a key to success. Each particular external interaction will have an execution model from the inputs required to maximize the potential value of the collaboration, the processes in place to execute the strategy, and the outputs such as the quantity and quality of ideas generated. For collaboration projects with universities, IBM tracks the quality of the people involved, the meetings that take place, the achievements throughout the project, the quality of the ideas generated, and the follow-up work undertaken.

The third leg of a healthy idea generation process is a clear strategy backed up with access to competitive knowledge that is used to direct and catalyze innovation. One of the purposes of strategy is to clarify what efforts are within the bounds of the company's playing field and therefore should be pursued. By clarifying these boundaries, the company focuses creativity and energizes action.[19] Assessments of the types of ideas and projects combined with employee surveys can provide a good indication of whether the organization understands the strategic framework for innovation and uses it to generate ideas. Chrysler conducted assessments of the range of innovation efforts across its platforms, and measured employee attitudes and their understanding of the strategic framework to gain a better understanding of its innovation efforts.

The last lever of a healthy environment for ideation—the infra-structure element of the measurement system—should track whether adequate resources and processes are in place including:

- **Talent**, which measures the level and effectiveness of recruiting, training and resource allocation.

- **Money**, which measures funding available for ideation from the budgeting process and from discretionary pools within the company.

- **Knowledge**, which measures the development and use of effective knowledge management platforms to support internal and external groups.

- **Management systems** that track the quality of information, planning (such as strategic planning mechanisms), resource allocation, and incentive systems which reward ideas. These systems enable the "friction" that leads to creativity.

- **Communication**, which tracks the level and effectiveness of planning and constructive conversations regarding the need and direction of innovation.

Siebel Systems developed an internal knowledge management software, later commercialized as Employee Relationship Management Systems, to put relevant information at the fingertips of each employee, access to the people throughout the company's network, and targeted training. This software allowed the company to track how the company was using its network of people and training processes.

Table 6.1 describes other measures that are used to measure innovation input.

Table 6.1   Measures for Ideation

	Inputs	Process	Outputs	Outcomes
Culture	Percentage of qualified people per opening Mix of backgrounds Quality of new recruits Staff motivation	Training sessions Communication efforts Number of ideas from planning exercise	R&D staff turnover Employee suggestions Employee commitment External HR audits Change in core competencies	Cost of misbehavior Change in revenue per employee
Interaction	Research agreements with partners Percentage of R&D budget that is non-internal Quality IT infrastructure to support interest groups Individual networking skills	Innovation and creativity workshops Ideas fairs Conferences' attendance Interest groups Participation of suppliers in stage-gate process Number of contacts with partners Deal manager's team bandwidth	Quality of ideas funded Alliances to further develop ideas Investments in new projects Number of ideas from outside company R&D Deal options that are exercised	Percentage of sales together with partners Percentage of sales from ideas originated outside
Understanding of Strategy	Funding availability Knowledge depth	Communication workshops Competitive information Quality of development pipeline	Assessment of competitors' innovation investments Map of upcoming innovations to the market Understanding of company strategy Percentage of growth covered by innovation	Expected sales from incremental innovations against competitors Expected sales from radical innovation against competitors
Process and Systems	Quality of resource allocation process Quality of recruiting process Effectiveness of motivational systems Empowerment	Quality of training programs Quality of workshops Quality of external collaborators Quality of planning systems	Funds committed to innovation Effectiveness of planning systems Improvement in knowledge stock	Cost of developing and maintaining infrastructure Actual versus budgeted costs for planning and knowledge management

Measuring Your Innovation Portfolio

The purpose of *portfolio measurement systems* is to evaluate the balance of the various innovation efforts across several dimensions.[20] The typical portfolio tool is a graphic where two of the dimensions are plotted in the x and y axes and an additional two dimensions can be captured in the size of the bubble identifying each project and the color of the bubble. Figure 6.7 provides an example from an energy organization. The portfolio matrix for this organization positions each innovation in terms of risk, time frame, funding, and business line. In this example, the company has chosen to de-emphasize low-risk projects and focus its efforts on medium- and high-risk projects. This is a reflection of the innovation strategy that stresses taking appropriate risks in order to make significant advances.

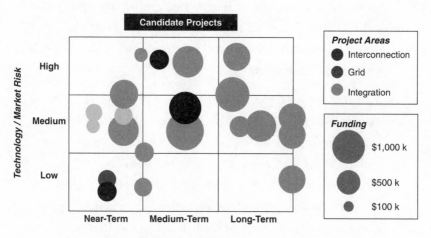

FIGURE 6.7   AN INNOVATION PORTFOLIO PERSPECTIVE.

Key measures commonly used in portfolios include:

- **Time to value**. Because of the forward-looking nature of innovation, portfolio analysis includes the dimension of time. This dimension refers to the time until the project achieves a significant milestone usually related to market release or turning cash flow positive. From a portfolio perspective, this dimension provides visibility into the development pipeline. Break-even time, a measure widely used in technology firms, is the time since inception of the project until it pays back the investment.

- **Risk**. Risk may be associated with risks of the technology, business model, or the execution of the project. Risks are typically measured through a subjective assessment based on previous experience and personal knowledge. For high-risk strategies, the risk dimension often receives additional attention through scenario analysis, more elaborate probability distributions, options assessment, and contingency plans. Portfolios provide optics to see and manage the risks inherent in the innovation strategy and execution.

- **Value**. Another dimension of the portfolio analysis is the economics of each project. This dimension can be limited to measuring the budget for a project, or it can be disaggregated to include other measures of value. In particular, value can be measured through expected profits, expected value added (profits minus the cost of the capital involved in developing and running the innovation), or likely measures as ROI or return on assets. More sophisticated measures may include option valuation methods that take into account not only the expected benefits from the current effort but also future benefits associated with the capabilities developed. This latter approach is especially relevant when evaluating platform products where the benefits come from the platform as well as future derivatives.

- **Type of innovation**. Another dimension is the balance between the incremental, semi-radical, and radical projects. This perspective is valuable in keeping the investments aligned with the innovation strategy.

- **Implementation stage**. In order to assess the projects in the pipeline, a useful dimension is to examine the stage of development of each project. Typical stages include pure research, development, demonstration, and commercialization. A good pipeline of projects will have projects distributed through the different stages, typically with more projects in R&D stages than in commercialization.

Finally, there are measures related to the dynamic dimension of portfolios. These measures address how fast the organization adapts its portfolio to changes in its execution plans or strategy.

Portfolio measures and diagrams are sophisticated analytical tools. However, they are only tools and the decision is always in the hands of managers. A common fallacy is that a "perfect measurement system exists and can be designed" which leads to decision-making being delegated to these analysis tools. This is potentially destructive. Every measurement system has limitations and nothing can replace good judgment.

In addition to portfolio maps, *innovation roadmaps* are another way of looking at an innovation portfolio. In contrast to portfolio maps, innovation roadmaps depict current and future innovation projects and link the projects to demonstrate the inter-relationships and dependencies. The development of new transmission technologies to solve the U.S. power outage problems is dependent on the development path of distribution technologies, demand response technologies, new business models by utilities, and federal policy development. Mapping these relationships provides a crucial strategic context. The roadmaps also make it clear that certain innovation efforts may not be financially attractive on their own, but could develop value that can be leveraged into the future. A leading medical device company with sales grossing more than $4 billion uses innovation roadmaps that describe the general evolution of certain internal and external technology developments to manage investments in services or products that may only be attractive in a future date when the market has evolved. Projects are planned, evaluated, and improved against this backdrop.

Research Bite: Innovation Measures at a Consumer Electronics Firm

A large consumer electronics company in our research described various distinct measures associated with innovation. At the project execution level, it measured the cycle time between a concept's start and the product's commercial release. Quality was measured as a function of field calls during the first year, effectiveness was measured using market share, brand index (market share in dollars divided by volume), and brand recognition. The company had recently completed the global standardization of processes and systems for product development with various objectives. Therefore, it also carefully measured design reuse.

At the functional level, measure included managers' opinions on the competency gap for current and future competencies, training, environmental performance, number of engineering changes, software defect density, hit rate (number of projects prior to funding commercialization), and the participation of the quality improvement teams.

Finally, the company carefully measured its progress against its roadmaps—technology, features and functions, products, and markets. The technology roadmap was seen as critical to developing technology platforms for new product families.

Measuring Execution and Outcomes of Innovation

In a business unit or company, typically a wide range of innovation efforts is going on at the same time. There are ideas that are still in the exploration phase, there are incremental innovation projects, there are semi-radical innovation projects that explore technologies and business models outside the current strategy, and there are radical projects that explore potentially disruptive innovations.

A good system for measuring the aggregate performance of all of these types of innovation efforts has four characteristics:

- Visibility over the evolution of the various projects being executed

- Informative about the relevant aspects of each particular project

- Capacity utilization

- Product platform leverage

The first characteristic of the execution measurement system is the ability to provide visibility into all these innovation efforts. This capability is intimately related to the information technology infrastructure that underlies the measurement system.[21] Managers must have the option to drill down into the measurement system to understand the evolution of each innovation effort. Good managers use this capability to be on top of the developments in their company and to be able to ask the right questions and take action when needed, but they avoid the precision to micromanage the organization.

The second characteristic of the execution measurement system is to give an informative picture of the innovation status of the organization. To achieve this, the measurement system has to aggregate the project level information into a higher level overview. For example, on-time performance is aggregated to provide an overall diagnostic of the company's performance in managing its projects on time. Current information technology has the flexibility to aggregate information in various ways and look at performance using different perspectives.

Matching a project's needs to the different types of resources over time leads to more efficient project execution. This is the third characteristic of the execution measurement system. A well-designed system has to clearly describe the various types of resources needed, the resource capacity available, and the allocation of resources to projects. This capacity utilization identifies potential resources that will be constrained (or oversupplied) and permits planning—especially important for resources that take longer to develop.

A leading company in external power supplies developed a measurement system following these design rules to track its product development projects. As a result, senior management had periodic, informative reports on how the company as a whole was performing in terms of schedule, budget, productivity of its engineers, and project changes. For finished projects, it also aggregated time-to-develop, budget, and market acceptance. This information was tracked over time to visualize the trend of R&D efficiency and effectiveness.

Product platform measures are the fourth execution measure.[22] These measures evaluate the effectiveness and efficiency of a product. Product platform effectiveness is defined as:

**Derivative development cost (or time) /
platform development cost (or time)**

Well-designed product platforms allow derivative products to be developed quickly and with low investment. Therefore, the lower the ratio the higher the leverage the development organization is getting out of the initial product platform. As the ratio starts to increase, the organization should explore whether to move to a new platform.

Measuring Sustainable Value Creation

The desired result of innovation efforts is *value creation*.[23] Within for-profit firms, value creation is measured through financial performance. Typically financial measures link value creation to the innovation. For non-profit firms, including government research and development organizations, value creation depends on the particular mission of the organization. The California Energy Commission (CEC) uses its specific program mission and goals as the basis for determining the value creation of its transmission and distribution research projects.

For incremental innovation projects, financial performance is relatively easy to measure.[24] Because the value that these projects generate is easily and rapidly captured, the value generated is the associated increase in revenues minus the associated change in costs minus the cost of the resources invested. This value can be measured as ROI or residual income (RI, also known as value based management)[25]—the latter having the advantage of being an absolute measure compared to ROI, which is a ratio measure.

Return on Investment

(sales − costs) / investment

Residual Income

(sales − costs) − cost of capital × investment

Limitations of ROI absent in the RI measure include the following:

- **Ignores the absolute magnitude of the investment**. But two projects returning 10 percent (same as ROI) are very different if the investment in one of them is $100 and the other is $1 million.

- **May lead to underinvestment**. A division with an ROI of 25 percent may reject a project with a 20 percent ROI because it would lower its ROI, even if the cost of capital (the adequate reference point) is 10 percent.

- **May lead to overinvestment**. A division with an ROI of 5 percent may reject a project with a 7 percent ROI because it would increase its ROI, even if the cost of capital (the adequate reference point) is 10 percent.

Figure 6.8 presents an illustrative cash flow over time of a project. This information is critical to have both at the individual project and the aggregate level. It depicts the financial risk of the project (and at the aggregate level the potential need to borrow cash); the time to recover the investment (the break-even point); and the value generated (the cumulated cash flow at the end of the product's life).

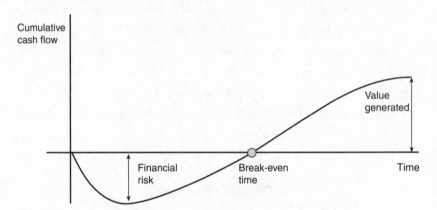

FIGURE 6.8   PROJECT CASH FLOW OVER TIME.

For radical projects, measuring value creation becomes more challenging. First, the overall value generated may take years before it is captured. Think about the time it took Amazon.com to start capturing the value (turn its original concept of selling business on the Internet into a cash flow positive business) that this initial concept had the potential to generate. FedEx, a radical business innovation when first started in 1971, received $90 million in venture capital (a quantity unheard of at the time) and did not turn cash flow positive for 26 months after accumulating losses of $29 million.[26]

Second, it is difficult to disentangle how much of the value is directly attributable to the innovation effort and how much of it is due to the execution of the strategy. How much of Google's value is linked to the original search code, and how much is associated with a skillful execution of the business model around the technology breakthrough?

Third, the project may develop capabilities that can be further extended through additional development efforts. The development of the minivan concept and the original Dodge Caravan not only saved Chrysler from a likely death but also created one of the most successful product lines in the auto industry, which is constantly improved. What were the financial returns as a result of the development of the first Caravan? Huge, but hard to quantify.

Finally, measuring value creation is difficult because the risk of failure is very high. Thus, value creation should be looked at not only at the project level but also more importantly at the portfolio level. Eli Lilly—one of the largest pharmaceutical companies in the world—bought a portfolio of medical devices' startups in the early 1990s. Some of them were unsuccessful, but a decade later these companies were spun off as Guidant Corporation with an initial market capitalization of $1 billion (that became $9 billion three years later).

Alternative value creation measures—such as experts' evaluation, development milestones, intellectual property creation, and patents—are more relevant especially in the early phases of radical innovation where the uncertainties are the largest and the time horizon is very long.

Table 6.2 provides examples of the components of a measurement system. These are presented as examples of what could work in your company, not as what would be best for your company.[27] You will find some that fit your situation well and some that do not. During this process, you may also think of some that are not presented here. Select and develop those that best fit your company.

Table 6.2   Examples of Measurements

Objective	Measures
Outputs	
Long-term corporate profitability	Stock price Projected sales growth Projected residual income
Short-term corporate profitability	Residual income growth Sales growth Return on equity Percentage of sales from new products
Outcomes	
Customer acquisition	New customers gained through innovation Number of customers through existing products/services who buy new products/services Number of new customers of new products/services who go on to buy existing products/services Market share
Customer loyalty	Frequency of repeat customers Average annual sales per customer Customer satisfaction with innovation activities Percentage of customer attrition Ratio of new visitors to repeat visitors
Value capture	Margin of product and services offered to customers Average of prices paid by customers Number of new product and service lines introduced Profitability of innovation operations Revenues generated through innovation efforts (total revenue, innovation revenue, revenue per innovation customer) Customer profitability
Process	
Portfolio	Percentage of innovation efforts devoted to radical, semi-radical, and incremental innovation Portfolio balanced over time, returns, risk, and technologies Alignment between innovation strategy and resource allocation
Execution	Product platform effectiveness Reduction in new product/process development time/cost Within target sales/profits Projected within time, budget, product performance targets

R&D productivity
Number of new patents granted each year
Number of gateway returns
Rate and quality of experimentation
Cost, development time, delivery time, quantity, and
price of products and services offered
Product and process quality score

Inputs	
Commitment and focus on innovation	Time dedicated to innovation Budget percent allocated to innovation efforts Performance-based compensation linked to innovation success Success of ideas passing through selection and execution processes Investment in training
Balanced innovation of networks inside and outside of organization	Level of innovation integration across business units and functions Mix of innovation sources Percentage of innovation projects outsourced Number of strategic alliances Number of experienced innovation team members Assessment of supplier capabilities
Coherent and aligned innovation strategy	Number, cost, price, and perception of new products offered from innovation projects Number, cost, price, and perception of new services offered from innovation projects Perception of brand Profitability of innovation operations Objectives for innovation efforts clearly communicated to senior managers and employees Competitive position within industry Number, complexity and size of competitors, customers, partners, and suppliers
Appropriate management infrastructure for effective innovation implementation	Percentage of performance measures and rewards aligned and linked to innovation activities Quality of IT infrastructure Quality of information for innovation Market and technology research resources Amount and quality of customer data acquired related to innovation Dollars of resources available for innovation Free time allowances for R&D employees Geographic diversity of production and sales Level of empowerment to Strategic Business Unit (SBU) and functional managers Cross-functional initiatives

CEO Sanity Check: How Well Are the Four Areas of
Innovation Measurement Working?

Assess the strength and weakness of the measurement system in
each area. Unevenness in one or more reduces the effectiveness of
the whole system.

- Ideation
- Portfolio
- Execution and Outcomes
- Value Creation

The Barriers to Effective Performance Measurement

There are seven basic barriers to having a measurement system in
place and functioning well:

1. **If the basic business model is flawed, the organization
   will focus on the wrong levers of value creation, and
   measure the wrong variables during development of
   the innovation**. Microsoft has shown time and again its ability to observe, learn, and change its business model to adapt
   to market and technology changes.

2. **Avoid measuring the wrong variables**. One company that
   we worked with reported every financial number down to
   the cent, but failed to measure crucial non-financial variables. For example, measuring time-to-market is important if
   the execution model is built on the assumption that first
   mover advantages are key to the strategy and the value creation proposition. However, for innovation projects following
   a low-cost product strategy, time-to-market must take a back
   seat and allow innovation around lowering costs rather than
   reducing time.[28]

3. **Objective measures are attractive, but in a lot of settings they are of limited use**. Subjective measures allow companies to capture intangibles and to adapt the information to the particular events of an innovation effort.[29] Citibank periodically evaluated the motivation and commitment of its branch managers to the company strategy, absent any reliable objective measures.

4. **Failure to use the power of the available information technology is a costly mistake**. The cost of measuring and communicating information has gone down significantly. Better information allows not only better management but also data mining capabilities to uncover new opportunities. Information technology can be more powerful than is usually assumed. Boeing used information technology to design the 777 airplane faster, better, and cheaper than traditional design approaches could have delivered.

5. **Another barrier to success is believing that IT is more powerful than it is**. No measurement system can replace the analysis and judgment of management. Measurement systems guide the attention to the information reported, raise questions, and frame the thinking process. However, the measurement system never provides the answers; managers do that.

6. **Using a management system the wrong way is a common mistake**. Using a system to monitor instead of to learn is damaging. A well-know business story describes a company in the baby food industry that continually monitored sales. Management noticed that the sales office in Florida consistently met its sales target. After many years of this phenomenon, someone in management went down to Florida to see what was happening. He found that in addition to babies, many aged people were also eating baby food because it was

easier to eat. The use of the measurement system to monitor blocked the communication and learning that would have brought this innovation quickly to headquarters and benefitted the whole company.

7. **The final barrier is using the wrong data**. Just as 'garbage in garbage out' plagues a company's manufacturing operations, the same phenomenon also hurts innovation.

Senior management should look very carefully at its innovation measurement systems and honestly assess which of these barriers are real or potential problems. It is management's responsibility to ensure that the innovation measurements systems are designed properly and in good working order; their company's future depends on it.

CEO Actions: Removing the Seven Barriers to Effective Performance Measurement

Identify which of theses are barriers to the effectiveness of your measurement systems:

- Wrong execution model
- Wrong measures
- Ignoring subjective measures
- Limited information technology capabilities
- Over-reliance on "facts" and not enough on "learning"
- Giving the system the wrong role
- Getting the wrong data into the system

Discover why the barriers exist—and then go after the root causes.

Measurement and the Innovation Rules

Managing and measuring go hand in hand. Thomas Edison managed his research team by measuring the number of innovations they developed every week. He set the innovation target at one small innovation per week and a big one every six months. This was a breakneck rate of innovation, and Edison's team called themselves "the insomnia squad."[30]

While Edison's measures seem overly aggressive and a little simplistic, he was on the right track; managers and teams need a small number of straightforward, effective measurements to guide and drive successful innovation.

There are several critical things to do when you design and implement innovation measurement systems:

- **Directly link the innovation measures to the innovation strategy and the innovation business model**. The majority of global companies surveyed recognized that they were deficient in measuring the strategic value of their innovation.[31]

- **Don't be rigid; build in enough variability to allow valuable measurement**. Different innovation processes and different organizational levels need different measurement systems, and these can vary over time. Projects need measures that are consistent with the business unit but different enough to capture project-specific innovation characteristics. The measures that are appropriate at the beginning of a project may not be adequate in the later stages.

- **Know the specific purpose of each type of measurement system; trying to achieve too many objectives will get you nowhere**. Dissect measurement systems to ensure that they are proving the right mix of planning, monitoring, and learning.

- **Keep it simple; too many measures can be more of a distraction than a help**. It is better to have five simple measures linked to the strategy and the innovation business model than 20-30 measures; even if the additional measures provide a more complete picture, they will overwhelm the decision-makers. In this case, quantity is the enemy of quality.

- **Stay in charge**. Be aware of the limitations of measurement systems. They enhance but do not replace good management.

Measurement is one of the most significant factors in successful innovation. Ironically, in many organizations, it is one of the least attended to.

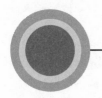

7

REWARDING INNOVATION: HOW TO DESIGN INCENTIVES TO SUPPORT INNOVATION

The Importance of Incentives and Rewards

Incentives and rewards are some of the most powerful management tools available. When Mobil changed its measurement system to support introduction of its new business model, it linked 30 percent of the bonuses of all salaried employees to these metrics. A significant part of Mobil's improved measures tracked the ability of the organization to learn better ways to execute the business model. At the corporate level, measures such as the growth in non-gasoline revenues were used to reflect the value of incremental innovations to the model. At the division level, the company measured new product ROI and new product acceptance rate. The result was Mobil moving to the number one position in the industry.

However, be careful what behavior you reward—you might just get it. A high-growth startup company just acquired by a large pharmaceutical company (let's call it ATH Technologies) faced the problem of motivating its employees to reach the sales and profit goals associated with the earn-out structure of the acquisition. Subjective bonuses, top management encouragement, and a performance-focused culture had been unsuccessful in reaching the goal. Then top management changed the incentive scheme of each employee in the firm. Everybody would receive a 30 percent bonus and a trip for two to Hawaii if the sales and earning goals were met. The incentive system linked to the financial goals was very effective, and the company reached its growth goals. However, after the trip to Hawaii, the FDA discovered significant quality problems in the products shipped, and the company was threatened with closure. Measures and incentives are powerful, but they should be carefully designed and balanced with the rest of management tools, including risk management.

Motivation

People engage in an activity because of:

- The expected incentives associated with the activity

- Their passion about the activity

- Trust that they will be appropriately recognized

- A vision that provides a clear sense of purpose

Designing adequate reward systems for innovation needs to take into account these four elements (see Figure 7.1).

Some important rewards do not happen through explicit management systems in the organization.[1] They happen within the realm of personal interactions: a casual conversation where the chief engineer praises the work of an engineer over a cup of coffee; the team leader's satisfaction when her team members are committed to the project, enjoy their work, achieve winning results, and grow as people; the boss that appreciates the effort in executing a risky project even though it does not succeed; or the personal satisfaction of seeing the results of one's effort implemented.[2] As one manager who we interviewed plainly put it: "One thing about technology people is money is important, but food is extremely important."

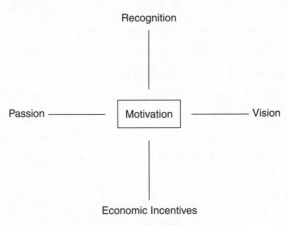

FIGURE 7.1   **THE FOUR ELEMENTS OF MOTIVATION.**

Different Strokes for Different Folks

Incentives are designed before an innovation effort starts, and they link performance measures and rewards.[3] Philips, the Dutch consumer electronics company, links the bonus of its product development teams to meeting release date targets specified before the project starts. The size of the bonus depends on the difference between the target and the actual release date. Volkswagen links the promotions of the design team to performance, including hitting the schedule and budget milestones.

In contrast, *recognition* is a reward that occurs after the outcomes of the project are available, even if there was no prior contract in place linking performance to rewards. Recognition rewards are based on subjective assessments of the value generated. Inviting a development team to a hockey game after they have successfully finished the project even though the "contract" did not require it is part of the recognition system. Assigning the manager to a more important project or simply enabling peer recognition is another way of recognizing a project manager's performance.

A European company had been researching for several years a new material for brain surgery clips that are used to temporarily close blood vessels during surgery. Conventional metal clips were affected by magnetic fields and moved during brain scans. The improved clip they were searching for needed to have the same ability to close blood vessels as existing clips but be non-responsive to magnetic fields. The head of the research team said that an important part of what kept the team going during the long search was the internal drive to solve the problem and the strong interest that the CEO showed.

Some people innovate because they have a passion about what they do and not because of extrinsic rewards. People who are deeply interested in their work are self-motivated and are less influenced by external factors.[4] An R&D manager in one major car company described his development teams being heavily motivated by their strong interest in car technologies and their desire to get the best ideas incorporated and seen brought to market.

Formal reward systems are well-suited for incremental innovation, such as increasing the efficiency of a manufacturing plant or improving quality through quality circles. Incremental innovation projects have a clear problem to solve. The solution to the problem can be translated into targets and linked to rewards. For instance, when the problem is that a product is too expensive, the solution is to incrementally redesign the product to achieve a 30 percent cost reduction. This specific target can then be linked to rewards, providing strong reinforcement to solve the problem.

Incentives are much harder to use for radical and semi-radical innovations because the targets are not well-defined and often change during the course of a project. Radical innovations rely more on recognition as a reward. Art Fry's recognition as the father of Post-its is a major, long-lasting part of his reward. Using recognition to reward radical innovation gives an organization the flexibility to adjust the reward to each individual project, team, and person.

The rise and fall of the dot-com bubble was partly attributable to too much focus on incentives. People started companies with their eyes on the prize of a successful IPO (initial public offering) rather than the value and excitement connected with the development of a semi-radical or radical innovation.[5] It was not the passion for creating something new that drove the teams; it was the downstream financial reward. Now that the bubble has burst, venture capitalists are going back to their roots: investing in new technology and business models led by individuals and teams that are passionate about their innovations.

A Framework for Incentive Systems' Design

An incentive system should reinforce a company's innovation strategy, whether it is Play-to-Win or Play-Not-to-Lose. It is vital to design incentives so that they motivate people to work together to where the company wants to go. Nikon, the Japanese camera manufacturer, defines very clear goals for the teams designing the cameras for the upcoming season. The goals specify the release date, product size, image quality, and most importantly, cost. Nikon uses target cost goals and incentives to ensure the profitability of the product. Figure 7.2 presents the key elements of incentive systems' design.

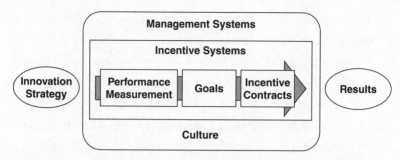

FIGURE 7.2   A FRAMEWORK FOR INCENTIVE SYSTEMS' DESIGN.

The goals for more radical innovations are less specific. When Guerrino de Luca took over as CEO of Logitech, the world leader in computer peripherals such as mice, the company had reached a sales plateau of $400 million. His goal was to take the company beyond the current sales plateau, and he was encouraged to use new business models and consider new technologies. During the next seven years, he complemented the company's main (and almost only) product—computer mice—with a host of new products: keyboards, webcams, cordless peripherals, joysticks. He moved the company from being mostly an OEM supplier to becoming a household name, and expanded its marketing efforts worldwide. Through small acquisitions and lots of internal innovation efforts, Logitech reached sales of $1.26 billion in the end of fiscal year 2003.

Different projects need their own distinct goals. Applied Materials' integrated circuits manufacturing machines work with technology at the edge of existing particle physics' knowledge. Intel—one of Applied Materials' main customers—requires its production lines to be 100 percent flawless—exact replications of the first one installed to produce a certain chip. This is because the underlying physics are not fully understood, and even minimal changes may have horrible effects on productivity. The main criterion at Applied Materials is performance—at almost any cost. This is a significantly different cost priority than Nikon uses.

Once goals have been set, team and individual incentive contracts are defined to establish the formal link between performance and rewards. The incentive contract can be based on a formula that links performance against goals and prescribes payoffs. For instance, being on time has a $1,000 bonus for each team member. However, it is also common to use performance against goals as an input to a subjective performance evaluation. At Johnson & Johnson Medical Devices and Diagnostics, product development leaders are chosen from different business functions. Leading a development team is only one of the tasks that they do throughout a year. At the end of the year, a product development leader's supervisors gather to evaluate the person and decide his or her reward. The performance as leader of a development team is only one input to their evaluation and how it will be weighted is left to the evaluation committee.

The advantage of subjective performance evaluation is that it allows for an interpretation of the information that the measurement system provides and adjusts for events that are not adequately reflected in the "hard" numbers. A formula-based incentive system cannot adjust for the negative impact of the unexpected bankruptcy of a key supplier of technology. A subjective incentive system can account for it and reward the manager more fairly.

The final step in the design of incentive systems is defining the actual rewards. There are multiple ways of providing rewards: bonuses, prizes, stock options, and promotions, just to mention a few. Larger companies tend to rely on cash bonuses to a larger extent compared to a startup that relies on stock based rewards. Each one has its advantages and limitations, and there are no hard and fast rules about which to use when. Management needs to ensure that they have been combined optimally.[6]

Incentive systems do not work in isolation; they act inside an organization in the context of its own culture and management systems. Incentive systems have to be aligned with the culture and systems to be effective. One startup company in Silicon Valley that was in a hurry to get to market simply copied the incentive system from a competitor. The employees of the startup rebelled because they felt the incentive system was inherently unfair; it did not fit their operating style and culture. The company was forced to start from scratch and design incentive systems that fit their situation.

Setting Goals for Measuring Performance

Without clear goals, innovation metrics lack a clear reference point from which to evaluate progress, and the power of the incentives is blunted.

Goals vary across several dimensions:

- Specific versus broad

- Quantitative versus qualitative

- Stretch versus realistic

- Success-driven versus loss-avoidance

Specific Versus Broad Goals

Goals can be specific, such as "reduce the cost of the mousetrap by 7 percent," or broad, as in "build a better mousetrap." Both have their place. Goals for incremental innovation projects should be specific, such as Nikon's focus on a specific camera at a pre-determined cost.

With clear, specific goals, incremental innovation projects can be managed by exception—when managers intervene only if there are significant deviations. An exceptional deviation (either good or bad) is investigated to understand the underlying cause. It may indicate the existence of risk that was underestimated or perhaps bad execution.

Exceptional deviations are not always a "problem." They may actually lead to larger innovation opportunities. Once identified, these opportunities can be pursued within the current project or, as happens in most cases, spun-off into a new innovation project. Post-its was an instance where an unexpected discovery led to an unanticipated innovation. While 3M's researchers were searching for a super-strong adhesive, many less than satisfactory adhesives were developed. That is par for the course in material research; you need to create many unacceptable experiments before you find the right solution. One of these "less-than-satisfactory" adhesives caught the eye of Art Fry who was looking for a material that would allow someone to affix a paper multiple times without leaving any adhesive residue. He had gotten the idea when his choir bookmarks fell out; he wanted a bookmark that would stick and not hurt the book. The new adhesive performed better than expected in the bookmark role. That intersection of the less-than-acceptable adhesive and Art's concept for marking his place in the choir notes was the beginning of Post-its.

As product development initiatives take on more risk and shift towards radical innovation, goals necessarily become broader and less specific. Think about Logitech's new CEO's goal of moving the company beyond its current sales plateau. Radical innovation requires experimentation, trial and error, openness to new ideas, and exchange of knowledge. Such freedom can only be achieved with goals that give managers flexibility.

Broad objectives stimulate constructive conversations between the project team, partners, other groups in the company, and top management. These discussions help the team better understand the strategic intent of top management. They also help senior management understand new strategic opportunities that were not easily articulated earlier in the process when the broad objectives where first described. Logitech's development of the IO Digital Pen—a pen that memorizes whatever it writes exactly in the place it was written and downloads it into a computer-readable file—is an example in point. Logitech's CEO defined the company's product space as "last-inch" interfaces between humans and technology. With this broad definition, marketing and engineering went around the world interacting with suppliers, customers, or simply interesting people. They bumped into the technology behind the IO Digital Pen in a fair in Europe. At the time, the technology was applied to a totally different product, but the Logitech team saw how it could be transformed to lead to a "last-inch" product. Ongoing interactions among various groups in the company distilled the product concept, created a business model unique to the characteristics of the product, and provided a clear, specific example of the broad "last-inch" goal—one that was not evident at the onset.

Quantitative Versus Qualitative Goals

Goals can be quantitative or qualitative. As a rule of thumb, incremental innovation projects tend to be more amenable to goals that can be easily quantified, such as time-to-market, level of resource consumption, and incremental changes in product performance. Quantitative goals for innovation usually have a specific time horizon: "Develop LCD screen TV by 2002."

Goals for radical and semi-radical innovation use more qualitative criteria because of the inherent uncertainty. Relying too much on quantitative goals may narrow the scope of the innovation effort and preclude the much-needed room for experimentation. Examples of qualitative goals that are being pursued today include "developing a cure for AIDS" or "create a viable business model for photovoltaic energy generation that does not rely on government subsidies."[7]

Stretch Versus Expected Goals

Goals also vary in terms of how demanding they are. Incremental innovation projects should have goals that are clearly attainable and realistically set. When Citibank first started to demand and reward branch managers on customer satisfaction, it set a target of 80 percent. This target was chosen to be demanding but feasible. Having set the target at a very aggressive level of 100 or even 95 percent would have been so hard to hit that it would have been de-motivating; managers would either ignore it or overinvest trying to reach it.

Goals for radical innovation projects should be *stretch goals*. These goals demand more than what most people would consider to be easy to attain or even realistic (in the sense of being easy to imagine and expect). When Microsoft spelled out its original vision of "a PC in every home," it did not expect to reach the goal in the near future. Its goal was to inspire employees but also customers and society to think about the importance of the PC and how to make it available to everybody.

Radical innovation goals have to be inspirational. The people in the team (or organization) must feel as if they are part of something special, part of a feat that has never been accomplished. The goals must spark an internal drive to succeed that does not exist within business as usual. Stretch goals should be used to stimulate discussion, exploration, experimentation, and exchange of ideas. They should force people to ask questions like: What is the right way to think about this? What kinds of experiments will move us closer to understanding how to do this?[8]

Success-Driven Versus Loss-Avoidance Goals

The last dimension includes *success-driven goals* versus *loss-avoidance goals*. When Applied Materials was designing its 65 nanometer (nm) chip manufacturing machines, success was defined as achieving the 65nm performance level, at required quality levels, on time. These are success-driven goals (meaning, they defined success). They are based on the key success driver of the project, whether it is time-to-market, product cost, or product performance.

In addition to the on-time success-driven goals, Applied Materials' products must be developed within a certain budget and within a certain product cost to be economically sound. These are loss-avoidance goals. As long as they are not exceeded, they are a marginal part of the innovation process. However, if the project reaches the limits set by one of these goals (such as product cost), then the project is running into a dangerous zone where it may achieve the key success-driven goals but fail because it exceeded one of the loss-avoidance goals.

Loss-avoidance goals are usually tighter for incremental innovations where the margin to redefine a project is smaller. Radical innovations, because of their inherent uncertainty and the larger payoffs if successful, have more slack in their loss-avoidance goals.

In summary, radical innovations typically employ goals that are broad, qualitative, stretch oriented (that is, aiming beyond what is thought to be attainable through normal effort), and success driven. Figure 7.3 depicts the range of characterizing goals for radical and incremental innovations and summarizes this discussion.

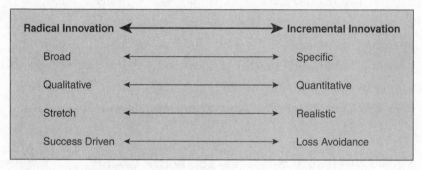

FIGURE 7.3   CHARACTERIZING GOALS.

Research Bite: A View on Incremental Versus Radical Innovation

A corporate manager described the challenges of radical innovation as follows:

"There are four risks in innovation. The traditional ones are technology and market risks. These are the ones that most often put incremental innovation at risk. But there are two additional risks: funding and people. Will I have the funding? And will I have the right people? These questions are irrelevant to incremental efforts, but they are critical for breakthroughs. If I have the funding and the right people, I'll have the technology and market understanding. Companies like

Cisco have huge networks inside and outside to know where technology and the market are going. If they don't have the talent to pursue an opportunity, they go out and buy it. Venture capitalists focus on funding and people; project managers focus on technology and markets. The key for breakthroughs is not to run a project but to create innovative technologies and business models; it is not about hurdle rates but about creating intellectual capital. It is not about filling a pipeline, but being exposed to deals and managing risks—do I want to share the risks and with whom? Radical innovation comes from breaking the project mentality."[9]

Performance Evaluation and Incentive Contracts

Goals are the reference point to evaluate performance during project execution and when the project is complete. In evaluating performance, several issues should be considered:

- The balance between team and individual performance measures

- Subjective versus objective performance evaluation

- Relative versus absolute performance evaluation

Team Versus Individual Rewards

Innovation projects are team efforts. Team members have a common objective: achieving the goals set out at the beginning of the project. They should have an incentive to collaborate and support each other's work. However, many companies block the effectiveness of teams by having inadequate incentives.[10] On the other hand, the individuals on teams may deserve rewards because of their performance. The performance evaluation system cannot ignore important individual efforts—otherwise, the system is perceived as inequitable, dissatisfaction will grow, and the innovation effort will be adversely affected.[11]

Team effort and spirit may be undermined if certain team members carry most of the load while others have a free ride. As one manager described her experience: "I was working more than 15 hours a day most of the time seven days a week, I was doing the analysis of every single project performance; I quit because I thought it was unfair to do all the work and then everybody getting the praise."

To avoid the possibility of a "free rider" (a team member who does not do his or her share of the work), the team leader should be empowered to choose team members or at least to replace a team member that he or she does not feel is contributing to the group. Another option is to complement team-based measures with evaluation and incentives for individual members. But while objective performance measures typically exist for teamwork—for instance, whether the project was on time, on budget, or on-specifications—they are almost non-existent for individual team members. Individual performance evaluation needs to rely on subjective assessments. The team leader may evaluate the performance of each of his or her team members or use a 360 degrees evaluation mechanism, where the people who work with a person evaluate her. These individual evaluations will help to avoid the free-rider problem.

Incremental innovation typically uses formula-based team incentives supplemented with individual performance evaluations and incentives. A development team working on a new energy technology received a cash bonus upon successful completion of the project. In addition, the individual team members were rewarded in the annual review process with bonuses and salary increases and in some cases promotions.

Companies could also offer profit sharing or gain sharing mechanisms. *Profit sharing*, used when the team is the division, encourages collaboration throughout the division. As the size of the division increases, the effect of profit sharing to motivate project teams decreases. For large divisions, excellent innovation team performance may end up uncompensated because the rest of the division performed poorly. Think about the Marks & Spencer store that significantly improved its operating performance in the early 2000's; what would have been the reward to the manager if the only performance measure used to determine the bonus was company performance? Given the poor performance of the British retailer during that interval, the bonus would not have reflected the store's outstanding performance. Such dislocation between performance and rewards is very common when stock-related compensation is used in large companies. While the team at the store may feel some kind of psychological solidarity with their co-workers, it also feels unfairly compensated.

Gain sharing links the value that an innovation project creates and the compensation of the team. Gain sharing typically leads to rewards throughout several years—as long as the effort is creating value. The longer time horizons of gain sharing mechanisms have the advantages of measuring actual value creation rather than a leading measure that is never a perfect predictor. On the other hand, the gains not only depend on the effort of the innovation team, but also on the efforts of the people that implement the innovation. Over time, other events impact the gains, and the initial effort is diluted among these other events.

Product profitability is a better measure of value creation than whether the product was designed on time or on budget. Most product development teams are rewarded based on hitting certain targets at the date of market release. However, product development teams could be more effectively rewarded on product profitability over time. The rub is that using profitability measures to reward performance requires more collaboration between the innovation team and the operating groups that manage the innovation in the commercial arena. That additional collaboration can be a good thing for the company because it provides a more seamless path from innovation development through to commercialization. However, the development team has less control over achieving the reward and depends on the quality of execution from operations.

Research Bite: Team and Divisional Incentives

The reward system for product development teams in a technology company in our research had an interesting approach to motivate collaboration. The teams were evaluated based on traditional project-related measures such as meeting milestones, budgets, and product specifications (including performance as well as quality). But in addition, the division manager chose a milestone from a project at a particularly important point in its development. An important piece of the quarterly bonus for everybody in the division was based on meeting that project's milestone. A manager described it as: "if you are not working for that particular project, then you try to help even if you are not directly responsible; however, the next quarter it may be your project that is selected." This is an interesting approach to rewarding teams that breaks with the normal approaches. What is unanswered is if this will produce the desired effects.

Subjective Versus Objective Evaluation

Objective measures are the bread and butter of incentive systems, but they have limitations:

- **They leave out important value levers**. The main contribution of the original Honda U.S. team was not the initial sales of large motorbikes but the team's identification of a major market segment, small motorbikes, that was totally overlooked from Japan.

- **The more value levers that an objective measure captures, the more that uncontrollable factors distort it**. Stock price, under the efficient markets assumption, is the only measure that summarizes all the value created. However, stock price includes a lot of factors outside the control of the company from interest rates to economic, social, and political events. For divisional managers, stock price includes the value that other divisions create, which they hardly control.

Subjective measures of performance should be used to complement objective measures. There are several advantages to subjective evaluation:

- Managers can include information not foreseen before the project started.

- Managers can observe actions and decisions of the person evaluated.

- Managers can evaluate tasks that are hard to quantify and judge, whether they are beneficial to the company.

- Managers can discount the effect of uncontrollable events.

- Managers can adjust the importance of different measures and observations with changing priorities for the innovation effort.

- Because people interact in various issues and over time, the manager can use what he or she knows about the person evaluated to better assess her performance.[12]

Subjective measures have their own limitations. They rely on the availability of information and the ability, knowledge, and effort of the person doing the evaluation. Subjective evaluation also relies on the supervisor having the right incentives to give a fair evaluation. This is not always the case. In fact, often there are incentives to give good evaluations regardless of performance in order to avoid the personal costs of an unhappy subordinate.[13] Grade inflation at universities reflects this problem. Professors have no incentive to give a low grade because it leads to unpleasant interactions with students and potentially lengthy administrative processes. But grade inflation is not unique to universities; as a human resource manager described the process to us, her company had five different levels of performance but 95 percent of employees ranked in the top two levels.

Probably, the most severe limitation of subjective measures is that they rely on the reputation, fairness, and ability to judge of the evaluator. A person without credibility will hardly lead to satisfactory

evaluation (unless every single subordinate gets the top grade).
Without them, subjective evaluation is worse than objective evaluation. Figure 7.4 illustrates this idea. Subjective evaluation can be the
best—when the person evaluating is competent, trustworthy, and
committed—and the worst performance measure—if any of these
conditions are not met.

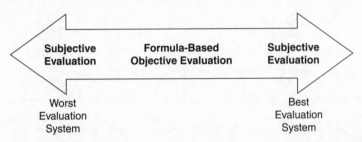

**FIGURE 7.4 THE ROLE OF SUBJECTIVITY IN PERFORMANCE
EVALUATION.**

Creating a mix of objective and subjective measures for evaluation is the best approach. Over-reliance on either one distorts incentives and behavior.

Relative Performance Versus Absolute Performance Evaluation

Goals can be set relative to the performance of other projects or initiatives—either inside or outside the organization. Relative goals are
perceived as tangible and less "made up" than absolute goals. They
also filter out uncontrollable events that affect the project and its reference target. When Mobil introduced a new measurement system,
performance goals were set relative to competitors. Financial performance—ROCE (return on capital employed) and EPS (earnings per
share)—was measured against Mobil's top seven competitors.
Bonuses associated with non-financial measures were linked to
Mobil's ranking in the industry.

Performance evaluated relative to peers inside a company motivates destructive competition. The Latin American division of a large software firm suffered from competition among its countries' managers. Aware that the manager who showed better financial performance would get the division's top job, countries competed against themselves. While competition was a good stimulus to improve within country performance, the division lost various deals that involved cross-national customers. The sale was booked to the country where the sales process was closed, regardless of the other countries' involvement.

Relative performance evaluation also depends heavily on the existence of a comparable set of projects. This is more likely to happen for incremental projects, where the performance of other projects can come directly into the relative performance or into the definition of goals; it is unlikely to happen in radical projects.

Incentive Contracts

Companies need to decide the right percentage of compensation to make variable and the right mix of economic rewards. Organizations have different types of economic rewards available; most relevant are bonuses, salary increases, stock ownership and stock option plans, and promotions.

Compensation has four components:

- Expected level of pay
- Shape and slope of the performance-pay relationship
- Timing
- Delivery of the pay

Expected Level of Pay

The expected level of pay is the "market price" for a particular type of job. Compensation consulting firms develop reference tables for industries and regions that define "market prices" and companies use to set their level of pay. The inputs to these "market prices" are the characteristics of the job including skills, knowledge, and competencies required. Some companies add a premium based on the characteristics of the person in addition to job requirements. When pay is based on personal characteristics, the mechanisms used to determine the level are also based on skills, knowledge, or competencies.

The Shape of the Pay-Performance Relationship

The second characteristic is the shape of the pay-performance relationship. For instance, Citibank used three different levels of pay: below par, par, and above par (as shown in Figure 7.5). Step changes are inferior to smooth linear relationships. A manager who knows that he is going to get par, but sees very improbably that he would be able to move to above par may decide to limit his effort. A linear relationship would not generate this behavior, where even small improvements are rewarded.

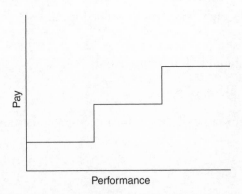

FIGURE 7.5   PROBLEMATIC PAY-PERFORMANCE RELATIONSHIP.

Most compensation systems are linear or close to linear. A *linear relationship* rewards and penalizes proportionally to the performance, and therefore provides a constant incentive to improve performance. For instance, a distributor of electronic material facing problems with late deliveries put together a team to work on ways to improve its service. The goal for the team was to achieve 95 percent of the orders delivered within 24 hours. If the goal was achieved, the team would receive a bonus of 10 percent of its salary. For each percentage point above or below the target, the bonus would be modified by another 1 percent. The team mapped the process and investigated the various causes for late deliveries, ranging from the organization of the orders, the packaging people, logistics, and product availability. They gave top management a list of recommendations that were implemented to move the service to a 99 percent level.

This particular company had a lower bound on the shape of the bonus contract. Any performance below 85 percent led to no bonus. Having a lower bound is intended to protect against very negative performance. These lower bounds are set to protect managers from very negative outcomes that are mostly outside the control of the manager (if the manager is responsible, the outcome is dismissal of the person). In some cases, the shape also includes a ceiling that limits the upside potential. This avoids rewarding for favorable factors that are outside the manager's control. A Canadian pharmaceutical company faced a problem associated with a lack of an upper bound. One of its divisions was the leader in a market with one other major competitor and a myriad of smaller ones. Competition between the two main players had kept margins low. The landscape changed when the FDA closed the production facility of the main competitor and left the division as the leader with little competition. Margins soared, and the division increased its yearly profits by 400 percent. Things would go back to normal the following year when exiting and new competitors added new capacity to grow in such a lucrative market.

The division's manager bonus on a typical year was around 30 percent of the salary, but that year it was 350 percent of the salary (a similar proportion applied to other top managers). To make the problem even more acute, profit became the goal for the following year. Thus, the top management for the division was certain that the following year would have no bonus. An event that, to a large extent, was out of the division's control was responsible for a windfall in bonus.

In addition to the shape, the slope of the relationship is another relevant parameter. Steeper relationships provide more incentives to deliver performance. On the other hand, too much pay-for-performance puts too much risk upon the manager's shoulders and leads to risk-averse decisions. Researchers in basic science seldom work under steep incentive schemes, favoring recognition systems. Research is too uncertain and too unpredictable. Rather, the opposite is more common. Research contracts are *cost plus*—where a client such as the government reimburses the costs that the team incurs in the project. Cost plus contracts remove economic incentives, and the team can focus its efforts on creating. Steep slopes also focus the manager's attention too much on the performance dimensions included in the formula at the expense of other relevant issues. The ATH Technologies case described earlier in this chapter, where employees sacrificed the quality of the imaging systems to reach sales and profit goals, is a vivid example of how steeper slopes have to be carefully integrated with an appropriate culture and risk management systems that limit the temptation to innovate in a way that is detrimental to the company.

Timing Incentives

Another characteristic of the incentive system is timing. Two issues are at play. One is retention of key employees that can be enhanced through deferred and long-term compensation. One of the virtues of stock options is their vesting period, usually over five years. In Silicon

Valley gatherings, it is common to hear managers sticking with a particular firm because their stock option plan has not fully vested. The other is the fact that the value which an innovation creates—especially radical innovation—happens over long time horizons. The value of a radical innovation such as Virgin Galactic's venture into space tourism cannot be assessed on the basis of whether its development was on time or on sales in its first year but on its impact over the next five or even ten years.

Stock option plans or restricted stock ownership plans vest over several years with the objective of both retaining key employees and linking their incentives to the long-term performance of the company. Bonus payments can also be based on future performance. For example, the bonus associated with a process improvement innovation project may be a percentage of the cost savings that the company realizes over time. Again, this timing links incentive compensation to a measure closer to value creation and enhances employee retention.

Finally, there are more sophisticated schemes where bonuses for excellent years are not fully paid out but kept in the employee's "bank account" and paid over future periods if performance remains above expectations. If the performance falls in a particular year, rather than cutting the employee's salary (a negative bonus), the company is paid out of the employee "bank account."

Delivery of Compensation

The most common forms of delivering compensation are cash (through bonuses) and stock-related mechanisms. Cash incentives are better at motivating and rewarding actions that have short-term consequences such as meeting milestones. Stock options and (restricted) stock awards are better at motivating a long-term perspective into the decision-making process and rewarding events that can only be measured after a long period of time, such as the success of a particular technology.

Another important issue relevant to stock compensation is its relevance in large companies. In large companies, the potential impact of the actions of a particular manager on stock price is almost negligible. Therefore, stock compensation is, for economic purposes, unrelated to the performance of the individual. How much can the controller of the Greece sales office affect the stock price of a Fortune 500 company? This person could as well get any other stock in the Fortune 500 list and be as well off because his or her effort has an imperceptible effect on the stock price of the company. The only benefits in these large organizations are the potential psychological effect related to "being owners." This is especially true for incremental innovation, while for radical innovation the impact may be more significant or the innovation can be spun out into a smaller company.

CEO Sanity Check

Talk to some of your best innovation teams and get a read on your reward systems' main components to see how they are driving behavior and performance.

- Expected level of pay
- Shape and slope of the performance-pay relationship
- Timing
- Delivery of the pay

Odds are, some of these are not working well and frustrating employees. Get a team together to tune these four elements to achieve significantly higher levels of innovation.

Key Considerations in Designing Incentives Systems for Innovation

The problem of most innovation incentive systems is that they reward the wrong behavior and provide disincentives for the right behavior. Add to that the powerful effect of economic rewards, and you end up with a dangerous force working against the objectives of the organization. In an effort to stimulate innovation, a bottling company decided to reward each suggestion with a small amount of cash; not surprisingly, it received lots of suggestions but none of them useful. Most of the arguments against using incentives are based on this idea: Badly designed incentive systems are worse than nothing.[14]

The Danger of Over Use

Incentive systems can fail because they are overused. Putting too much emphasis on pay-for-performance without considering the risks involved may lead managers to shy away from risk-taking behavior. This, in turn, could lead to more incremental and less radical innovation in an organization.

Research Bite: Economic Incentives—What Is the Effect of Too Little or Too Much?

Our research addressed the question of how important are economic incentives in product development. In the course of our study, we asked product development managers in medical device companies about their incentive structure as well as the perceived performance of their projects. If economic incentives are always a plus, we would expect a linear relationship between pay-for-performance and actual performance. On the other hand, economic incentives may kill the intrinsic motivation—the internal curiosity that drives engineers to innovate—and decrease performance. Which force dominates? The promise or the limitations of economic incentives?[15]

Figure 7.6 reproduces the relationship that we found. The y axis is project performance, and the x-axis is the percentage of variable compensation if the project meets expectations. Pay-for-performance appears to lead to better performance when variable compensation was a small part of overall compensation. However, the relationship became less intense as the percentage of variable compensation increased until it reached 18 percent, when increasing the importance of variable compensation actually leads to worse performance.

The particular number where the peak happens is the least important piece of information—it may vary across industries, types of projects, people, etc. The important issue is that more incentives, even if appropriately designed, may lead to lower performance. The curve suggests that providing some incentives is good, but too many decreases performance.

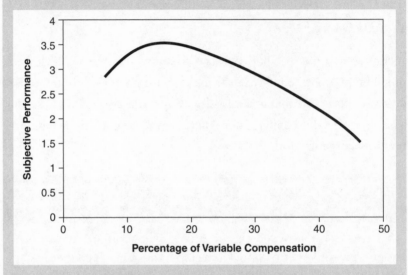

FIGURE 7.6 THE RELATIONSHIP BETWEEN PERFORMANCE AND ECONOMIC INCENTIVES.

The Negative Effect on Intrinsic Motivation

An additional challenge with innovation incentive systems is their potential negative effect on intrinsic motivation. *Intrinsic motivation* is the internal drive that a person has to do something purely because he or she loves it. This is a factor in all innovations and especially in semi-radical and radical innovations. The manager who led the team that developed the brain clips that did not react to magnetic fields did it because of the challenge of the project and his passion to create something new, not because of the potential economic rewards. Sometimes the most important reward for performance is the act of doing the job itself.

Social psychology research as early as the 1950s found that external rewards could undermine intrinsic motivation.[16] Research into intrinsic motivation in innovation has yielded similar results. A senior manager described it as, "Research employees are often less excited about bonuses than about peer recognition." Extrinsic rewards can actually drive away intrinsic motivation.[17] In this case, a rewards system may have the effect of focusing product development managers' attention away from relevant dimensions: "Planning and rewarding for schedule attainment are ineffective ways of accelerating pace."[18]

The promise of money if certain goals are met does not help creativity.[19] It cannot make a job more interesting or enjoyable for an employee, and in some cases generates a negative impression because it is perceived as a bribe. It is important to understand that genuine interest in the work is usually the launch pad for creativity.[20] This interest in doing something exciting with new technology is what drove Steve Jobs and Steve Wozniak to develop the first personal computer in their Homebrew Computer Club—and ultimately to found Apple Computer.

Fear, Failure, and Fairness

The level of risk-taking that a company encourages is an important issue to consider in addition to measuring and rewarding. Risk-taking behavior is necessary for successful innovation, but it can be killed if failure is punished either economically or socially. In one company, a team of innovators was publicly abused by the CEO because an initiative was apparently failing. They were publicly threatened with no promotions or worse. No amount of financial compensation could offset the message that sent to the entire organization about innovation: "Do not fail or you will be humiliated and punished." This created near paralysis in the organization, and innovation efforts ground to a halt. Laying off innovation staff when a business downturn occurs also sends strong signals to the organization about the value placed on taking risks.

> ## CEO Action Plan: Avoid These Common Mistakes
>
> - Choosing the wrong goals or the wrong measures is a formula for disaster.
>
> - Over-use can dampen the effect of rewards and even produce a backlash.
>
> - The wrong rewards can kill the intrinsic motivation of truly creative people.
>
> - Rewards must be designed to address employees' fear of taking risks, concern that project failure could jeopardize their careers, and the desire to be treated fairly.

Incentives and Rewards, and the Innovation Rules

So far we have considered innovation to be a positive force: Companies want more innovation because it leads to value creation. But there is a dark side: Innovation can also be value destroying (see Figure 7.7).

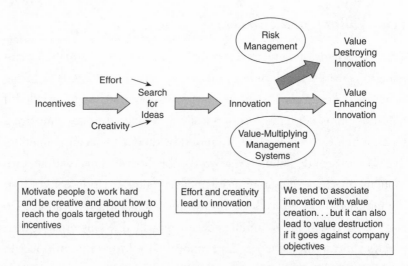

FIGURE 7.7   INNOVATION AS A POSITIVE AND NEGATIVE FORCE.

Innovation, driven by goals and incentives, can add value and create growth. Unchecked and unbalanced, innovation can have a dark side that can put a company at risk. Kidder, Peabody, the oldest investment bank at the time of its demise, disappeared because of too much innovation. One of its traders was innovative enough to find a clever way to generate "profits" that did not exist but for which he was handsomely rewarded. Unfortunately, the company ignored various warning signals until it was too late. The cumulative losses led to the death of a venerable bank. A strong set of ethics may help take care of a situation like this, but it is also necessary to put risk management systems in place to provide checks and balances.

Cash-based incentive systems using performance measures with a large component of formula-based evaluation are best when innovation initiatives have short-term results, smaller impact on overall organization, easily measured performance, and are relatively easy to describe expected performance. As innovation initiatives incorporate a larger amount of radical innovation, incentive systems should be based on long-term incentives (stock-based incentive systems) and subjective evaluation.

Figure 7.8 summarizes the major differences that should be considered when designing incentive systems for radical versus incremental innovation.

For radical innovation initiatives, recognition systems play a much larger role. In particular, managers participating in these projects need to feel rewarded for taking the risk even if the project was not successful, or alternatively they must feel that they receive a fair share of the value generated from the project if it is successful. Because effort, risk-taking, and value generated from a project can only be fairly judged once the project is finished, incentive systems are ill suited for this task. Reward systems are better suited to this purpose.

Incremental Innovation Projects ←————————→	Radical Innovation Projects
Incentive systems more relevant	Reward systems more relevant
Cash-based compensation more relevant	Stock-based compensation more relevant
Formula-based incentive systems emphasized	Subjective evaluation emphasized
Performance measures play a significant role in compensation	Performance measures play a minor role in compensation
Outcome-based performance measures more relevant	Input and process-based performance measures more relevant
Local performance measures	Company-level performance measures

FIGURE 7.8 SUMMARY OF DIFFERENCES IN INCENTIVES AND REWARD SYSTEMS FOR INCREMENTAL AND RADICAL INNOVATION.

Incentives provide a major impetus for behavior change. Without measures and incentives, organizational antibodies are released that resist innovation and block organizational change.[21] Incentives can also cement in place beneficial behavior, creating a solid foundation for innovation.

LEARNING INNOVATION: HOW DO ORGANIZATIONS BECOME BETTER AT INNOVATING?

The Importance of Learning

In fast-changing environments, the ability to learn faster, better, and more cheaply than your competitors could mean the difference between retaining market leadership and barely surviving.[1] In Silicon Valley, it became clear to major venture capital companies that ramping up the sales volumes in startups always took longer and cost more than was projected. Sometimes the result was slower-than-expected growth, but often it resulted in the failure of the startup because of poor cash flow. Reviewing the successes and failures of startups led to the development of the Sales Learning Curve to guide better, faster, and cheaper sales growth in the crucial early days. The *Sales Learning Curve* concept says that the time it takes to achieve cash flow breakeven is reasonably independent of sales force staffing. It is, instead, entirely dependent on how well and how quickly the *entire* organization learns what it takes to sell the product or service while incorporating customer feedback into the product itself.[2]

The key to learning is not to avoid making mistakes but to learn from them.[3] Microsoft has made learning from mistakes a virtue. Version 1.0 of its products is "good enough," but the company improves the product relentlessly until it dominates the market. It does not wait to have the "best" product, and knows that to improve the product it needs to listen and see how the product is used. However, organizations are not usually adept at learning. Many organizations do not learn from their mistakes regarding innovation, and are stuck repeating the same errors and feeling the same frustrations.[4] The key to organizational learning is to have systems in place that enable people to learn better, faster, and with less associated expense.[5] You can often tell that an organization suffers with innovation learning disabilities after seeing several symptoms. They are disbelievers in the effectiveness of innovation; they stumble on execution of innovation projects, favoring only incremental innovation, and they are constantly amazed that others invest in innovation at levels higher than theirs.

Company A (the name is meant to keep it anonymous) suffered from significant learning disabilities that hampered its innovation. The company had a poor track record of innovation successes—a few winners and a bunch of losers. The company's managers exhibited a penchant for rampant incrementalism, and scoffed at other companies that invested in major innovation initiatives. The company was locked in a downward spiral driven by a lack of learning where organizational antibodies attacked every innovation. There was a lack of meaningful metrics for innovation, and therefore efforts to learn what they did right and what they did wrong were frustrated. And, no special efforts to learn from its own innovation actions or those of competitors could be launched because the management team did not believe innovation was worthwhile. The downward spiral went like this: Because they did not innovate successfully in the past, they did not believe in the value of innovation. Because they did not believe in it, they did not learn about it. Therefore, they did not do it well. For the record, this company performed very badly relative to its industry counterparts and was eventually purchased at a discount.

Company B had similar learning disabilities. The company had a mediocre track record for innovation, a culture that tended to dismiss the value of innovation and a high level of organizational antibodies that attacked change and innovation. In addition, the management had no useful metrics or learning systems in place to assist the innovation processes. However, this company's management team saw the long-term implications of this handicap, and directed the staff to diagnose the situation, identify the sources of weakness in its innovation approach, and to fix them. The analysis led to an overhaul of the innovation approach. Changes included the development of a measurement system to help change behavior and improve learning, improved innovation processes and organization, and specific efforts to combat the organizational antibodies that frustrated innovation in the company. The result was a rejuvenated company that began to develop and implement important innovations. Currently, the company has one of the highest levels of profitability in its industry, and is often held up as the standard for long-term success.

Organizational learning and changing go hand in hand. Because innovation is all about change—incremental, semi-radical, and radical change—learning is an intrinsic part of innovation. Properly conceived and executed, organizational learning can unleash powerful forces of creativity and the development of processes to focus them into successful commercial realities.

CEO Action Plan: You Can't Ignore Learning

You can't improve any part of innovation—not the framework, strategy, processes, organization metrics, or incentives—and expect to see good results unless you make sure that your organization knows how to learn and change.

Learning in an innovative organization has these characteristics:

- Specific processes for learning and change link to strategy and embody explicit and continual efforts to improve. The product development manager in one company sat with each development team twice for learning purposes. Before the project, start to adapt the process to the needs of the project. Then, at the end of the project, sit down again to investigate how the process could be improved.

- A systems approach to complex organizational dynamics, where actions and reactions are understood in terms of causal loops (actions, reactions, and effects) rather than linear cause and effect.

- Shared vision—alignment in the organization resulting from shared understanding of what is important for the organization (as opposed to what is important for *my part* of the organization)—is critical to minimize the appearance of organizational antibodies.

- Flexibility and agility that enhance changes and create an environment that is conducive to ongoing innovation. IDEO, the design company renowned for its unique product solutions, constantly renews its teams with people having very different backgrounds.

- Timely at anticipating challenges and threats rather than responding to crises. Often, change comes from within the organization rather than from the top. Intel's shift from memories to microprocessors happened at the middle level, and top management recognized it only when the change was inevitable.[6]

- Collaborative but challenging environment that maximizes creative tension and minimizes destructive tension.

A Model of Learning

There are two major types learning: *Learning to Act* and *Learning to Learn*.[7]

Learning to Act

This type of learning includes collaborative assessments of how the current systems (including the structure, processes and resources) are working, a development of shared understanding of strengths and weaknesses, and a proactive effort to improve them.[8] This type of learning takes the current strategic objectives as given and does not question them. *Quality circles*, where team members brainstorm about making the current manufacturing process better, are a classical example of learning to act. The team does not question whether the company should be producing PDAs or whether it should be produced in-house or subcontracted. Taking these decisions as given, the team looks for ways to improve the efficiency of the existing plant.

At a strategic level, most planning systems extrapolate the current business models into the future. This extrapolation represents Learning to Act, where the planning effort focuses on incrementally improving the current actions. This type of planning is key to move the company along the current strategic trajectory. However, it may run the risk of becoming a ritualistic exercise, with little if any value added—the worst case of bureaucracy. Becton Dickinson, one of the largest medical devices companies in the world, had a strategic planning process that ran from December through September. It incorporated strategic, operational, and financial plans. Throughout the cycle, there was significant flow of information along the organizational hierarchy, with frequent meetings. The outcome of the process was a thick book with detailed strategic analyses, plans, and financial commitments. The nature of the process and the relevance of financial plans led to a strategic plan that projected a conservative picture of the current business model into the future and incremental innovations.[9]

Learning to Learn

This type of learning consists of structured processes to assess how well the organization learns and changes. This big picture perspective is critical to ensure that the investments in innovation are yielding maximum return and that the organization is building sustainable innovation. The Learning to Learn cycle questions the current processes as the best way to innovate. By questioning what is pursued and how, the organization is more open to new ideas and taking educated risks (the type of risks that can have large payoffs). At the process level, reengineering does not try to improve the way processes are currently performed. Reengineering efforts do not improve what is already done; rather, they question the assumptions behind what is currently done to come up with potentially very different ways of executing the same tasks.

A high technology company used strategic planning as a Learning to Learn exercise. The planning cycle had two processes going on at the same time, culminating in an annual off-site meeting. The first day and a half of the meeting focused on the financial goals and programs for the upcoming year—much in the same way as a traditional strategic planning process.[10] The last part of the meeting focused on exploring new technologies, market trends, and any ideas that any manager thought of relevance. Each lead was examined, and teams were formed to further explore those that were judged to be more relevant.

Innovation relies on both learning cycles; incremental innovation relies to a larger extent on the Learning to Act cycle, and radical innovation uses the Learning to Learn cycle more often.[11] Both types of innovation use different types of knowledge. Incremental innovation is grounded on knowledge that is widely shared in the organization. People know what the problem at hand is; they know what potential solutions exist out there, what the current process intends to do, why it is in place and how it works, and they can easily communicate ideas. Knowledge that is widely available and easy to communicate is called *explicit knowledge.* It can be stored and retrieved from knowledge repositories. Consulting firms such as Accenture encourage their project teams to write up the main features of each project—what was the problem, how did the team approach the solution, and what was the final recommendation. The objective of this knowledge management process is to make existing knowledge available throughout the company. Rather than starting from scratch, new projects can reuse existing knowledge, coded in an intranet, to provide better service to the client.

Radical innovation relies to a lesser extent on explicit knowledge. Because it dives into unexplored territory where knowledge is not well-articulated, it is raw knowledge in the heads of people that crystallizes through their interactions. Management may know that it has a potentially great idea, but it is often unable to fully articulate it or find hard numbers to back it up. It is intuitive.[12] This type of knowledge is called *tacit.* Radical innovation is not only hard because of the novelty of the idea, but also because communicating it so that other people understand it is difficult.[13] SpaceShipOne developers could not specify exactly how many and what types of people would buy their commercial space flights; however, it was intuitively obvious to them that there was a business there.

Learning Systems for Innovation

Systems interact with the learning process of an organization at four different levels. The first two are more amenable to incremental innovation, while the latter two are more relevant to radical innovation:

- **Systems for delivering value**. These systems reflect what the organization knows and make this knowledge explicit in processes that can be controlled and acted upon if deviations happen. Learning is embedded in the design of the process and the responses to the deviations.

- **Systems for refining the current model**. These systems move the current business model into the future. They embed the learning to act cycle that forces constant improvement.

- **Systems for building competencies**. These systems facilitate the learning associated with new capabilities. Top management uses these systems to induce the organization to experiment and develop capabilities needed for future strategies. Theses systems guide the knowledge creation process in the direction of the chosen capabilities

- **Systems for crafting strategy**. These systems encourage and capture knowledge outside the current business model that emerges throughout the organization. Ideas happen all the time, and these systems make sure that they are not wasted or go into creating value in a different company.

Systems for Delivering Value

The first set of systems distills what the organization knows and applies it to a new event. For example, product development roadmaps synthesize what the organization knows about the product development process. Texas Instruments' product development process is described in a booklet. It details the various stages that a project goes through from validation of the idea, technical specifications, execution, and market introduction. The booklet specifies the requirements at each stage, what is evaluated at the review points, and who gets involved.

These systems capture explicit knowledge coded into systems that govern the innovation process. Their purpose is to make sure that the innovation effort has the highest chance to *deliver* the value it is intended to generate. Learning happens through the adaptation of the systems to the needs of each particular effort.

Research Bite: Limited Learning in Product Development

We explored how companies used the product development processes. One of the companies we looked at had what seemed to be a structured and well-designed product development process. The manual described specific stages with clear targets to be met, clear definitions of who had the authority to do what, clear procedures intended to liberate development teams' attention from routine activities, and checklists to coordinate the support activities of all departments. The process was on the upper quartile in terms of design quality. However, the project managers in the company had a different opinion; they saw the process as controlling and unsupportive. The manager overseeing product development projects and who was responsible for the use of the process saw her job as disciplining the project teams to follow the routine, and she was a stickler for detail. She made sure that all the documents were in place, that every stage gate was properly documented, that every step in the process was carefully followed. Her objective was to maintain the routines as if they were a rigid, immutable ritual—strict adherence was required. The company's product development manual was static, outdated for the team leaders' needs, and the perfect target for a reengineering effort. The system was more of a hindrance to innovation than a help.

These systems give visibility into the future of the innovation project. This type of learning is *anticipatory*—it accrues from planning ahead of time, from examining the different alternatives before the team dives into the execution of a project, from outlining a path that, even if flexible, it provides direction to the innovation effort. The learning involved in these systems is mostly incremental in that it usually ensures that the project develops knowledge along the expected path.

Systems for Refining the Current Model

The second level at which systems interact with learning is through their own improvement and the improvement of organizational processes. During the execution of a particular project, there is learning about the process itself that is captured. In other words, there is learning not only about the particular innovation, but also about how the company can improve its innovation processes. Systems here have the purpose of *refining* processes. Semiconductor manufacturing equipment relies on very high technology. When products are introduced, they meet very demanding technical specifications. However, products' costs are not sustainable as competition erodes prices. The product development teams rightly focus their attention in solving electron-related problems. But over time, lowering costs is necessary. Applied Materials, the leader in the market, addresses this problem by having a department with the objective of reducing product costs after product introduction. The department has a set of procedures to identify, prioritize, and address cost reduction opportunities. In one case, the department redesigned a sub-system made of 17 different parts into one part, at one-ninth of the cost, and better lead-time and quality.

The learning here is not as much anticipatory but experiential. Team members draw on their experiences to identify problems and envision solutions. The learning process may often incorporate knowledge from other organizations—through visits, the use of consultants, or hiring external experts. Knowledge is tacit—it does not exist before the problem is solved and usually develops through the effort of a team. In a way, the knowledge it dispersed in the heads of people and teamwork makes it into coherent knowledge that is made explicit.

Research Bite: Experiential Learning in Product Development—Another Approach

Compare the role of the product development manager described in the previous sub-section who saw her role as maintaining a rigid ritual to that of the manager in the same position in a different company. This manager saw her role as supporting the development teams and the process as a flexible tool to help in the task. She sat down with project teams to tailor the process to the project's needs, to make sure that the routine provided value to the teams. Not only was the knowledge adapted to ensure that the best value was delivered; most importantly, the manager reviewed each finished project with the project team to update the product development manual and make it even more helpful the next time. This was a live manual, constantly evolving and incorporating learning. The product development manager saw learning at two levels: deliver value as well as refine the process.

We have identified the main learning purpose of each of these two systems. It does not mean that these systems cannot fulfill different roles. A system to deliver value may lead to review and refinement of the process itself. That may lead to identification of a radical innovation prospect. The framework presented here is meant to help in design and execution, but it is not meant to be a forced straightjacket.

Systems for Building Competencies

Certain systems interact with learning through their role in *building* future competencies. Top management oftentimes drives strategic renewal. It asks the questions and comes with novel answers for the design of the company's strategy. Top management senses the need for a new approach—for lack of current performance or anticipation of future threats to the current model.[14]

The process of building competencies is much more complex than that of evolving current knowledge. It requires both anticipatory and experiential knowledge. *Anticipatory knowledge* happens through strategic thinking and planning. Merrill Lynch had to design a new strategy to respond to the emergence of online brokers such as E*TRADE or Charles Schwab. The market forced Merrill Lynch's top management to think creatively and respond to an important threat to its business. It could not wait for something in the organization to solve the problem; the company had to develop new competencies to adapt itself to the new market. But new things cannot be fully brewed in the laboratory. Developing new strategies requires experiential knowledge that happens through the experience in developing the competencies. Barnes & Noble, the successful book retail chain, quickly learned that responding to Amazon.com was not only a matter of reproducing Amazon.com's web site. It required learning how to use the strength of its physical presence in the online world. Both types of knowledge constantly interact as new information requires a redesign of the plan.

This constant back-and-forth between vision and action benefits from periodic meetings, revised goals, and deadlines. In contrast to incremental innovation, where systems to deliver value compare plans with progress to make sure that the project is on track, systems to build competencies use the periodic deadlines to pace the organization and to bring together different players to exchange information and crystallize knowledge. When Sony began the development of its magnetoscope line (the earliest video recorders), the first goal that Masaru Ibuka, Sony's founder, gave to Nobutoshi Kihara, the manager of the product line, was to produce a working product. The first video was the equivalent at the time of $55,000.

Once the product was developed, Ibuka asked Kihara to develop one that would sell for $5,500. As the cheaper version was introduced to the market, Ibuka went back to Kihara, this time he asked for a $550 color video for the Japanese market. The product was later known as Betamax.

These types of meetings are comparable to board meetings in startups. Board meetings pace the organization, force management to leave tactics and look at the strategy, and bring together people with different backgrounds to give a fresh new look at the company.

Systems for Crafting Strategy

Finally, systems interact with learning to *craft* the future strategy and business models. Innovation often emerges from unexpected places in the organization. The idea of the PlayStation did not emerge from top management, but from a middle manager who did not find support and had to sell the idea as a way to sell more CDs. Intel's transition to microprocessors happened because of middle managers' decisions. Siebel, Salesforce.com, and Business Objects are all successful startups founded by Oracle managers.

These are unplanned discoveries that initially may grow outside the span of attention of top management. If the organization does not identify them, they will move and thrive as independent companies (and potential competitors). This type of radical innovation has attracted most of the attention—because of its uniqueness, the appeal of the story when successful, and the attractiveness of making it happen even if odds were against its success. In contrast to the proactive process of building competencies for a new business model, this type of radical innovation has a larger reactive, improvisational component.[15] Figures 8.1 and 8.2 summarize the four interactions with learning systems.

Incremental Innovation				
Systems' Purpose	Systems	Leading Process	Type of Learning	Knowledge
Deliver Value	Planning systems Roadmaps Exception reports	About outcomes	Anticipatory	Explicit
Refine Model	Process improvement Customer feedback Product tests	About the process	Anticipatory/ Experiential	Tacit to explicit

FIGURE 8.1   INCREMENTAL INNOVATION.

Radical Innovation				
Systems' Purpose	Systems	Leading Process	Type of Learning	Knowledge
Build Competencies	Strategic planning Strategic control Project management	About what should be done	Experiential/ Anticipatory	Tacit to explicit
Craft Strategies	–Skunk works Idea management Internal venture management	About what can be done	Experiential	Tacit

FIGURE 8.2   RADICAL INNOVATION.

How to Make Learning Work in Your Organization

Learning is captured through a proactive approach. Several tools have proved to be valuable in helping crystallize learning so that it can be used by the organization.

Knowledge and Ignorance Management

The management of innovation requires *knowledge management* (using what you know to the best effect) as well as *ignorance management* (being aware of what you do not know and of the implications of that ignorance). Knowledge management is useful in incremental innovations. Ignorance management is most valuable in semi-radical and radical innovations.

Knowledge Management

Knowledge management systems are important elements to code data and give it a structure that makes it useful throughout the company. These systems rely heavily on information technology. They store particular executions of organizational processes that can help current projects to be more efficient. Their value depends on their design—how easy is to store and retrieve information, how is the database structured—and the discipline of the organization to code learning histories of the projects.

British Petroleum designed *peer assists* as a mechanism to leverage the knowledge dispersed throughout the company. Business units lent people in their organization with certain knowledge to another business unit facing a specific problem where this expertise was required.[16] McKinsey & Co. developed its *Practice Development Network* documenting the company's experience with its clients and published its Knowledge Resource Directory—with people's expertise and other key documents—that was quickly adopted throughout the company. By 1996, the Practice Development Network had almost 12,000 documents with 2,000 downloads per month.[17]

Ignorance Management

Incremental innovation builds on data about established technologies and existing markets, and uses the process of knowledge management and data mining to move forward. For radical innovation, ignorance management replaces knowledge management. Managers familiar with incremental innovation feel massively uncomfortable when ignorance dominates. Data are hard to find, and must be generated from ignorance management.

When Salesforce.com first introduced its concept—sales force management delivered through the Internet—there was little knowledge to rely on. Little was known about how small and medium companies would use the system, which ones would adopt the system faster, what features were most useful, or how to approach its potential clients. Decisions were based on managed trial and error. During this early period, the company carefully collected data about its customers and how they used the product. As the company matured, the analysis of this data became the source of improvements to the product and redesign of the strategy. One of the studies of the data uncovered that large companies were also using the product. The study concluded complexity of the business rather than size was a better way of segmenting the market.[18]

Ignorance management is the process of identifying the most important things the team does not know and designing an approach to help reduce that ignorance to a level that allows forward movement. Experiments are great ignorance management tools. They help resolving technological decisions but also business model design. Approximation is another ignorance management tool. Rapid prototyping puts in front of potential users the existing concept of a product and provides quick feedback about its design. Educated guesses are needed to advance through radical innovations. It is always better to have something good enough than to wait until the perfect product has been designed.

The Project Roadmap

Project roadmaps assist management in understanding how different innovation efforts reinforce each other. A roadmap visualizes how the learning in a particular project becomes the basis for a new project. Projects are not isolated efforts that compete against each other as in ranking systems. They form a whole, where learning cumulates to make possible alternatives otherwise unfeasible.[19] Motorola has effectively used project roadmaps to plan and develop its line of products. Robert Galvin, its legendary CEO, was a big supporter of the process: "The fundamental purpose of Technology Reviews and Technology Roadmaps is to assure that we put in motion today what is necessary in order to have the right technology, processes, components, and experience to meet the future needs for products and services."[20]

Figure 8.3 describes the product roadmap (a particular application of project roadmaps) for a medical device company. This particular map was developed at the strategic level, and then was detailed within product divisions. The roadmap projected the evolution of technologies, markets, and how products would be brought into the market as technologies and markets created opportunities. The technology roadmap includes owned technologies as well as technologies that the company knows are being researched outside. Finally, the product roadmap is more detailed early on. As it moves into the future, it outlines expected products and synergies.

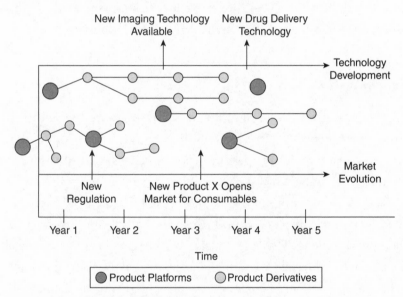

FIGURE 8.3 PRODUCT ROADMAP FOR A MEDICAL DEVICE COMPANY.

Failures as Part of the Process

It is impossible to predict in the beginning of the creative process what ideas will be successful and which won't; however, it's important to realize that failure is part of the creative process. Viagra was born from an apparent failure to treat heart disease. A logistics software company found out who would buy its products through experimentation and failure. Initially it targeted medium-sized companies. This

strategy seemed adequate because software firms did not have logis-
tic products for this segment of the market. Despite the selling
efforts, the software was moving slowly. The software was too expensive for them, and logistics was low in their priority list. Luckily, the
vice president of marketing tried to see how the concept would come
across in a division of a large firm that happened to be located in the
neighborhood. The selling process went very smoothly. The software
performance and price point suited perfectly the need of large companies.

Learning what does not work often leads to what does.[21] If organizations do not recognize "'failure value," then people will be dis-
couraged from experimentation through the fear of failure.

Learning Histories

Learning histories is a term of art for stories that are specially con-
structed to uncover the truths about how an organization innovates.
Learning histories review past projects, initiatives, and situations to
identify in as unbiased way as possible what really happened, what
worked, what did not, and what the possible root causes were. In
story form, they speak to individuals in the organization better than
slide presentations. They use a historian's perspective to gain crucial
perspective and insights. Learning histories are not designed to highlight specific actions, people, or events but recurring themes—to
answer the questions "What do we as an organization do repeatedly
that impacts our performance positively and negatively?" and "What
are the consequences; and why do we do it?" Frito Lay used learning
histories to better understand the root causes of success and failure in
its innovation efforts when it developed its strategic plan for growth;
knowing what made its innovation engine run well was important
before placing its strategic investments.

The purpose of the learning history process as a whole is to spark new insights both in the people who took an active part in this experience and in others within the organization who could benefit from sharing in this learning. The purpose is not to assign blame or credit; it is to try to *learn* from what these people are willing to share with others about their experience.

> ### CEO Sanity Check: Learning Histories
>
> Conduct a learning history of several major innovation successes and failures. Take a dispassionate look at what you learn about your organization's abilities—positive and negative—in order to innovate. Share this with the innovation leaders, and identify what needs to change to help the organization learn and change.

The Dynamic Nature of Innovation Strategy

As an industry moves through its lifecycle, the learning that supports innovation varies. Figure 8.4 illustrates the level of change in different parts of the industry lifecycle. The y-axis indicates the level of turbulence. Turbulence starts at a low level, peaks, and then goes back to a low level. The highest threat to survival for an incumbent at a particular stage happens when turbulence is highest. A lower level of turbulence indicates a lower threat, but not the absence of risk. Ice-makers in the 19th century were improving the efficiency of ice harvesting to beat each other while a new technology was emerging that wiped them out in less than two decades. Coca-Cola was focusing on more effective marketing campaigns to beat Pepsi, while startups were coming with new beverage concepts for market segments totally overlooked by the two main players.

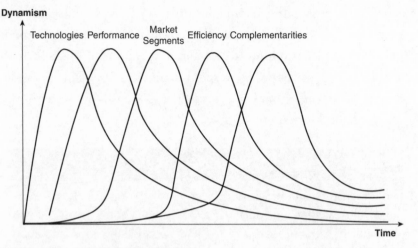

FIGURE 8.4   LEARNING LIFECYCLE.

The Technology Stage

Early in the lifecycle of an industry, technology innovation often dominates. This is a very fluid stage, where different companies bet on different technologies—a risky environment typically populated by startups. Learning focuses on exploring new technologies and generating new solutions. Learning systems focus on building the capabilities to develop the technologies that top managers have in mind or on crafting new ideas that may radically change the technology. In the late 19th century, car companies were numerous. Each one was trying different ways to put together a car, some of them used gasoline engines, but lots of them were betting on steam engines similar to the ones used in railroads. The personal computer industry in the late 1970s was a myriad of companies, each one understanding the PC as solving different needs. More recently, the customer relationship management (CRM) software market was populated with several hundred startups. Each one had a different solution to the management of customer information. Today, several groups in large and venture-backed companies are competing to grab the Voice over Internet Protocol (VoIP) market.

The outcome of this first lifecycle stage is the emergence of a technology that dominates the market. In the car industry, it was the gasoline engine; in the PC market, the WinTel structure became the dominant solution; in the CRM market, Siebel Systems emerged as the dominant software solution. The many companies that bet on the wrong technology disappear.

Large firms may create the technology and drive this first stage. Sony did that in developing the technology and business model for the Walkman. But often, companies rely on learning from outside. Their corporate venture capital arms establish links with the startup community to scout the environment. Their objective is to spot promising new technological solutions. This learning strategy—where the crafting of new innovations happens outside the firm—supports acquisition of those innovations that are complementary to the current strategy or amenable to be brought inside the company into a new business unit. Intel capital supports startup companies with technologies that complement Intel products. This support happens not only through funding, but helping the companies leverage the resources and contacts available at Intel and its partners.

Research Bite: The Main Source of Ideas

International R&D managers in our survey of innovation practices ranked the importance of various sources of ideas for new products. Table 8.1 reports the average ranking of different sources. The most common sources are the internal R&D and marketing functions; interestingly, the third most-important source is technology partners before field support and sales.

Table 8.1   Average ranking of different constituencies as sources of ideas

Constituencies	Average ranking
R&D function	1.69
Marketing function	2.47
Technology alliances	3.46
Technical and field support function	3.62
Sales function	3.70
Marketing alliances	4.03
Manufacturing function	4.35
Manufacturing alliances	5.17
Distribution alliances	5.72

The Performance Stage

After a dominant technology emerges, performance begins to improve quickly. Radical innovation in the underlying technology is still possible but much less likely than in the previous stage. A few companies may still bet on a new technological solution that would radically change the market. But most companies invest in improving the performance of the technology as quickly as possible. At this stage, performance is measured primarily on a single dimension—for example, image resolution in digital cameras or uptime for network providers. Competition is often focused solely in this dimension.

The competitive advantage goes to the company able to execute the learning cycles faster. Market share shifts quickly to the product that performs better. In the late 1980s and early 1990s, defibrilla-tors—medical devices implanted in the chest of patients that only stimulate the heart when it detects a problem—entered the perfor-mance stage. Guidant and Medtronic were the main players. The main limitation that defibrillators had was their size. Bulky devices could not be implanted close to the heart (as pacemakers were), and had to be implanted in the belly. A belly implant had two main problems: one was the reliability of the long cables going to the heart, and the second one was the patient's comfort. Doctors and patients did not care much about other performance dimensions—both companies delivered excellent performance—but size. Each learning cycle by one of the companies meant a smaller device, and each time a new product entered the market, the market share moved to this product. Both companies were excellent at executing their learning cycles, and market share kept on shifting from one to the other as new products were introduced. The performance cycle ended once both companies were able to get a small enough defibrillator that it could be implanted next to the heart. At that point, size became just one of the many performance dimensions relevant to customers. The industry moved to the market segmentation stage, with different customers valuing different things.

The Market Segmentation Stage

As product performance improves, certain customer segments are happy with the level achieved and start valuing different product dimensions—price, availability, cost of ownership, aesthetics, style, and so on. A new stage in the innovation process starts.

In the previous stages, the challenge from the business side had been to design a business model to deliver the technology. Compared to the fluidity of the technology, the market was stable. Now the technology stabilizes and fluidity moves to the market. Customer needs evolve quickly, and new segments appear at a fast pace. The investment in learning moves to develop market knowledge. The winners are those companies that are able to "read" the market and understand the differences across market segments.

The medical imaging division of a large European company suffered because it missed this transition. The division had been the leader in market since its inception. They had commanded the market

through constant improvement of the quality of the image. The resolution of the image had been the main performance dimension for a
significant period of time. As image quality improved, market segmentation began including the evolution of a price-sensitive segment that
was willing to sacrifice performance for price. This segment saw the
division's products as offering too much performance and being too
expensive. New entrants quickly captured that market segment, and
others and reversed the division's dominant position.

The Efficiency Stage

As market segments stabilize, competition shifts to efficiently create
more value to customers—whether in the supply chain, in design, or
in marketing. At this stage, efficiency becomes critical, and the winner is the company that becomes more efficient. Winning can happen
in this stage via superior learning on how to make a steady flow of
incremental innovations. Toyota's early lead in the post-1970s auto
market came from its ability to constantly learn how to become better
at quality. It was not a single event but the intersection of various
management practices that led to its success.

At this stage, as in previous ones, most of the innovation game is
played around a particular theme—but surprises can occur and disrupt
the focus. A new technology, a quantum leap in performance, or a new
segmentation of the market may redefine the industry and move it to a
new lifecycle. Airlines in Europe were competing at how to be more
efficient when the low-cost carriers—such as Ryanair or easyJet—
entered the market with a radical proposal along the price dimension.

The Complementarities Stage

In the last stage, the focus shifts to managing complementarities. This
capability comes from the ability to maximize the synergies among
different products and businesses within a company. It also comes

from establishing a network of partners that can substantially enhance the value proposition to the customer. Competition shifts from identifying the value proposition for each market segment to managing interactions and complexity. The success of FMC Corporation—a diversified chemical company—resides on its ability to manage the synergies among its three main businesses: agricultural, industrial, and consumer. Competition among game console's manufacturers—Sony, Microsoft, and Nintendo—is mostly about creating and maintaining a network of software companies that come up with blockbuster games for their consoles.

As industries evolve incrementally through these lifecycles, radical innovations can move the industry to a new lifecycle at any time. Unless a company has a strategic imperative to invest part of its portfolio in radical innovations, the processes and culture solidify around improving the status quo and leave the company vulnerable to radical changes in any of these dimensions.

Learning and the Innovation Rules

In a healthy innovative company, leadership supports learning and puts in place the systems for it to happen. This includes quick-and-dirty diagnostics that are run to provide critical insights into problems and opportunities, as well as more complex learning systems that operate continually to provide feedback and guidance, such as planning tools. Driving innovation into the business mentality requires learning and change. Dell learned what was important to succeed in its innovation strategy, and worked hard to ingrain the learning into the business mentality and culture.

Managing the balance between creativity and value capture requires learning systems. Otherwise, despite best intentions, one always becomes dominant over the other and the correct balance is lost. Apple suffered from too much creativity and not enough value capture, despite a strong focus on innovation processes. Learning what went wrong with that balance and fixing it was one of the things Steve Jobs made happen when he returned as CEO.

In addition, innovation networks are fairly dynamic. Managing them requires information and learning to remodel and update the structure. Without learning, the networks become bureaucratic, cumbersome, and ineffective. Many companies that have established strong networks have failed to maintain the levels of learning and change required to keep them current, and the networks have become weak and fallen into disuse. A major global equipment company did not maintain its networks during a growth spurt that lasted for the better part of two years. It was distracted by the opportunities at hand, and resources were committed to other activities. Once the growth rate decreased, the innovation networks had deteriorated and were not in shape to support the level of innovation required to fuel the next round of growth; the company's growth rate began to decline.

Finally, learning is one of the most important elements in combating organizational antibodies. Preventing the antibodies requires learning systems and activities that allow the organization to differentiate good change from bad change. Otherwise, the organizational antibodies become unselective and they attack and disrupt all change. In that state, innovation is dead. Company A described earlier had severe learning disabilities. There was not enough learning to counteract the organizational antibodies, and the company was in a death spiral. Company B had similar learning problems but engaged in focused learning on its innovation approach and broke the spiral.

Innovation learning changes over time, as the business and industry evolve from an initial technological focus for innovation through to a mature stage where efficiency is the focus of innovation. However, the importance of learning does not change—it stays a high priority throughout an organization's involvement with innovation.

9

CULTIVATING INNOVATION: HOW TO DESIGN A WINNING CULTURE

How Culture Affects Innovation

Layered on top of and spread throughout the organization, a company's systems and processes are a network of social interactions—the organizational culture. Culture, comprised of unwritten rules, shared beliefs, and mental models of the people, affects the effectiveness of the innovation tools we have described. The mightiest company in the computer industry, IBM, nearly disappeared in the early 1990s. The company's culture prized homogeneity and conformance, and the company could not deal with the rate of change going on around it. Only a risky and forceful change driven by a new external CEO put IBM back on the success track.

Figure 9.1 depicts how these two elements interact and influence each other, and affect the outcome of the innovation effort.

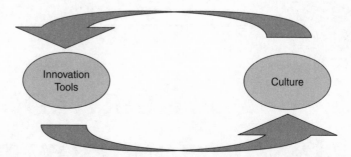

FIGURE 9.1   THE INTERACTION BETWEEN MANAGEMENT TOOLS AND CULTURE.

Culture is not static; it continually evolves. New systems and processes, new symbols and organizational values can be designed to evolve company culture.[1] Dell's CEO Kevin B. Rollins launched a concerted effort in 1997 to understand and grow Dell's culture into a strong competitive asset. The goal was not to create a different culture for Dell but to adapt and enhance its positive elements. Dell's Human Resources Director Paul McKinnon said, "We just aspired to do better." He said that he and the CEO asked themselves the question, "What would a new winning culture look like here at Dell?"[2]

Is Innovation the New Religion?

Innovation in some companies is more than a strategy, it's a way of life—a religion almost. Companies such as Virgin and Southwest Airlines have imbedded innovation into their company cultures.[3] Virgin CEO Richard Branson expects innovation and rewards it. He has put systems in place to keep innovation alive and a part of the business mentality.

People in organizations, ones that are riding a high due to successful innovation, believe intensely in what they are doing, so much so that the intensity is palpable when you are near them. They are zealous and energetic in espousing their commitment to innovation and their processes that surround it. They think others would benefit from innovation if they only saw the light. Employees at 3M, for instance, can seem almost surprised when visitors to the company don't have a special creative or innovative interest area of their own.

The cultural anthropologist in us asks, "What is going on here? Why this intensity of belief? Why do innovation processes sometimes become icons?" An example of such an icon is 3M's "15 percent free-time" policy, which states that all employees should spend 15 percent of their time on their own projects and ideas. 3M employees hold this policy in such high esteem that they do not believe the company could survive without it. Likewise, Google, another place where innovation is deeply imbedded in the culture, is going down the same road and has upped the ante, allowing 20 percent free time for innovation.

Innovation's mystical aspect is tied to two phenomena:

- Harnessing creativity

- Renewal of the company

In an organization that harnesses creativity, employees celebrate that accomplishment. People treat proper management of creativity with a spiritual intensity that is akin to religious belief. For them, creativity in business has an element of luck, and certain organizations are more likely to get it. The uncontrollable nature of luck leads some people to attach a mystical aspect to creativity. You are likely to see in the workspaces of such an organization calendars and signs that promote an "idea a day," or think and rest areas, such as the play rooms some software companies maintain. In general, the air is more abuzz with a sense that you are more alive and vibrant when being creative. Innovation in these companies is not an obsession—where everybody is worried about how to be more innovative—it has become a way of life ingrained in their business mentality.

Case Study: British Airways

British Airways (BA) is an excellent example of a company that, by proactively changing the culture, fostered innovation and a whole new way of doing business, and in doing so transformed itself into "Best in Class" for most of its routes. In the 1970s, BA was notorious for poor service. In the recent past, it was one of the most respected airline companies. What changed? Fundamentally, BA changed its culture. It redefined itself, changing from being a transportation provider to being a *service* provider. How did BA achieve the change? It reeducated its entire workforce. BA provided training for all employees on the new company culture, and as a result created an environment that fostered innovation. Following that transformation, BA achieved many process innovation successes as a result of the new culture. For example, the company changed its baggage-handling procedures with such dramatic increases in efficiency that this soon became one of the areas that separates BA from its competitors.

Interestingly, BA is more recently wrestling again with some of the same cultural problems that hampered its performance in the 1970s. This change is an indication that culture is not static; it is dynamic. You can change from a culture that does not support innovation to one that supports and enhances the innovation and performance. But by the same token, you can shift from a leader in innovation to a poor performer if proper care is not given to maintaining the culture that supports innovation.

The outcome of innovation is renewal and growth for the organization and for all the people within. Successful innovation is viewed differently from other management functions because people perceive that it creates ongoing life for the company. Without innovation, a company succumbs to competitors or market shifts and eventually disappears. As a result, some people in an organization see innovation as securing their futures. For them, innovation is a crucial element of survival, and it needs to be held in high regard and protected.

These phenomena reinforce the power of innovative culture in a company. They can be a vital source of competitive energy as well as an energizing force for the people in the company.

The Danger of Success

Paradoxically, the biggest threat to innovation is success. The very organizations that are riding high on the success of their innovation efforts, and whose employees believe fervently in the organization and the doctrine of ongoing innovation, are often the organizations most at risk. The risk comes in two forms: complacency and dogma.[4]

Successful organizations tend to become complacent and conservative in order to preserve their core competencies—those things that lead to their success. This is logical and largely advantageous in the short-term. Paradoxically, the things that led to their success could be the very things in the long-term that pull them into failure. The danger is that the organization's managers may become complacent in examining and evaluating their systems and culture because of the performance advantage they enjoy. While enjoying the sensation of success, they may lose the drive that got them there in the first place. Paul Otellini, Intel's CEO, faced this dilemma when he realized that Intel's success would not depend on what they had always done well—namely, stamp out faster and faster processors. "The history of the industry was the better-mousetrap syndrome: You build a faster thing and the word will beat a path to your doorstep. But as the industry matured, that no longer became the best way to look at the problem." Otellini decided that the future would belong to the creative, not the fast. He led the charge to create better, more creative products to run the high-end machines in corporate data centers and make deeper inroads into new consumer markets.[5]

Success is intoxicating, and people can become very attached to the things they believe cause the success. They become resistant to change, trapped in their own practices. In successful organizations where complacency has set in, it is often very difficult for new ideas and businesses to attract enough resources to get off the ground.

CEO Sanity Check

Success is one of the most dangerous threats to innovation. Once an organization feels successful, it falls into ways of thinking and acting that are corrosive to successful innovation. This is the trap that every successful innovator faces: The Enemy Within.

It is the CEO's job to identify the bad behavior and demand change. Complacency at the top leads to complacency within.

Sometimes this complacency results in a shift to a Play-Not-to-Lose strategy, even though the company's situation would favor a Play-to-Win strategy. People start to play more conservatively, dulling the sharpness of the Play-to-Win innovation strategy. Despite their innovative strengths and relatively strong competitive situation, the companies gradually slide into a Play-Not-to-Lose strategy. Digital Equipment Corporation (DEC) was IBM's main competitor in the mainframe market in the 1980s, with more than 100,000 employees. It was a highly admired company. In contrast to IBM, which had migrated to the computer market, DEC had been a computer company since its inception in 1957. DEC was one of the few companies that could threaten the almighty IBM at the time. Its success was its innovative products, from the successful PDP series in the 1960s, to the famed VAX series in the 1980s. However, DEC was unable to adapt to the market. Two forces changed the market. First, customers started to demand open architectures, but the company kept offering DEC-centric products. Second, PCs had gained performance power to eat on DEC's mainframe market. DEC's new products were engineering masterpieces in line with the previous generations that had made the company so successful. But they were designed for a market that did not exist anymore. After a decade of losses and turmoil, the company was acquired in early 1998.

In addition, as complacency grows, organizational antibodies become more prevalent. Good ideas are attacked because they would require more change, and the organization is complacent—so complacent that it encourages rather than fights organizational antibodies. A highly successful European manufacturer of electronic components saw how its market started to deteriorate in the last part of the 1970s and early 1980s. Its traditional customers had been European consumer electronic manufacturers that were being swept by Asian competitors. Rather than looking for new business models, the company was stuck to its traditional way of doing business. Top management saw new ideas as either too risky for the firm or too difficult for the firm to execute on them. It saw the destiny written in stone: to die with its customers. It was not until a new top management team took over and redefined the company as a distributor that its future was again bright.

Some of the companies that we have used as examples of innovation leaders—Apple, Nokia, GE, IBM, Genentech—currently face the challenge of maintaining their innovation leadership. Their success has led them into a dangerous situation where they could lose what they once had that made them great. To avoid that loss, they will need to avoid complacency, fight organizational antibodies, keep the strategy carefully honed, and maintain a culture that supports innovation.

Sometimes, the threat from success is not complacency, but that firmly held cultural values turn into dogmas. Toyota challenged the long-held cultural dogma of lifetime employment in Japan when it decided that company salaries should be based on capability rather than seniority, and they opted to reward strong performance with bonuses.

Values represent a company's belief system. They give employees direction in their day-to-day activities and in decision-making. However, these beliefs often harden into rigid principles and orthodoxy. Managers follow these principles as unquestionable truth, without thought or evaluation. While they may have been effective when initiated, they will not remain so, especially in a fast-changing business and market environment. The very values that initially promoted innovation and success in an organization can be the demise of that same organization if they are not evaluated and adjusted on an ongoing basis. Organizational learning plays a key role in fighting dogma.

Take the example of Arthur D. Little, an international management and technology consulting firm headquartered on the Charles River in Cambridge. A.D. Little was proud of its heritage as an innovator, being more than 100 years old and the oldest consulting company in the world. It had a long history of innovation in consulting services and in technology. The culture favored constant innovation, and many consultants at the company used to feel that the innovative problem-solving approach should be improved every time a new project was started; the net effect was that the same approach was seldom used twice. Consequently, innovation was rampant. A.D. Little learned it is very expensive to innovate *everything, all the time*.

Organizational Levers of an Innovative Culture

Managing innovation while delivering performance is a paradoxical process. The organization has to be stable in its identity and strategy and yet open to constant change:

- Focused on the things that make it successful in the present market, and yet diverse in the areas it explores for opportunities.

- Conservative to perpetuate the best-practices that exist and yet willing to take risks on new and better things.

- Controlling to ensure the innovation investment is well-used, but trusting enough to allow employees the freedom to create, explore, take risks, and innovate.

Some companies may choose to avoid this paradox; by doing so, they risk reducing innovation to the minimum, and failing to fully capitalize on their innovation investment. Alternately, some may avoid the paradox by maximizing innovation and reducing their performance. Neither is recommended.

Success requires managing this paradox by recognizing and managing the levers of culture that affect innovation.

The Levers of an Innovative Culture

Managers have different levers to create the culture that the innovation strategy needs. These levers locate the company in a position between conflicting goals. The particular position depends on the culture that management wants to create. Figure 9.2 lists these levers.

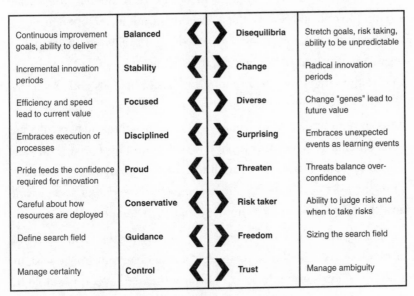

Continuous improvement goals, ability to deliver	Balanced		Disequilibria	Stretch goals, risk taking, ability to be unpredictable
Incremental innovation periods	Stability		Change	Radical innovation periods
Efficiency and speed lead to current value	Focused		Diverse	Change "genes" lead to future value
Embraces execution of processes	Disciplined		Surprising	Embraces unexpected events as learning events
Pride feeds the confidence required for innovation	Proud		Threaten	Threats balance over-confidence
Careful about how resources are deployed	Conservative		Risk taker	Ability to judge risk and when to take risks
Define search field	Guidance		Freedom	Sizing the search field
Manage certainty	Control		Trust	Manage ambiguity

FIGURE 9.2   LEVERS OF AN INNOVATION CULTURE.

An innovative culture embraces balance and disequilibria. A balanced culture permits the peace that creativity and value creation need. At the same time, the organization needs to move forward, and only challenges and surprises will move the company forward. Microsoft culture provides stability to people working on its long-term projects such as the .NET initiative, while at the same time gives a sense of urgency to people closer to the strategic game played in the market.

Innovation also requires periods of stability and periods of change. Constant revolution is an unproductive state because the company is unable to fully capture the value of its innovation effort. Toyota's introduction of the hybrid automobile Prius changed the direction of the industry. Subsequently, Toyota followed with a series of incremental innovations and withheld additional disruptive innovations. A period of incremental innovation (the constant refinement of an idea) should follow each radical innovation in order to maximize the value extracted from the radical innovation.

The challenge for top management is to time periods of stability with periods of change—that is, to be aware of and to orchestrate around the ebb and flow of these. An organization cannot be in a constant change process; it needs periods of stability to regroup and regain energy. It needs stability to fully extract the value of innovation. But, at the same time, the organization has to be constantly ready for change. This requires that there be a constant underlying sense of urgency, an imperative for change. The environment may create this need for change. Webvan, even if one of the most expensive failures of the dot-com area, became a threat to existing supermarket chains that were forced to evaluate how to respond to its eventual success and how to embrace the new technology that Webvan was leveraging.

Sometimes, the environment may not create the required sense of urgency because the company has a significant advantage sustainable in the foreseeable future or because the market is very stable. In this case, the disequilibria needed to prompt an episode of radical innovation needs to come from inside the organization. BP's CEO Lord Brown saw that the company needed to be prodded out of the complacent equilibrium that had affected BP and the other leading companies in the oil industry. He spearheaded the change to focus BP on non-traditional energy issues including renewable energy. Management plays a critical role in moving the company out of a stable and attractive equilibrium and challenging the organization to innovate. This internal sense of urgency can be communicated through stretch goals—in the form of financial targets (double sales in two years) or as non-financial targets (enter new geographical markets or grow into new technologies). Stretch targets alone are not enough, though. They need to be supported by a credible strategy that devotes adequate resources to innovation, by systems that encourage innovation, and most importantly by a top management team that is committed to innovation.

Research Bite: Combining Incremental and Radical Innovation

A medium-sized medical company in Northern Europe that we studied exemplifies the ability to stay on-course and break into new areas. The company produced medical instruments for surgery rooms. Its main families of products had a clear positioning—highest quality—and new products within this strategy had clear selection criteria. Its traditional products generated healthy cash flows. This strong financial position allowed the company to fund long-term projects, sometimes close to five years (compared to a regular project for a new product of a few months). These projects explored new product markets, new geographical markets, and new technologies, and were highly regarded in the firm. The CEO devoted periodic attention to them, and project managers for these initiatives had a direct line to the CEO. These managers were granted significant freedom, with loose goals and schedules. Supervision came directly from the CEO (together with the appropriate functional manager) who spent time understanding the project, its risks, and its potential upside. The result was a healthy core group of products with periodic additions of radical and semi-radical innovations that drove the big increases in top- and bottom-line growth.

Focus and diversity is another paradox that successful companies master. Focus provides the efficiency and speed that keeps a company ahead of competitors during evolutionary times. In stable environments, the winners are those companies able to execute—that is, to serve customer needs more efficiently. Focus brings the ability to execute. The virtues of a focused strategy have been praised in management thinking for two decades now. But being overly focused leads to myopia and the inability to see potentially important changes in the environment, or becoming inflexible and unable to react to these changes. Focusing on what it knew best left Levi's unable to react to new trends in the jeans' market; focus on cash registers' technology that it knew best brought NCR to a very turbulent period.

Embracing diversity in people, ideas, and methods ensures the organization will thrive in periods of change. The organization has to be attentive and invest in related opportunities. It has to diversify away from what it knows very well and try promising ideas. 3M is constantly experimenting, often outside its traditional markets. Microsoft has diversified progressively from its core PC software to take advantage of market opportunities and has brought entirely different types of people into the company.

An innovative culture embraces discipline and surprise. The second one creates value, the first one captures it. Without discipline, great ideas do not become valuable. Every company successful at innovation follows great ideas with disciplined processes that translate them into value. Philips Electronics, the only European consumer electronics company that has thrived in a market which eliminated all its local competitors, has very detailed processes that have created a sense of discipline together with a sensitivity for new ideas within and outside the company.

Another paradox to manage, and where culture is critical, is to have a proud organization that also feels threatened. Pride provides the confidence to embark in risky projects with a potentially large payoff. However, pride may also lead to complacency, dismissing the abilities of competitors or potential entrants. Thus, pride needs to come with a sense of uneasiness, a sense of threat that keeps the organization on its toes. The "HP way" created a company in which every employee felt proud and lucky to be part of HP. The pride and the commitment of its people were beyond what any large company had ever achieved and closer to the unity of religious groups. The "HP way" drove the company from its founding. When Carly Fiorina took over, HP's performance was starting to lose its brightness. Pride seemed to be feeding complacency. Fiorina dramatically changed the emphasis toward the threats that faced the company and each employee. The sense of threat had been losing ground in HP culture, and she brought it back to enhance performance. The culture shock displaced a significant number of employees. The recent demise of Fiorina and the dismal performance of HP stock can be attributed to various reasons; but the move away from the "HP way" and the attempt to refocus the culture away from the sources of the pride required for innovation certainly explain part of these events.

This sense of threat can be real, coming from the market or enacted through the culture of the organization. But in both cases, it provides the balancing force to the potential overconfidence required to address innovation.

An innovative culture is conservative and risk-taker at the same time. Vodafone, the leading European mobile phone service provider, is known for its constant innovations in products, services, and marketing. Its leadership is based on being ahead of its competitors in these dimensions. But Vodafone combines this appetite to try new things with a strong financial control. Risk-taking is balanced with attention to measuring and managing risk. Salesforce.com combines new approaches to market its products with careful analyses of its returns. The *Red Herring*, one of the leading publications in the business of technology, keeps its innovation appetite with a cost-conscious culture that emanates from its CEO.

The conservative mindset ensures that employees are aware of the importance of the resources with which they have been entrusted. Every investment and every expense has to be viewed from the perspective of ROI. A culture that supports unquestioned spending, with little regard for the value of the resources, leads to a company that fails in innovation. A conservative culture values risk and carefully evaluates the pros and cons of each innovation opportunity.

Innovation requires freedom, but freedom alone seldom leads to innovation. Real Madrid, one of the best soccer teams in Europe, had a disastrous season in 2003-2004 when the talent it had amassed was the best in the world. Each star player wanted to shine more than the others and played to do precisely this. The coach was unable to guide the players' desire to be creative into a coherent effort. The 2003-2004 Lakers in the NBA suffered from a similar problem when they lost the finals to a team with much less talent. Too little guidance dilutes the power of freedom into unrelated efforts that ignore each other and do not build a coherent set of abilities going forward. In contrast, too much guidance leads to rejecting good ideas.

Top management needs to outline the "rules of play." Sony Founder Masaru Ibuka gave a clear direction to the company when he described the mission as:

1. Establishing a place of work where engineers can feel the joy of technological innovation, be aware of their mission to society, and work to their heart's content.

2. Pursuing dynamic activities in technology and production for the reconstruction of Japan and the elevation of the nation's culture.

3. Applying advanced technology to the life of the general public.

This mission permeated the company since inception and provided guidance for decision-makers. No guidance leads to paralysis; people may find too much freedom crippling because they don't know what they can do next. But very narrow search fields leads to local searches unable to move the company to a new paradigm.

The final paradox is between control and trust. Innovation requires both elements. On the one hand, control is required to make informed decisions about resource allocation, strategy development, and performance evaluation. On the other hand, the early stages of innovation are usually hidden to top management; they happen throughout the organization and they grow with the support of the local department. An idea that is exposed to the scrutiny of the whole organization too early may easily be killed. Top management needs to trust the systems, people, and culture of the organization to nurture ideas with good potential, even if these ideas are outside the traditional view of top management. Post-its was successful because it was supported by mid-level managers through the early development stages. Had the innovation been exposed to senior-level scrutiny earlier in its early stage, it would have lacked sufficient development and supporting market information to further its development, and the idea probably would have been killed.

Legends and Heroes

A large force in shaping culture is the stories that circulate around the organization.[6] These stories illustrate extreme manifestations of the culture. As stories circulate from person to person, though, they become distorted. The protagonists become heroes that achieve goals unheard of. The stories get detached from reality and become legends. Every organization has legends and heroes that communicate the culture.

Nordstrom—one of the most successful retailers in the United States—has a very strong culture around customer service. This culture is reflected in stories of regular employees who went beyond their call of duty to serve the customer—from driving in the snow to deliver a pair of shoes on time, buying a tie from a competitor to have the perfect suit for a customer, or changing the tire of a customer who could not do it by himself.

Legends and heroes emerge as stories circulate, but management can affect which stories are emphasized and what aspects are highlighted. Electronic Data Systems developed a history of the company's problems and successes, and an outline of the plan going forward that provided the framework for specific stories that described the emerging culture of the company. This was important in garnering support in the organization, and was an integral part of the cultural change and revitalization that was launched in 2004.

The Physical Environment

The indirect effect of physical environment on creativity is substantial.[7] Features in buildings such as colors and shapes have been shown to have an effect on creativity.

This does not mean you should completely redesign your office building, but there are ways to promote a more creative environment through use of color, light, and space. IDEO's top performers say they "joined not only because they lead their industry but also because of their physical and cultural environment."[8] The IDEO office spaces make innovation happen because they are visually and mentally exciting. IDEO's CEO says that what distinguishes IDEO from its competitors is not their processes but their ability to *see* better. He claims they see the market situation and the customer need better; they see the trends and discontinuities better; and they see solutions better. If clarity of vision is key, if *seeing* is at the heart of success, then the visual environment of the innovators is a key success factor.

Different Country Cultures Breed Different Innovation Cultures

Understanding and managing organizational culture takes on a new dimension when your organization crosses geographical borders. For managers in multinational and global organizations, the challenge of managing the culture to foster innovation begins with the challenge of understanding how local culture affects the values and beliefs people hold, and thus affects how they think, behave, and contribute. As an HP engineer located in Spain described it, the concept of being on time to a meeting is different in Spain from the concept in the U.S. While in the U.S., it is totally acceptable to finish a conversation to be on time to a meeting, this engineer described how in Spain it was unacceptable to leave a conversation if the other person had not finished his or her point; even at the expense of being late to a meeting.

It is important to be aware that a person's cultural background has a fundamental impact on how he or she responds to organizational culture. Furthermore, most of the elements that make up a culture are not visible or easily discernible. Figure 9.3 is used by Shell Oil to educate its employees on this point.

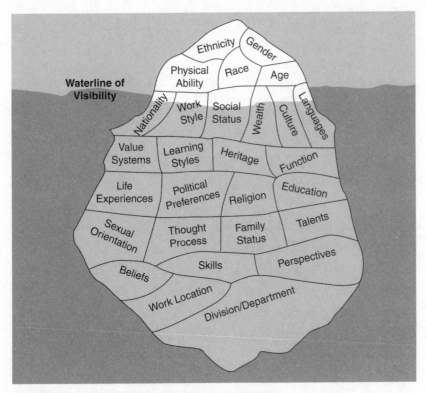

FIGURE 9.3   THE FOUNDATIONS OF CULTURE.

Research Bite: Geographical Differences in Innovation

An interesting finding from our survey of R&D managers is how different regions in the world perceive the key strategic dimensions of innovation.

For Asian companies, **technology leadership** was perceived as the most important dimension going forward.

For American companies, **product performance** was the most challenging dimension.

For European companies, **time-to-market** was the key strategic dimension.

In addition, Europe and America give much more importance to product cost than do Asian companies.

This divergence in preferences reflects what these different regions perceive to be their limitations in innovation. While they may capture real weaknesses, these contrasting opinions also reflect the consensus about these weaknesses that emerges as part of the formation of the regional cultures.

These differences suggest different perceptions about the source of innovation.[9] Asia focuses more on the *resources* and being able to have the right technology that will put the right products in the hands of the customers. The innovation of these companies focuses primarily on managing the resources of the innovation process. In contrast, American companies manage the *results* of innovation as reflected in product performance. American companies use a *pull* strategy for innovation where market demands drive innovation, while Asian companies favor a *push* strategy where innovation happens in the company and it is then driven to the market. Europe follows a mixed strategy, closer to the American pull strategy, but with more of an emphasis on managing the innovation process.

People and Innovation

It is the people in an organization who adopt, adhere to, change, or reject a culture. They are the vehicles through which a culture has impact and through which innovation (and everything else) happens. Therefore, the human resources strategies of an organization are critically important to building and maintaining innovation.

This section examines the most important elements of people management, including recruiting the right people in the first place, managing them to ensure satisfaction and ongoing motivation, and ensuring the leaders of the organization fulfill a role that promotes innovation.

Recruiting to Build an Innovative Organization

To foster innovation in your organization, you need to attract and recruit people who will be innovative. It may seem that what you need to do is develop techniques and instruments to identify innovative people, and then hire them. However, it is not that simple. While it may be true that some people are more naturally innovative than others, it is the interplay between the person and their environment that will ultimately determine their level of innovativeness. Even a person who has a proven ability to be innovative, if put in a culture and situation that does not foster the creativity within him or her, will find it difficult, if not impossible to be innovative on an ongoing basis. The culture could stifle his or her innovation, either because it is so comfortable for him or her that it does not prompt them to think of new approaches, or because it is so foreign and uncomfortable that it disrupts that person's ability to work and contribute.

A software firm was famed for using a very top-down command and control approach. Each employee had clear goals on his or her objectives for the quarter, and these goals were tightly linked to each other. The result was a machine so well tuned to execute on its strategy that quickly gained a commanding position in the market. The success attracted very talented employees, and the company appeared to be in a virtuous cycle. However, the talent it was attracting was excelling at execution, but its creativity was unused and even punished—a classic case of unbalanced creativity and value creation. One manager described how she proposed to adapt the software to an Asian market. Her supervisor reluctantly accepted the idea and, because of her insistence, accepted to have the project as part of her goals. The problem was that the objective contributed 5 percent to her performance. Enough to be a worry, but not enough to devote the time required to make it a success. The company began to suffer from a monoculture that suppressed creativity and favored value capture.

Turn Your Recruitment Strategy Upside-Down!

The norm for human resource departments the world over is to find the "right people" with the "right fit" for the organization. However, research into hiring for innovation suggests that a more effective strategy may be to sometimes hire the *wrong* people, the people who make some people feel uncomfortable during interviews, the people perceived not to fit perfectly into your organization's culture. This recruiting policy will find people who will challenge the status quo, increase diversity and creativity, and bring higher levels of innovation to the organization.[10]

There are many examples of success stories in which people have been hired because of their lack of knowledge about the industry. Their lack of preconceived ideas or specific topic knowledge permitted them to explore ideas and see opportunities that others could not. Jane Goodall and her groundbreaking research on chimpanzees is a good example of this. Louis Leakey, the famous anthropologist, offered Goodall the job of researching chimpanzees in Africa. She was reluctant to take the job due to her lack of knowledge and scientific training. However, this was exactly what Leakey wanted—no preconceived ideas of chimpanzee behavior to cloud observation of Goodall's findings. Goodall's results were a major breakthrough, and Leakey later commented that, "If she had not been ignorant of existing theories, she would never have been able to observe and explain so many new chimp behaviors."[11]

CEO Action Plan

Identify what types of innovative people you need to meet the strategic objectives. Then set specific hiring objectives and an approach to get them on board ASAP. This will surprise the organization and send a clear message that you understand and care about the innovative culture.

However, it can be difficult to hire people who do not fit comfortably in your organization's preconception of what an employee should be. Remember that you will have to manage the resulting tensions that arise. To hire "outside the mold" to stir up innovation, consider doing some of the following:

- Hire people you think will *not* fit in but would contribute to creative tension.

- Hire people you don't like who have significant capabilities and knowledge.

- Invite people from other companies as visitors, and let them tell you what is right and wrong with your innovation.

- Look for people who lack some of the knowledge required for the post, but who have some significant level of compensating qualities.

- Hire those who will question rather than accept.

When you think about it, the characteristics listed here perfectly describe Christopher Columbus. By all accounts, he did not fit in, always questioned the norm, was not well liked, and made a pest of himself in courts across Europe. Spain's Ferdinand and Isabella gave him a special task, one that put his obstreperous personality and dogged determinism to good use. It also put him far away from others that found him too difficult to stomach. The net result was the discovery of new lands, the accrual of massive wealth, and the recognition of Spain as the leader in world exploration. Columbus perhaps represents the best example of innovative hiring in the history of the Western world.

Hiring the *wrong people* requires that you hire carefully. Hire skilled people who bring a different perspective, with the qualities required to do an excellent job in their assignment. The aim is to create a team that is creative and can rise to the challenge. Hiring *wrong* still requires that people hired are team players and have the basic capabilities to be a good match to the prospective job or assignment.[12] The old adage, "People are your most important asset," is wrong. *The right people are your most important asset.*[13]

The Role of Senior Management

If the top managers do not understand the inevitable challenges of innovation, the effort is doomed to failure even as it starts. Thomas Edison knew that people were an important part of innovation. He referred to his team—the army of researchers that developed the ideas, and the scientists and machinists who created the prototypes—as *muckers*. The odd term came from the job title of workers who cleaned out the stables; Edison even referred to himself as the "head mucker." His metaphor for the people involved in innovation left no doubt about the no-nonsense, hard-working approach he had to innovation.[14]

Leading Innovation

Innovation leadership should provide:[15]

- **An aspiration that challenges the complacency and demands the organization to go beyond its current performance; to search, create, and surprise the customer**. Sony's founder constantly challenged his engineers to do things that had never been done before, such as new ways to create an image on a TV screen (the Trinitron tube) or very cheap video (the Betamax system).

- **A vision that tells the organization where it is going**. Johnson & Johnson's credo, which has guided the company for more than 60 years, starts by saying, "We believe our first responsibility is to the doctors, nurses, and patients, to mothers and fathers and all others who use our products and services." This vision makes Johnson & Johnson's reason to exist transparent to employees and other constituencies: Its main mission is to make the life of doctors, nurses, and patients better.

- **A leadership commitment in terms of resources**. Without this commitment, aspiration and vision are not taken seriously. The new products group at a major consumer goods company was told by senior management that innovation was vitally important and that higher levels were required to meet growth targets. To support this innovation initiative, senior management sent a clear signal of its commitment. They assessed the adequacy of the resources to meet the challenge, identified several critical gaps, and quickly filled them. The resource allocation process serves as an important communication tool to begin to translate long-term strategic plans into actions that people in the organization understand.

- **An innovation strategy and a set of processes and management systems to support the strategy**. It does not make sense to cheer for innovation and then reward, emphasize, and pressure employees for short-term performance—a common situation in many firms. As a manager described it: "We are behind in product design and product quality, and a big reason for it is the bureaucracy that we have."

- **Leadership by example**. When people see the team at the top doing what it says, the message becomes credible. Examples come in very different flavors, from acquisitions that move the organization into new territory, to remodeling the top management team, or to enhance the visibility of innovators within the organization.

- **A clear sense of command**. Business is about trade-offs, and innovation is no exception. The top management team is where the chain of command ends and where certain decisions have to be made. In the 1980s, PC companies were faced with the decision of having proprietary systems or bending to the IBM standard (that later became the Wintel standard). The decision was not easy, and most of those companies that did not adopt IBM's standard disappeared (only Apple survived, and not without problems).

- **A culture receptive to new ideas and change**. Jeffrey Immelt, CEO of GE, stepped up to this challenge when he took charge; he engaged the company in a reassessment of the direction and level of innovation. He challenged norms of behavior and showed that change was necessary for survival.

These are the collective responsibility of senior management. However, the CEO has special responsibilities.

The Role of the CEO

One of the key roles of the CEO is to make innovation part of the culture of the company. Putting the innovation strategy and systems in place is not enough. The CEO needs to work on and in the innovation culture. IDEO, one of the world's leading industrial design firms and a company known for its innovative culture, says that methodology alone is not enough to create innovation in your organization. According to the CEO David Kelley, "Some companies seem more comfortable going through the methodological motions than making the cultural commitments that ongoing innovation demands."[16]

Earlier innovation approaches attempted to kluge together the business and technology parts of the organization, but the effect was always suboptimal. If the technology group was in charge of innovation, then business management was included in the oversight and management of the process (in other words, a stage-gate process). Likewise, if the strategy and business people were driving innovation, then the recommendation was to invite the technology people to the table. The goal was to achieve balance and collaboration between the two groups. However, this missed the essential point—innovation is based on managing both functions effectively and in concert. Unfortunately, the business functions in an organization cannot effectively manage the technology side, and vice versa. The CEO needs to make certain that collaboration occurs and becomes part of the culture. Steve Jobs works this critical cultural angle at Apple by being the clear leader of innovation and pushing hard to ensure that there is effective collaboration between the technology and business folks.

Culture and the Innovation Rules

We have come full circle, and returned to the point where we started the discussion of the seven rules in Chapter 1—the role of the CEO as leader. The culture of an organization has many components, but one of the most important is leadership. The CEO has significant impact on the innovation culture that grows in the organization. Marc Benioff, chairman and CEO of Salesforce.com, said, "The difference between success and failure in innovation is leadership." He said that culture is the most important ingredient that aligns the company and allows it to make its numbers.[17]

The innovation culture provides the business mentality for innovation. That is the reason why many attempts to improve innovation focus on culture; it is the cross-cutting element that threads its way across all of the innovation rules. But these views tend to see innovation as only amenable to soft, elusive, almost mystical actions. An innovation culture interacts with the very tangible performance measures and incentives. These are crucial management tools for changing and forming the appropriate innovation behavior, and those changes take place inside of the culture. Even organizational antibodies have a cultural component, and different organizations have different types of responses to try and thwart change. Certainly, managing the balance between creativity and value capture has a cultural component. All of these are important aspects of changing culture.

You don't change culture by going at it directly. You get people to change how they do things, how they think about things, and how they talk about things. And these changes seep into and become the new culture. Dell's CEO Rollins used this approach: He worked to have important new values added to the way the people thought about their business, and he pushed to have those values—codified in a document called "The Soul of Dell"—become the norms of action, and influenced the thinking and the discussions within Dell.[18]

Remember: *How you innovate determines what you innovate.* Culture is an important variable in that equation. It is not just differences in the processes, organization, leadership, performance measures, or incentives that separate the innovation leaders from the others; it is the *culture*.

10

CONCLUSION: APPLYING THE INNOVATION RULES TO YOUR ORGANIZATION

Combining Creativity with Commercial Savvy

> "The key to the whole game is to innovate and to make a profit."
>
> —Kevin Rollins, CEO, Dell[1]

If a CEO overemphasizes innovation, it can spell disaster. Durk Jager at Procter & Gamble found out the hard way that too much emphasis on innovation can displace the focus on the profitability of the business. Jager's over-zealous pursuit of innovation created significant disruptions in the organization and the business faltered: The profits, company morale, and the share price all declined.

A.G. Lafley, the CEO who replaced Jager at P&G, did not abandon the emphasis on innovation and has successfully moved P&G toward significantly improved innovation. Under Lafley, the company continues to shift its center of gravity toward higher-growth, higher-margin businesses such as healthcare and personal care. It increased its emphasis on innovation, increased the speed of getting new products to market, and reduced its over-reliance on incremental innovations. Lafley said that Jager attempted too much too fast, and indicated that the push toward higher levels of innovation alienated some people. He said, "We don't want to be pushing something out of an ivory tower somewhere."[2]

Lafley has slowed the rate of change and regained profitability. He has demonstrated that he has a firm grasp on the innovation *and* the operational side of the business, and he has led people in the company to recognize that innovation and profitability can coexist. Executing to improve innovation requires good operations.

Lafley slowed the rate of innovation to regain profitability; however, it is possible to achieve very high levels of innovation and not upset the profit of a business. In the rapidly changing world of the fashion business, where each company introduces new product innovations several times a year, Giorgio Armani has been steadily profitable for 30 years. Margins for his ready-to-wear fashions are among the best in the industry, and he has diversified into new lines without cheapening his brand. He has combined creativity with commercial savvy and led his industry.[3]

Sir Richard Branson has kept the Virgin group profitable, growing and maintaining high rates on innovation. In October 2004, he announced plans to enter space tourism with a new company, Virgin Galactic; unveiled a new online music store; and an airline in Nigeria that will become the nation's flag-carrier. At the same time, Virgin Rail's new high-speed tilting trains were being inaugurated on the London-to-Glasgow run. He has demonstrated that new ventures can be launched while existing businesses can be profitably managed.

Smart Execution

Successfully executing improvements to innovation is relatively straightforward. The seven Innovation Rules provide the basis for effective execution:

1. Exert strong leadership defining the innovation strategy and designing innovation portfolios, and encourage truly significant value creation.

2. Match innovation to the company business strategy including selection of the innovation strategy (Play-to-Win or Play-Not-to-Lose).

3. Make innovation an integral part of the company's business mentality, and ensure that the processes and the organization support a culture of innovation.

4. Balance creativity and value capture so that the company generates successful new ideas *and* gets the maximum return on its investment.

5. Neutralize organizational antibodies that kill off good ideas because they are different from the norm.

6. Create innovation networks inside and outside the organization; networks, not individuals, are the basic organizational building blocks of innovation.

7. Implement the correct metrics and incentives to make innovation manageable and to produce the right behavior; many companies have disincentives or poor incentives to elicit the appropriate innovation behavior.

CEMEX's CEO and senior management team took a hard, honest look at the company's overall historic performance, analyzed the specific performance of its innovation systems and organization, and identified their vision of the role that innovation needed to play in the businesses in the future. They selected the overall portfolio of investments, defining the mix of business models change and technology change. By using the diagnostic of the innovation systems and culture, the management team identified gaps in the role that innovation needed to play versus the role it had played. They saw areas of under-performance in the company's systems and organization, and identified the parts of their culture—including the leadership style—that would need to change. Then they developed an execution plan that defined the changes that needed to occur, the teams that would lead the changes, and the schedule for completion.

The Role of Leadership

The lesson from the most innovative companies is that leadership— particularly the CEO's leadership—is the crucial difference in creating and sustaining successful innovation. Marc Benioff, chairman and CEO of Salesforce.com, said that it is the CEO's role to lead the company to develop new models—business, technology, and leadership models—that will drive innovation to fuel growth and profitability. He has used this approach to lead Salesforce.com to quickly become an innovative leader in the rough-and-tumble competition of the software industry.

There are three initial activities that the leadership team should undertake to set the context for any change to innovation.

Leadership Must Define the Innovation Strategy and Link It to the Business Strategy

The leadership team should design the innovation portfolios and identify the role of business models and technology change to lead to truly significant value creation. Upon succeeding Jack Welch, GE's CEO Jeffrey Immelt critically reviewed the company's business plans and identified the need for new levels and types of innovation in each business area. Immelt identified the role that innovation would play. He identified the level of incremental innovations needed to maintain their current businesses. He identified the new business models and technologies that GE needs to systematically develop within the next decade, and prescribed increased levels of semi-radical and radical innovation to spur growth and create entirely new lines of business.

Faced with lagging innovation and a depressed stock price, Kraft—one of the leading packaged foods company—launched a new innovation initiative led by an Innovation Leadership Team consisting of the CEO and five senior executives. Among other activities aimed at giving new impetus to innovation, the Innovation Leadership Team oversaw the development of the portfolio and the allocation of resources for innovation efforts. This put the leadership in the driver's seat, and sent strong positive signals to the organization about management's desired emphasis on innovation and their commitment to the initiative.

Innovation Must Be Aligned with the Company Business Strategy, Including Selection of the Innovation Strategy

Here again, the leadership team plays a pivotal role. Although few companies in Japan come anywhere close to matching GE's impressive record of innovation and growth, Sanyo Electric has been compared favorably to the U.S. conglomerate. The consumer electronics maker has recently transformed itself from an industry also-ran, best known for low prices, to a technology powerhouse focused on businesses where it has global markets. The transformation was led by the CEO and chairman; the Play-to-Win innovation strategy resulted in a string of new and improved products that raised operating profits 21 percent.

In 2004, Sanyo had transformed itself into the world's largest maker of digital still cameras with 30 percent of the market. The company led the global market in optical pick-ups—key components in DVD and CD players—with 40 percent market share, and Sanyo's rechargeable batteries dominated the market and were in half the world's cell phones. Yukinori Kuwano, Sanyo's chief executive, along-side of Satoshi Iue, chairman, were successful because of selectivity about where to place its resources. "Unless you choose what to focus on, you will not be able to survive," said Kuwano. In addition, Kuwano and Iue directed the portfolio of investments and identified the areas that were ripe for investment. "That is the interesting thing about manufacturing," said Kuwano, "As soon as the technology breaks through or as soon as you change the business model, (something that appeared to have no future) can stage a comeback." Sanyo's leadership selected the Play-to-Win strategy, and identified the roles of business model innovation and technology innovation in each of its business areas.[4]

Leadership Must Define Who Will Benefit from Improved Innovations

It is leadership's responsibility to make it very clear to the team who are the targets for value creation from innovation. Otherwise, the company will not be aligned.

Innovation almost always focuses on maintaining or increasing profitability by delivering value to the consumer. Dell's CEO Kevin Rollins says, "The true test of R&D value is 'Does it make a profit, and does it benefit the consumer?' You've got to have both."[5]

Gillette learned the hard way that it is not always easy to deliver the right value to the consumer. Gillette wrongly applied the "blade-and-razor" strategy to its Duracell battery business. Build a better battery, they reasoned, and consumers would trade up. There was just one problem. Most consumers did not want better batteries; they wanted cheaper ones. "Gillette made a major error in bringing innovations that the consumer did not want. It was a flawed strategy," said Gillette CEO Jim Kilts.[6]

Innovation can have several other recipients. In 2004, Kraft's big focus was on innovation, not only to persuade consumers of superior performance of its products but also to maintain the relationship with powerful global retailers such as Wal-Mart, Tesco, and Carrefour.

Roger Deromedi, CEO of Kraft Foods, said, "The success of Wal-Mart requires us to do more in terms of bringing true innovation to the consumer. If you are not bringing that to the retailer today, then what do they need your brand for?"[7]

Wall Street also can see value in innovation. In the 1990s, Dow Chemical found that its patent and intellectual property assets were not recognized by Wall Street. Dow sent the clear message that it was spending wisely on R&D and innovation, that it was creating innovations, and that it was a stronger company for it—today and in the future. Wall Street saw the potential value of innovation to the company, and stock prices subsequently increased.

Innovation can also be important to the network of suppliers and partners. In the 1990s, a major automobile manufacturer was considered the most innovative by the tier-one suppliers. The manufacturer's investment in innovation, its use of innovation platforms to spur incremental and more aggressive innovations, and its heavy reliance on internal and external innovation networks made it the perceived leader. The suppliers preferentially brought their innovations to that manufacturer because partnering with that company was more likely to result in a profitable new product.

Finally, innovation can also be a powerful force to attract, retain, and energize the best employees for a company. The most innovative companies are often recognized as the best companies to work for. Google's reputation for innovation made it a magnet for the best and the brightest.

Diagnostics and Action

After these three initial steps, the leadership team should assess the company's innovation capabilities and its current situation.

Leadership needs to ensure that innovation is an integral part of the company's business mentality. Carly Fiorina, HP's former CEO, said about innovation, "You institutionalize it. It is a mindset and a set of capabilities. It is about technology. Also inventing different business models."[8] Fiorina was able to state the concept of leadership correctly, but apparently her board thought her execution fell short.

Siemens' CEO Heinrich von Pierer launched a wide-ranging management initiative meant to instill innovation and the need to change as part of the business mentality. Investment analysts identified a link between Siemens' strong performance between 2000 and 2004 and the initiative. Called *Top*—Total Optimized Processes—it is credited with changing the culture of the company.[9] It has resulted in a steady flow of new products and the creation of managers who are able to effectively use innovation to solve the operational problems.

Likewise, the leaders in Google, Nokia, and 3M created a culture where innovation is built into the way the company thinks and acts. Innovation is a way of life in those companies. Ingraining it in the business mentality, through leadership and learning, has kept innovation as an integral part of their success formula.

Marc Benioff, CEO of Salesforce.com, requires that all new initiatives and products be reviewed using the *V2MOM* management tool. The V2MOM tool, developed during his time at Oracle and used at Salesforce.com since its founding, derives its name from the five elements of the tool:[10]

- **V**ision: What do you want?

- **V**alues: What's important about it?

- **M**ethods: How do you get it?

- **O**bstacles: What is preventing you from getting it?

- **M**easures: How will you know when you got it?

The executive committee develops a company-wide V2MOM annually. Subsequently, every department and individual develops its own that supports the company V2MOM. The tool is used to align the entire organization from individuals to the company–level. Benioff believes that the CEO should set the context for innovation and should supply the overall mandate to allow the organization to take risks; this provides the basis for incremental as well as semi-radical and radical innovations.

Before launching an initiative to improve innovation by using pre-selected tools, it is important to conduct a diagnostic assessment of the innovation processes to assess the effectiveness of the key elements that maintain innovation in the business mentality: the company's understanding of the strategy, processes, and organizational structures that support innovation. The P&G senior management team launched a diagnostic before establishing its plans to change and improve innovation in the company. This type of diagnostic provides leadership with fresh understanding of the current state of the components of innovation, gaps in actual versus desired performance, and priority areas for change.

Diagnostics vary in scope. The diagnostic should fit the need. If the leadership team needs to characterize general performance and broad areas for improvement, it should rely on high-level diagnostics that address some of the major components of innovation, such as overall performance against goals and staff identification of perceived problem areas. If the management team is looking for specific targets for every aspect of the innovation process (for example, ideation, idea evaluation tools, selection parameters, team interactions, project management, and effectiveness of the strategy) it should rely on detailed diagnostics targeted to these objectives. Some typical diagnostic areas are included in Table 10.1.[11]

Table 10.1   Diagnostics

Strategy

Strong strategic alignment between innovation initiatives and business strategy.

Widely understood innovation strategy and clear management support.

Strong, well–developed innovation platforms.

Very clear understanding of customer needs.

Clear and strong approach to valuing innovation projects based on incremental, semi-radical, and radical taxonomy.

Processes

Strong market information and customer insights gathering.

Visioning and idea generation processes.

Effective idea screening process.

Good project management discipline.

Fast, fluid innovation process.

Good process improvement constantly underway.

Resources

Business and technology departments aligned and collaborating on innovation.

Strong, cross–functional teams using most appropriate staff rather than just using staff that happens to be available.

Actively hiring staff with non–traditional perspectives.

Effectively building core competencies and partnerships to meet innovation needs.

Organization

An incentive system that rewards people for innovation.

High degree of constructive interaction and cooperation across functions.

Explicit senior management responsibility for innovation results.

Effective leadership.

Because the innovation culture of a company is such an important part of the business mentality, leadership sometimes includes an assessment of the Innovation Climate to determine employees' perception of how well innovation is ingrained in the business mentality. Understanding the perceptions of innovation across the organization and the cultural norms associated with innovation can be critical to understanding the obstacles to innovation. Typically an Innovation Climate survey diagnostic is used across and through all levels of the organization.

One leading consumer goods company used an Innovation Climate diagnostic to understand how well innovation was ingrained in its business mentality. The leadership team had already launched a diagnostic regarding the adequacy of the innovation strategy, processes, resources, and organization. It had a wealth of information regarding each of those functions and had identified several areas that would benefit from improvement.

However, some in the leadership team wanted to dig a little deeper and understand the cultural health of innovation in the company. During the past few years, there had been instances of significant friction between the business and technology functions regarding what innovations were most important to the business. The leadership team wanted to understand what was behind that friction and ensure that the improvements they were about to undertake would not be undone because of some overlooked cultural issues. They fielded an Innovation Climate survey across the company with a particular focus on the brand management and technology areas where the acidic conflicts had occurred.

The result of the Innovation Climate assessment was sobering. Most people in the company felt that despite spending heavily on innovation and having good processes, resources, and strategy, senior management did not truly support innovation. As a result, people in the organization—especially the marketing department— had adopted the attitude that innovation was a nice-to-have element but was not crucial to the company's survival. The technical community had developed a sub-culture that favored incremental changes to exiting products. The diagnostic demonstrated to the leadership team the power of culture; its portfolio of investments, clear innovation strategy, and the strong innovation systems had not been enough to integrate innovation into the business mentality. Something was missing from the culture, and it stopped meaningful collaboration. The leadership team identified the missing elements—including stronger senior involvement in innovation decision-making—and selected the priority areas that needed to change. They launched an initiative to change the prevalent mentality, reestablish a culture of collaboration, and improve the innovation climate. In addition, they committed themselves to periodically reassess the Innovation Climate to ensure that they were making sustained progress.

Figure 10.1 presents an example of an Innovation Climate survey. Applied across the company, the survey requires the respondent to identify two ratings for each of the identified elements:

- Company best practice for that element (what level should the company strive for)

- Actual company performance for that element

This information identifies important employee perspectives about what is desired in the company's culture as well as how well the company performs.

GE realized that, given CEO Immelt's strong focus on innovation, the culture in GE needed to be changed. The training center in Crotonville, the bastion of culture management in GE, added five new leadership traits to the idealized GE job description: external focus, clear thinking, imagination, inclusive leadership, and confident expertise. These additions reflect GE's recognition of the need to change its culture via training.

1.	Management is looking for short-term profits.	Management is prepared to wait for big payout.
2.	Management explicitly looks for innovation.	Management does not explicitly look for innovation.
3.	Management has high tolerance of innovative "mavericks."	Management has low tolerance of innovative "mavericks."
4.	Planning focuses on rationing resources.	Planning focuses on identifying opportunities.
5.	Management is not tolerant of failure.	Management is tolerant of failure.
6.	Leaders put little emphasis on the management of people and their interactions.	Leaders put strong emphasis on the management of people and their interactions.
7.	Company offers no career ladder with appropriate power and titles for innovators.	Company offers a career ladder with appropriate power and titles for innovators.
8.	Departure from the corporate norm is encouraged.	Sticking to the corporate norm is valued.
9.	It is no fun working here.	It is very fun to work here.
10.	Management has low tolerance for uncertainty.	Management has high tolerance for uncertainty.
11.	Formal vertical communications within the organization are the norm.	Informal horizontal communications within the organization are the norm.
12.	Management encourages the systematic use of independent task forces for special purposes.	Management discourages the use of independent task forces for special purposes.
13.	Management decides without much input from other levels of the organization.	Management actively seeks and considers recommendations from many levels of the organization.
14.	Decision process is elaborate and formal.	Decision process is short and informal.
15.	Specific incentive mechanism for innovation exists.	No incentive mechanism for innovation exists.

16.	The organizational culture is planning-oriented (analysis/ paralysis syndrome). <--|---|---|---|--- ---|---|---|---|-->	The organizational culture is action oriented.
17.	Management has an open attitude regarding external alliances, supply partnerships, and acquisitions. <--|---|---|---|--- ---|---|---|---|-->	Management has an open attitude regarding external alliances, supply partnerships, and acquisitions.
18.	Management expects people to be totally devoted to the development of the corporation. <--|---|---|---|--- ---|---|---|---|-->	Management encourages people to work towards their personal development.
19.	The management philosophy favors decentralization. Decisions are made very close to where the action is. <--|---|---|---|--- ---|---|---|---|-->	The management philosophy favors centralization. Decisions are made by the hierarchy.
20.	Few resources are available for new ventures (in terms of budget, personnel, time, and so on...) <--|---|---|---|--- ---|---|---|---|-->	Resources are generally available for new ventures (in terms of budget, personnel, time, and so on...)
21.	Individual project championing is encouraged and rewarded. Individual accountability is the norm. <--|---|---|---|--- ---|---|---|---|-->	Team-wide project championing is encouraged and rewarded. Team accountability is the norm.
22.	Innovative successes of the company are neither publicized nor discussed. <--|---|---|---|--- ---|---|---|---|-->	Innovative successes of the company are widely publicized and discussed.
23.	Innovation budget is much less than the competition. <--|---|---|---|--- ---|---|---|---|-->	Innovation budget is much more than the competition.
24.	Company is able to make balanced choices between global and local priorities. <--|---|---|---|--- ---|---|---|---|-->	Company does a poor job of balancing global and local priorities.
25.	Management has a clear vision of the role and focus of innovation in achieving its objectives. <--|---|---|---|--- ---|---|---|---|-->	Management has not defined a clear innovation strategy and focus, relying instead on entrepreneurship.
26.	Project failures are systematically reviewed and analyzed for lessons. <--|---|---|---|--- ---|---|---|---|-->	Project failures are buried and nobody talks about them (too painful).
27.	Product and service managers are very much attuned to the market. <--|---|---|---|--- ---|---|---|---|-->	Product and service managers are far removed from the market.

28.	Product and service managers tend to under estimate and under-use technology. <--|---|---|---|--- ---|---|---|---|-->	Product and service managers tend to understand and use technology well.
29.	Outsiders (customers, experts) are never associated directly with the innovation process. <--|---|---|---|--- ---|---|---|---|-->	Outsiders (customers, experts) participate systematically in the innovation process.
30.	High value ideas are plentiful. <--|---|---|---|--- ---|---|---|---|-->	High value ideas are scarce.
31.	Management sets reasonable result expectations on new projects. <--|---|---|---|--- ---|---|---|---|-->	Management sets unrealistic result expectations on new projects.
32.	Our innovation knowledge is inferior to that of our competitors. <--|---|---|---|--- ---|---|---|---|-->	Our innovation knowledge is superior to that of our competitors.
33.	Our knowledge of real customer needs is inferior to that of our competitors. <--|---|---|---|--- ---|---|---|---|-->	Our knowledge of real customer needs is superior to that of our competitors.
34.	The people I work with have very little confidence in the direction our company is going. <--|---|---|---|--- ---|---|---|---|-->	The people I work with have high level of confidence in the direction our company is going.
35	The people I work with are highly self-motivated. <--|---|---|---|--- ---|---|---|---|-->	The people I work with are not at all self-motivated.
36.	The senior management group is working at cross purposes— a lot of conflict exists. <--|---|---|---|--- ---|---|---|---|-->	The senior management group is working in concert—very little conflict exists.

FIGURE 10.1 INNOVATION CLIMATE DIAGNOSTIC.[12]

GE also realized that they needed to pay particular attention to the balance between creativity and value capture. This critical balance allows the company to generate successful new ideas *and* gets the maximum return on their investment. Under Jack Welch, GE had become very proficient at operational execution but had lost some important parts of its ability to create new products. When he became CEO, Immelt saw that GE's value capture and commercial execution had become stronger than its creativity. He had inherited a company that had become extremely skilled in operations; "One that could stop on a dime and deliver results," said Bob Corcoran, the current director of GE's legendary learning center, Crotonville, and a long-standing human resources manager at GE Medical Systems, the business Immelt ran before becoming CEO. "Now the question is how to develop the top line (defined as new products, markets and lines of business)."[13] This imbalance threatened Immelt's plans to aggressively grow GE via innovation, and he launched an initiative to reinvigorate the creativity functions and increase the rate of idea and deal flow.

Leadership teams looking at the balance of creativity and value capture need to look carefully at the project management systems used in the company. There are four very different types of innovation management approaches—stage-gate systems, venture capital models, technology innovation model, and time-driven systems—and each has its own creativity and value capture biases.

Stage-Gate Systems

Incremental innovation projects often rely on some version of *stage-gate process* (Figure 10.2 depicts a stage-gate process), where the project is divided into stages and a gate governs the transition from one stage to the next. The sequential stages have an embedded cause-and-effect structure in which the success in executing a particular stage is a prerequisite to move to the next stage. The measurement model provides the information required to track the evolution of a project throughout the course of the stage-gate process. Exxon has used a gate process since the 1980s with great success. According to Exxon, it's been the best initiative it has undertaken in a decade; it has shaped the way it does business.

The project's progress is put under the magnifying glass at each gate. The measurement system enables monitoring to ensure that the project stays on track and is likely to meet or exceed the original expectations. At Cintas, every deal—no matter how small—is periodically scrutinized by a dispassionate executive, according to CEO Robert J. Kohlhepp. A CEO or other ranking executive who has no qualms about pulling the plug if a deal smells wrong.[14] Alternately, continuing a project that will create a competitor to an existing business requires a dispassionate decision-maker focused on the long-term success of the company. HP's ex-CEO Lou Platt noted, "We have to be willing to cannibalize what we are doing today in order to ensure our leadership in the future. It is counter to human nature, but you have to kill your business while it is still working."[15]

Properly implemented, stage-gate systems tend to produce balanced creativity and value capture. The beginning of the process focuses on creativity and transitions seamlessly to value capture via commercialization. However, it is often the case that cultural biases against creativity creep into the system. The result is an increase in the degree of scrutiny and rigor of analyses in the early part of the stage-gate process. When that happens, creativity can be strangled because good ideas that do not have clear financial payback are considered less worthy and discarded or treated as second-tier opportunities. However, some semi-radical and radical ideas do not have clear markets identified, reliable cost estimates, or highly reliable financial projections at their inception. These potentially attractive ideas can be discarded in favor of incremental innovations that have clearer performance measures. When this happens, the stage-gate system becomes very efficient at value capture and commercialization of incremental innovations but it lacks sufficient quality and quantity of creative ideas because they were dropped in the early stages. This imbalance of creativity and value capture results in rampant incrementalism, one of the best indicators of an out of balance innovation system.

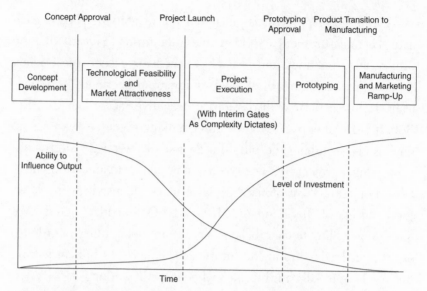

FIGURE 10.2   STAGE-GATE SYSTEMS AND INVESTMENT AND ABILITY TO INFLUENCE PROFILES.

The Venture Capital Model

This model relies on a venture team to interpret the fuzzy measurement information and make decisions at each stage of the investment process. It is widely used to manage semi-radical and radical innovations. The SpaceShipOne venture team working on commercial space flight made decisions even though there were no credible estimates of the market size or demographics for commercial space travel, and there were still major uncertainties in the technology and business model.

The venture team members bring together their experience and their instinct about the technology and market with the quality of people in the project and their progress. The role of the measures is to capture the most relevant aspect of the project to stimulate discussion. It is the richness of the interpretation of the information that adds value.

In the very early stages, when the ambiguity and uncertainty are the highest, concrete milestones are important measures of success.

Are the technology prototypes produced on schedule? Have the key elements of the business model been characterized and tested with key stakeholders?

In the later stages of development, the need to characterize the target market becomes greater. The measurement system focuses on identifying and characterizing the specific target segment that will drive the initial growth, the robustness of the technology to meet the needs, and the cost structure of the business model (customer acquisition costs, customer support costs, manufacturing costs).

The venture model deals fairly well with creativity; it allows consideration of radical new ideas in all stages of development. It especially favors creative solutions in the early stages of development. In the later stages of development, it requires more rigor of analysis and uses financial measures to guide decisions. However, the venture model can be biased toward creativity; it lacks the rigor of value capture commercialization contained in the stage-gate systems. It is often beneficial to blend a stage-gate methodology into the later stages of the venture capital approach to ensure the necessary balance between creativity and value capture.

The Technology Innovation Model

The *technology innovation model* describes radical innovation that is driven from the technology group within a company. Typically, the initial work is unstructured and relies on ensuring that technologists have time to spend on their own projects. 3M ensures that researchers have 15 percent free time to explore new ideas. Google and Genentech allots 20 percent for exploration.

The role of the measurement system in the early stages is limited; at most, it tracks inputs to the project including time and expenses. The initial stages rely on the intrinsic motivation and ingenuity of the particular technologist or team of technologists and the vision of management. There is no significant planning at this stage;

intangibles like trust, reputation, and "believing in the team" become more important in keeping people focused and motivated. As the innovation comes into sharper focus through experimentation and prototyping, the measurement model becomes more sophisticated, paralleling the venture capital model previously described.

Time-Driven Systems

For many incremental innovation projects, the key phrase is "schedule driven"—no matter the cost, "we must meet schedule." Time as a measure is popular because it is universally understood, simple to measure, and results are obvious; a project is simply on time or it is not. Projects that fall short are usually cut or significantly changed. One major car company executive reported that in his company meeting the schedule was significantly more important than meeting budget. Typically projects were always 60-70 percent over budget, but this was acceptable if there was not a schedule slippage.

However appealing this simplicity is, time-based systems are inherently biased toward capturing value; they do not lead to optimum use of creativity. Time-based systems favor getting the job done fast and encourage spread of rampant incrementalism. In addition, time-based measurements focus on outputs, not outcomes. To be truly effective, systems must incorporate all four types of measures: Input, process, output, and outcome. Using time as the only measure may appear expedient, but it runs the risk of leading to bad decisions. All things considered, time-based systems are inherently unbalanced and should be avoided.

The leadership team needs to neutralize organizational antibodies that kill off good ideas because they are different from the norm. One leading energy company did not curtail the organizational antibodies during its initiative to improve innovation. The antibodies showed in several different forms. Middle managers who resisted the changes did not provide adequate staffing and the innovation initiative was understaffed. In addition, several managers sent their second-string team members. The original project schedule was aggressive, signaling the importance and urgency of the initiative. However, schedule slippage occurred almost from the first day. In addition, managers often missed key meetings where important implementation decisions were made. All of these diminished the effectiveness of the initiative and signaled to the organization that there was significant resistance to the initiative. If that were not enough, some key players in the company began to nay-say the effort, casting doubt on its effectiveness and value. All of these antibodies could have been effectively countered if the senior management team had stepped forward, demanded appropriate actions being taken, and squashed the bad behavior. Unfortunately, that did not occur and the initiative failed.

Leadership should also ensure that the organization contains strong innovation networks inside and outside the organization. Networks, not individuals, are the basic building blocks of innovation. HP's former CEO Carly Fiorina said, "We focus our innovation where we can make the unique contribution and lead at the high bar, and we partner the rest."[16] Coca-Cola established networks that stretched throughout the global enterprise and focused them on their innovation platforms. To be effective, the networks have to be populated with a mixture of different types of people: idea generators, project managers, big-picture people, technical experts, and business strategists. Leadership should assess the caliber of the people in the network and the way they collaborate. One consumer goods company, prior to launching a major innovation initiative, conducted a skills inventory of its innovation networks and compared it against the technical and business challenges it faced. In addition, it assessed the collaboration and degree of alignment among the people in the network. This provided them with a clear indication of the networks' strengths and identified areas for improvement.

Finally, leadership should ensure that the company has the correct metrics and incentives to make innovation manageable and to produce the right behavior. CEMEX's management team created a balanced scorecard to drive the company's innovation teams toward the goals they set. Tetra Pak has made innovation a basic part of the company from its inception. It had never relied on measurement to help manage its innovations. However, Tetra Pak had evolved into a complex company with a broad portfolio of innovations. As a result, it recognized that it needed to add some additional incentives to help manage the innovation process and to prioritize its investments. The new metrics and incentives helped the company shorten time to market performance by more than 20 percent.

There are several rules governing metrics and incentives that the leadership needs to ensure are followed:

- Understand the strategy and business model of innovation for your company, and build a measurement system for innovation that is tied to both.

- Know what you want to achieve with each measurement system at each level of the organization. There are three options: communicate the strategy and the underlying mental models, monitor performance, and learn.

- Tailor the innovation measurement system to match the mix of incremental, semi-radical, and radical innovation.

- Ensure that the incentives provide the motivation to drive the innovation strategy.

ChevronTexaco recognized many years ago that metrics and incentives were crucial to innovation and change. It instituted a formal process (very similar to a stage-gate process) for all projects and innovation activities. The process includes the requirement to establish clear metrics that are tailored to the specific project. ChevronTexaco trains all of its employees on how to use the process, and it holds every team accountable for managing according to the metrics. Finally, the company uses the metrics to learn and improve its performance. This approach—coupled with strong, aligned incentives—has served it well throughout the years, and ChevronTexaco considers it one of its strengths in execution.

Organizing Initiatives

There are two basic types of innovation initiatives. *Fine-tuning initiatives* are designed to provide selective modest improvements. Many companies undertake fine-tuning exercises every one to three years to maintain the vitality of their innovation capabilities. *Redirection/ revitalization* initiatives are more aggressive, and their scope includes significant changes to their innovation capabilities. They occur less frequently. Companies undertake these types of initiatives when the situation requires more drastic action.

Fine-Tuning

Fine-tuning focuses on improvement of selective portions of the innovation strategy, portfolio, processes, organization and culture. Fine-tuning occurs when innovation is working relatively well (for example the gap between the desired and actual performance is relatively small), but improvements are required to improve performance and enhance competitiveness. Boston Scientific undertakes periodic assessment of its innovation processes to identify targets for improvement. Southwest constantly tunes its innovation capabilities; it is part of its culture.

Redirection/Revitalization

Redirection/revitalization initiatives are focused on major improvements to broad sections of the innovation capability. Redirection or revitalization is required when the innovation systems and organization are not delivering the correct types of innovations to adequately support the business strategy (such as when the gap between the desired and actual performance is relatively large). CEMEX undertook this type of initiative when it wanted significantly higher growth rates from innovation. Around 2000, Toyota recognized the growing importance of innovation in the automobile industry. It launched its redirection/revitalization initiative to capture the high ground in the highly competitive auto industry.

Generating Innovation Value

Every senior management team knows the drill: define a goal, identify the problem areas that limit attaining the goal, understand their root causes, develop a plan, send the signal to the company that this is important, and then work out the millions of little details that comprise execution. Innovation is the same. There is nothing to it but the basic blocking and tackling that all management requires.

What has frustrated many CEOs is that once they have executed improvements to their innovation capabilities—whether fine-tuning or redirection/revitalization—they don't get the results they hoped for. Admittedly, sometimes companies blow the execution of innovation improvements, but this is usually because they fail to neutralize the organizational antibodies that always come out when change is underway. Remember the energy company we discussed earlier that failed to neutralize the antibodies.

Far more often, companies fail because they do not understand the causal linkages between the parts of innovation. They launch efforts to fix some element of innovation and do not address the root cause of the problem. A household products division of a leading consumer goods company tried to fix their poorly functioning innovation effort by increasing the collaboration between the R&D and marketing group. The working relationship between those groups was rancorous and produced sub-optimal results, but the real problem was that leadership had not clearly identified the innovation strategy and defined the roles of business model change and technology change for the division. Without that leadership, each group made its own interpretation of what was important and the relative priorities to be assigned. Another company improved training on innovation in the hopes that everyone would improve. However, it did not address one of the key elements that needed to be changed—the cultural bias in the company against semi-radical and radical innovations. Through many years of leadership, the company's culture had grown to favor the incremental as opposed to the semi-radical. The company was brilliant at execution, but it killed off ideas that were anything but incremental. Training everybody about the tools for semi-radical and radical innovation would never produce the results the CEO desired.

There is no silver bullet for innovation, no one formula or structure for innovation that will work for every organization. The seven Innovation Rules provide the basis for executing improved innovation that creates value and growth.

ENDNOTES

Chapter 1

1 Often the original innovator fails to capture the market that it creates. For an excellent analysis of this phenomenon see Markides, C.C., and P. A. Geroski. 2005. *Fast second: How smart companies bypass radical innovation to enter and dominate new markets.* Indianapolis: John Wiley & Sons.

2 Wylie, Ian. How Nokia has tackled the ultimate creative act: Building innovation into the company's culture. *Fast Company*, Vol 70, May 2003; page 46.

3 Stevenson, Seth. 2002. I would like to buy the world a shelf-stable children's lactic drink. *The New York Times Magazine.* March 10.

4 Tomkins, Richard. 2002. Added spice. *The Financial Times.* April 5.

5 Drucker, Peter F. 1998. The discipline of innovation. *Harvard Business Review.* November – December.

6 CEO2CEO Conference Report, 2002.

7 For evidence on the underperformance of diversification, see Healy, P.M., K.G. Palepu, and R.S. Ruback, Does corporate performance improve after mergers? *Journal of Financial Economics* (31): 135-175. See also the classic study by Rumelt, R.P., 1974. *Strategy, structure, and economic performance.* Boston, MA: Harvard Business School.

8 Source: Navigant Consulting, Inc.

9   Similarly, the three criteria that the *Red Herring*—a leading business of technology magazine—uses to select the top 100 start-up technology firms are the quality of its management team, the firm's potential to disrupt an existing market or create a new one, and the quality of its execution strategy.

10 For more details on the concept of espoused theories and theories in use and their relevance to organizational learning and organizational blocks, see Argyris, C. 1993. *Overcoming organizational defenses: Facilitating organizational learning.* San Francisco, CA: Jossey-Bass.

11 On this line of reasoning, see Collins, J. 2001. *Good to great: Why some companies make the leap . . . and others don't.* New York: HarperCollins Publishers.

12 See the section titled, "Clearly Defined Innovation Strategy Defines Change," in Chapter 3, "Choosing Your Destiny: How to Design a Winning Innovation Strategy."

13 The two innovation strategies—Play-to-Win and Play-Not-to-Lose—are described in Chapter 3.

14 Palmisano, Samuel J. 2003. How the U.S. can keep its innovation edge. *Business Week*, November 17, page 34.

15 Amabile, Teresa. 1998. How to kill creativity. *Harvard Business Review*. September – October.

16 von Hippel, Eric. 1998. *The sources of innovation*. New York: Oxford University Press.

Chapter 2

1   Also, the academic literature focuses mostly on technological innovations. See Henderson R.M., and K.B. Clark. 1990. Architectural innovation: the reconfiguration of existing product technologies and the failure of established firms. *Administrative Science Quarterly*, 35(1): 9-30; Abernathy, W. and J.M. Utterback. 1978. Patterns of industrial innovation. *Technology Review*, 80(7): 40-47; Christensen, C. and R. Rosenbloom. 1995. Explaining the attacker's advantage: technological paradigms, organizational dynamics and the value network. *Research policy*, 24: 233-257.

2   Some authors have also included market as an additional dimension to technology to understand innovation (Afuah, 1998). We believe that focusing on the market unnecessarily restricts the locus of innovation to one piece of the business model.

3   Wal-Mart is currently focusing its attention on RFID (radio frequency identification) technology. The objective is to optimize even more of its supply chain. RFID will allow Wal-Mart to track the movements of every single item from the point of production until it reaches the final customer. This new enabling technology will be transparent to customers, but it will enable a much more efficient business model that will translate into further advantage for the retail giant.

4   Cane, A. 2005. The brain behind the brains at Big Blue. *Financial Times*, January 21.

5   Bucklet, N. 2003. Free deliveries help lift Amazon. *Financial Times*, October 22.

6   Dann, J. 2003. Can khakis really be disruptive? *Strategy & Innovation*, 3.

7   For the importance of process change, see Pisano, Gary. 1997. *The development factory: Unlocking the potential of process innovation*. Boston: Harvard Business School Press.

8 Examples of process improvements are numerous around the quality movement. See Cole, Robert E. 1998. Learning from the Quality Movement: What did and didn't happen and why? *California Management Review* 41 (1): 43-74. Also see Juran, J.M. 1992. *Juran on Quality by Design: The new steps for planning quality into goods and services*. New York: The Free Press.

9 There are various approaches to thinking about innovation. Gatignon, Hubert, Michael L. Tushman, Wendy Smith, and Phillip Anderson. 2002. A structural approach to assessing innovation: Construct development of innovation locus, type, and characteristics. *Management Science* 48 (9): 1103-1122. The Innovation Matrix is best suited for designing innovation strategies.

10 A more traditional way of looking at this matrix is using technology and market dimensions. See Meyer, Mark H. and Edward B. Roberts. 1986. New product strategy in small technology-based firms: A pilot study. *Management Science*, 32 (7): 806-822.

11 For this model, see Tushman, M. and P. Anderson. 1986. Technological discontinuities and organizational environment. *Administrative Science Quarterly*, 31: 439-465.

12 Utterback, J.M. 1994. *Mastering the dynamics of innovation: How companies can seize opportunities in the face of technological change*. Boston: Harvard Business School Press.

13 This is just one example of what are known as *disruptive technologies*.

14 See Bernstein, W. 2004. *The birth of plenty: How the prosperity of the modern world was created*. New York: McGraw-Hill.

15 The idea of incremental innovation has been applied to the technology innovation dimension. See Dewar, Robert D. and Jane E. Dutton. 1986. The adoption of radical and incremental innovations: An empirical analysis. *Management Science*, 32 (11): 1422-1433. Ettlie, John E., William P. Bridges, and Robert D. O'Keefe. 1984. Organizational strategy and structural differences for radical versus incremental innovation. *Management Science*, 30: 682-695. Green, Stephen, Mark Gavin, and Lynda Aiman-Smith. 1995. Assessing a multidimensional measure of radical innovation. *IEEE Transactions Engineering Management*, 42 (3): 203-214.

16 Incremental innovation is critical to sustain a firm's position in the market. See Banbury, Catherine M. and Will Mitchell. 1995. The effect of introducing important incremental innovations on market share and business survival. *Strategic Management Journal*, 16: 161-182.

17 Leading the way back: The CEO's role. CEO Conference Report, 2002.

18 Winning through incremental innovation. CEO2CEO Conference Report, 2002.

19 CEO2CEO Conference Report, 2002.

20 Semi-radical innovation is a common way to break away from incremental innovation but still rely on a subset of core competencies. See Utterback, James M. 1994. *Mastering the dynamics of innovation: How companies can seize opportunities in the face of technological change*. Boston: Harvard Business School Press.

21 Henderson R.M. and K.B. Clark. 1990. Architectural innovation: The reconfiguration of existing product technologies and the failure of established firms. *Administrative Science Quarterly*, 35 (1): 9-30.

22 Existing firms typically survive waves of semi-radical innovation because of the existence of complementary assets. See Tripsas, Mary. 1997. Unraveling the process of creative destruction: Complementary assets and incumbent survival in the typesetter industry. *Strategic Management Journal*, 18: 119-142.

23 Radical innovation has a higher degree of inherent risk and higher impact to the organization than semi-radical innovation. See Cooper, Arnold and Clayton Smith. 1992. How established firms respond to threatening technologies. *Academy of Management Executive*, 6 (2): 55-70. Also see Damanpour, Fariborz. 1996. Organizational complexity and innovation: Developing and testing contingency models. *Management Science*, 42 (5): 693-701. Also see Foster, Richard N. 1986. *Innovation: The attacker's advantage*. New York: Summit Books. For the high level of unsuccessful radical innovations, see Dougherty, Deborah and Cynthia Hardy. 1996. Sustained product innovation in large, mature organizations: Overcoming innovation-to-organization problems. *Academy of Management Journal*, 39: 1120-1153.

24 Radical innovation typically comes from architectural changes. See Henderson, Rebecca M. and Kim B. Clark. 1990. Architectural innovation: The reconfiguration of existing product technologies and the failure of established firms. *Administrative Science Quarterly*, 35 (1): 9-30. Also see Baldwin, Carlyss Y. and Kim B. Clark. 2000. *Design rules: The power of modularity*. Cambridge, MA: MIT Press.

    Radical innovation also comes from the destruction of current competencies. See Anderson, Phillip and Michael L. Tushman. 1990. Technological discontinuities and dominant designs: A cyclical model of technological change. *Administrative Science Quarterly*, 35 (4): 604-633. Also see Tushman, Michael L. and Phillip Anderson. 1986. Technological discontinuities and organizational environment. *Administrative Science Quarterly*, 31: 439-465. Also see Tushman, Michael L. and Johann P. Murmann. 1998. Dominant designs, technology cycles, and organizational outcomes. *Research in Organizational Behavior*, 20: 231-266.

25 These game changers have also been called *technological discontinuities*. Ehrenberg, Ellinor. 1995. On the definition and measurement of technological discontinuities. *Technovation*, 15: 437-452.

26 CNN News, June 2, 2004.

27 Radical innovation is frequently associated with startup companies that upset the current industry structure. For the problems facing incumbents when threatened by an external radical innovation, see Day, George S. and Paul J.H. Schoemaker. 2000. Avoiding the pitfalls of emerging technologies. *California Management Review*, 42 (2): 8-33.

28 Radical innovation also has a larger probability of being born in the interfaces of current business units requiring the participation of these various units—a concept called *white spaces* (Hamel, Gary and C.K. Prahalad. 1994. *Competing for the future*. Boston, MA: Harvard Business School Press)—with a significant chance of shifting the current strategy. The need for resources from various units and the strategic disruptive nature are labeled as "scope" and "reach" of the innovation (Burgelman Robert A. and Yves L. Doz. 2001. The power of strategic integration. *Sloan Management Review*, 42 (3): 28-38.).

29 Abrahams, P. 2002. Branching out. *Financial Times*, July.

30 Christensen, Clayton M. 1997. *The innovator's dilemma: When new technologies cause great firms to fail*. Boston: Harvard Business School Press.

31 Waters, R. 2003. Dell aims to stretch its way of business. *Financial Times*, November 13.

Chapter 3

1   Conference Board. 1999. The Business Innovation Conference, New York.

2   Chandy, R., J. Prabhu, and K. Anita. 2003. What will the future bring? Dominance, technology expectations, and radical innovation. *MSI Report*, 02-122 (Summer).

3   The problem of startups to grow beyond the first stage has been frequently associated with the difficulties that entrepreneurs have in becoming managers. See Chandler, G. N. and E. Jansen. 1992. The founder's self-assessed competence and venture performance. *Journal of Business Venturing*, 7: 223-237; Flamholtz, E.G., and Y. Randle. 2000. *Growing pains: Transitioning from an entrepreneurship to a professionally managed firm* (2nd ed.). San Francisco, CA: Jossey-Bass; Greiner, L. E. 1998. Evolution and revolution as organizations grow. *Harvard Business Review*, May-June: 55-64; Willard, G. E., D.A. Krueger, and H.R. Feeser. 1992. In order to grow, must the founder grow: A comparison of performance between founder and non-founder managed high-growth manufacturing firms. *Journal of Business Venturing*, 7: 181-195.

4   Artne, F. and A. Weintraub. 2004. J&J: Toughing out the drought. *Business Week*, January 26, 84-85.

5   Palmeri, C. 2003. To really be a player, Mattel needs hotter toys. *Business Week*, July 28, 64.

6   Markides, C.C. and P.A. Geroski. 2005. *Fast second: How smart companies bypass radical innovation to enter and dominate new markets.* Indianapolis: John Wiley and Sons.

7   Deutsch, C. 2002. G.E. research returns to roots. *The New York Times*, December 26.

8   Roberts, D. 2004. Voyage of discovery: G.E. stakes its future on the innovation of it scientists. *Financial Times*, October 11.

9   Weisman, R. 2004. G.E.'s sandbox for scientists. *Boston Globe*, March 15.

10 Schrage, M. 2000. Getting beyond the innovation fetish. *Fortune*, November 13.

11 Brown, S. and E. Eisenhardt. 1998. *Competing on the edge*. Boston, MA: Harvard Business School Press.

12 Buckley, N. 2002. Revolution with a relaxed approach. *Financial Times*, August.

13 Hamel, G. and P. Skarzynski. 2001. Innovation: The new route to wealth. *Journal of Accountancy*, November, 65.

14 The research literature that identifies internal non-transferable assets as key to a sustainable competitive advantage has a long history. See Prahalad, C. K. and G. Hamel. 1990. The core competence of the corporation. *Harvard Business Review*, 68: 79-91; Wernerfelt, B. 1984. A resource-based view of the firm. *Strategic Management Journal*, 5: 171-181; Zollo, M. and S.G. Winter. 2002. Deliberate learning and the evolution of dynamic capabilities. *Organization Science*, 13: 339.

15 For example, see Leonard-Barton, D. 1992. Core capabilities and core rigidities: A paradox in managing new product development. *Strategic Management Journal*, 13: 111-125.

16 Hamel, G. and P. Skarzynski. 2001. Innovation: The new route to wealth. *Journal of Accountancy*, November.

17 Simons, J. 2003. The $10 billion pill. *Fortune*, January 20, 58-68.

18 Barrett, A., J. Carey, M. Arndt, and A. Weintraub. 2003. Feeding the pipeline. *Business Week*, May 12, 78-82.

19   According to Goldman Sachs, as cited in *Financial Times,* October 24, 2002.

20   http://www.fda.gov/cder/reports/rtn/2003/Rtn2003.pdf

21   Geoff Dyer, G. 2002. Sagging morale, departing scientists, a dwindling pipeline: when will GSK's research overhaul produce results? *Financial Times*, October 24: 13.

22   Harris, G. 2003. Where are all the new drugs? *The New York Times*, October 5.

23   Stipp, D. 2003. How Genentech Got It. *Fortune*, June 9: 81-88.

24   Mossberg, W. 2004. Steve Jobs: We're doing it all and we're having a blast. *Always On*, August 21.

Chapter 4

1   Christensen, Clayton M. and Tara Donovan. 1999. Putting your finger on capability. *Harvard Business School*, note #399148.

2   Markides, C. 1998. Strategic innovation in established companies. *Sloan Management Review*, 39 (3): 31-42.

3   Thomke, S.H. 2003. R&D comes to services: Bank of America's pathbreaking experiments. *Harvard Business Review*, April: 71-79.

4   Shelton, R. 2001. Developing an internal marketplace for innovation. *Prism,* 1.

5   Ibid.

6   O'Brien, G. 2000. The Triumph of Marxism. *The New York Review of Books*, July 20, 47 (12).

7   For a detailed study of the options under a corporate venture capital structure, see Block, Zenas and Ian C. MacMillan. 1995. *Corporate venturing: Creating new businesses within the firm.* Boston: Harvard Business School Press.

8   There has been a lot of debate in the academic literature about the right way to structure innovation, from having a completely separate structure (Christensen, Clayton M. 1997. *The innovator's dilemma: When new technologies cause great firms to fail.* Boston: Harvard Business School Press.), a new venture division (Burgelman, Robert A. 1984. Designs for corporate entrepreneurship in established firms. *California Management Review*, 26 (3): 154-166. Chesbrough, Henry. 2002. Designing corporate ventures in the shadow of private venture capital. *California Management Review*, 42 (3): 31-49.), a corporate venture capital arm (Chesbrough, Henry. 2002. Making sense of corporate venture capital. *Harvard Business Review*, 80 (3): 90-100.), or within existing divisions (Sykes, Hollister B. and Zenas Block. 1989. Corporate venturing obstacles: Sources and solutions. *Journal of Business Venturing*, 4: 159-167.).

9   An important piece of external structures is managing partnerships and alliances. There is extensive academic literature on the topic; see Arino, A., J. Torre, and P. Smith Ring. 2001. Relational quality: Managing trust in corporate alliances. *California Management Review*, 44 (1): 109-132.

10   Chesbrough, Henry W. 2003. A better way to innovate. *Harvard Business Review,* July: 12-13.

11   www.innocentive.com

12   Greene, Jay, John Carey, Michael Arndt, and Otis Port. 2003. Reinventing corporate R&D. *Business Week,* September 22, 74-76.

13   London, S. 2004. Good old fashioned innovation. *Financial Times*, March 12, 10.

14   Thomke, Stefan and Eric von Hippel. 2002. Customers as innovators: A new way to create value. *Harvard Business Review*, April: 5-11.

15   von Krogh, G. 2003. Open-source software development. *MIT Sloan Management Review*, Spring: 14-18.

16   Chesbrough, H. 2003. A better way to innovate. *Harvard Business Review*, July: 12-13.

17   Quinn, James Brian. 2000. Outsourcing innovation: The new engine of growth. *MIT Sloan Management Review*, 41 (4): 13-28.

18   www.bigideagroup.net

19   Adapted from Navigant Consulting, Inc. Also see www.strategos.com.

20   For a completely different innovation from CEMEX, see Prahalad, C.K. 2005. *The fortune at the bottom of the pyramid*. Upper Saddle River, NJ: Wharton School Publishing.

21   Doughtery, D.J., and E.H. Bowman, 1995. The effects of organizational downsizing on product innovation. *California Management Review*, Summer.

22   Source: Navigant Consulting, Inc.

23   Buderi, R. 2003. GE finds its inner Edison. *Technology Review*, October: 46-50.

24   Block, Z. and I.C. MacMillan. 1995. *Corporate venturing: Creating new businesses within the firm*. Boston, MA: Harvard Business School Press.

25   Source: Navigant Consulting, Inc., and Arthur D. Little, Inc.

26   Tushman, Michael L., and Charles A O'Reilly, 1997. *Winning through innovation: a practical guide to leading organizational change and renewal*. Boston, MA: Harvard Business School Press.

27   The idea of combining incremental and radical innovation within one firm is also discussed under the definition of "complex strategic integration." In Burgelman, R.A., and Y.L. Doz. 2001. The power of strategic integration. *Sloan Management Review*, 42 (3): 28-38.

28   A study (Cooper, Robert. 1998. Benchmarking new product performance: results of the best practices study. *European Journal of Management* 16[1]: 1-7.) found that businesses with a strong resource commitment have a 40 percent higher new product success rate. Resource commitment is also strongly correlated to the impact and profitability of a business's new product efforts. Resources should not be perceived as just budgets. Human resources are also important in the success of new product development. In Cooper's study, it was found that although organizations had the right processes in place, its people were sometimes assigned to six different projects or were assigned to R&D in addition to their "real" jobs.

29   Flaherty, J. 2003. In handling innovation, patience is a virtue. *The New York Times*, September 29.

Chapter 5

1   For the importance of systems such as scanning, planning, and strategic controls, see Barringer, Bruce R. and Allen C. Bluedorn. 1999. The relationship between corporate entrepreneurship and strategic management. *Strategic Management Journal*, 20: 421-444.

2 The spark that initiates the innovation has received significant attention, but the process by which this spark translates into value has been less studied. Woo, Carolyn Y., Urs Daellenbach, and Charlene Nicholls-Nixon. 1994. Theory building in the presence of "randomness:" The case of venture creation and performance. *Journal of Management Studies*, 31: 507-5023.

3 Palmisano, Samual J. 2003. How the U.S. can keep its innovation edge. *Business Week*, November 17, page 34.

4 The fact that structure and systems are in place does not mean that the random and chaotic nature of innovation disappears (Garud, Raghu and Andrew H. Van de Ven. 1992. An empirical evaluation of the internal corporate venturing process. *Strategic Management Journal*, 19: 1193-1201; Polley, Douglas and Andrew H. Van de Ven. 1996. Learning by discovery during innovation development. *International Journal of Technology Management*, 11: 871-882), but instead it facilitates managing these uncertainties.

5 The importance of managing innovation rather than treating it as a mysterious event has been highlighted in the academic literature: Block, Zenas and Ian C. MacMillan. 1995. *Corporate venturing: Creating new businesses within the firm*. Boston, MA: Harvard Business School Press; Burgelman, Robert A. 1985. Managing the new venture division: Research findings and implications for strategic management. *Strategic Management Journal*, 6: 39-54.

6 The problem is not associated with the systems and processes per se, but the inability to change them when they are not useful anymore. The obsolescence of competencies and the inability to renew them but rather keep investing in them is called the *competency trap*. Levitt, Barbara and James G. March. 1988. Organizational learning. *Annual Review of Sociology*, 14: 319-340.

7 The reliance on structure and controls in innovative firms has been frequently highlighted. Cameron, Kim S. 1986. Effectiveness as paradox: Consensus and conflict in conceptions of organizational effectiveness. *Management Science*, 32: 539-553; Leonard-Barton, Dorothy. 1995. *Wellsprings of knowledge: Building and sustaining the sources of innovation*. Boston, MA: Harvard Business School Press; Miller, Danny. 1990. *The Icarus Paradox: How exceptional companies bring about their own downfall*, New York: Harper Business.

8 A subset of management systems are strategic and financial controls both related to innovation. Barringer, Bruce R. and Allen C. Bluedorn. 1999. The relationship between corporate entrepreneurship and strategic management. *Strategic Management Journal*, 20: 421-444.

9 Systems are critical to create the strategic flexibility required to combine executing the current strategy and designing long-term value. Burgelman, Robert A. and Yves L. Doz. 2001. The power of strategic integration. *Sloan Management Review*, 42 (3): 28-38; Raynor, Michael E. and Joseph L. Bower. 2001. Lead from the center: How to manage divisions dramatically. *Harvard Business Review*, 79 (5): 92-100.

10 Source: Navigant Consulting, Inc.

11 See the discussion later in Chapter 6 regarding electronic collaboration.

12 See for example Jolly, Vijay K. 1997. *Commercializing new technologies: Getting from mind to market*. Boston, MA: Harvard Business School Press.

13 While the process is described as linear, it moves in non-linear cycles. Moss Kanter, Rosabeth. Swimming in newstreams: Mastering innovation dilemmas. *California Management Review*, 31 (4): 45-69. A better way of thinking about it is a set of concentric circles indicating that once a stage is entered, it remains in the process until the end.

14 The depiction of innovation as a funnel is widely used and accepted. Clearly, it has certain merit in describing the certain aspects of flow from idea to commercial realities. However, it is not a complete picture of the flow and interactions involved in innovation. There is an opportunity for a new depiction of innovation. This could be very valuable to the management of innovation, because it could stimulate fresh insights and better management actions. We note the need but do not offer the improved picture of innovation. Our comment is meant to catalyze among innovation practitioners and researchers a new, improved graphic and mental model for depicting innovation (such as to innovate the innovation model and graphic).

15 Source: U.S. Patent and Trademark Office, U.S. Department of Commerce.

16 Derived from private communication with Southern California Edison and Moore, G. 1991. *Crossing the Chasm*. New York: Harper Business.

17 There is a general agreement on the stage nature of innovation processes, although the stages and their labels have varied over time. Dougherty, Deborah and T. Heller. 1994. The illegitimacy of successful product innovation in established firms. *Organizational Science*, 5: 200-218; Stopford, John M. and Charles W.F. Baden-Fuller. 1994. Creating corporate entrepreneurship. *Strategic Management Journal*, 15: 521-536. Our three stage model adds simplicity to capturing the most salient stages.

18 The idea of an intended process and a fortunate process has been discussed in the strategy literature under various labels such as intended strategy, emergent strategy, or autonomous strategy. Mintzberg, Henry. 1987. Crafting strategy. *Harvard Business Review*, 65 (4): 66-76; Burgelman, Robert A. 1985. Managing the new venture division: Research findings and implications for strategic management. *Strategic Management Journal*, 6: 39-54.

19 The strategic management literature has developed an elaborate model of these two sources of ideas within the strategic process concept starting from Bower, Joseph L. 1970. *Managing the resource allocation process*. Boston, MA: Harvard Business School Press; see Burgelman, Robert A. 2002. *Strategy is destiny: How strategy-making shapes a company's future*. New York: The Free Press; Burgelman, Robert A. and Andrew S. Grove. 1996. Strategic dissonance. *California Management Review*, 38 (2): 8-28.

20 For a list of potential sources for ideas, see Drucker, Peter F. 1985. *Innovation and entrepreneurship*. New York: Harper & Row.

21 For an elaboration of how to identify opportunities, see Colarelli O'Connor, Gina and Mark P. Rice. 2001. Opportunity recognition and breakthrough innovation in large established firms. *California Management Review*, 43 (2): 95-116.

22 Nussbaum, B. 2004. Design. *Business Week*, May 17: 87-94.

23 Source: Navigant Consulting, Inc., and Arthur D. Little, Inc.

24 Rothenberg, R. 2004. Ram Charan: The thought leader interview. *Strategy & Business*, Fall (36): 91-96.

25 Eisenhardt, Kathleen M. and Behnam N. Tabrizi. 1995. Accelerating adaptive processes: Product innovation in the global computer industry. *Administrative Science Quarterly*, 40: 84-110.

26 Leary, W. 2002. The inquiring minds behind 200 years of inventions. *The New York Times*, October 22, D4.

27 Source: Navigant Consulting, Inc.

28 Seikman, P. 2003. A long way from tiny time pills. *Fortune,* July 21: 126C-126H.

29 Kirkpatrick, D. 2003. How to erase the middleman in one easy lesson. *Fortune,* March 17: 122.

30 On the impact of technologies and the ability to execute innovation, see O'Hara-Devereaux, Mary and Robert Johansen. 1994. *Global work: Bridging distance, culture, and time.* San Francisco, CA: Jossey-Bass; Schrage, Michael. 2000. *Serious play: How the world's best companies simulate to innovate.* Boston, MA: Harvard Business School Press; Thomke, Stefan. 2001. Enlightened experimentation: The new imperative for innovation. *Harvard Business Review,* 79 (2): 67-75.

31 Von Krogh, Georg. 2003. Open-source software development: An overview of new research on innovators' incentives and the innovation process. *MIT Sloan Management Review,* Spring: 14-18.

32 Chesbrough, H. 2003. A better way to innovate. *Harvard Business Review,* July: 12-13.

Chapter 6

1 Private communication with R. Shelton, 2004.

2 Further discussion in Hertenstein, J.H., and M.B. Platt. 1997. Developing a strategic design culture. *Design Management Journal,* 8: 10-19.

3 A classic article on the dangers of a badly designed management system is Kerr, Stephen. 1975. On the folly of rewarding A while hoping for B. *Academy of Management Journal,* 18 (4): 769-784.

4 Frigo, Mark L. 2002. Strategy, business execution, and performance measures. *Strategic Finance,* May: 6-8.

5 The list of financial metrics range from simple ROI metrics to Net Present Value (NPV) calculations or sophisticated real options analysis. Amram, Martha and Nalin Kulatilaka. 1999. *Real options: Managing strategic investment in an uncertain world.* Boston, MA: Harvard Business School Press.

6 Within product development, these descriptive statistics have been provided by Hertenstein, Julie H. and Marjorie B. Platt. 2000. Performance measures and management control in new product development. *Accounting Horizons,* 14 (3): 303-323.

7 For a more detailed explanation of the turnaround at Mobil, see Kaplan, Robert S. 1997. Mobil USM&R (A1) and (A2), Harvard Business School Cases numbers 197120 and 197121.

8 Private communication with authors, 2004.

9 Monitoring is the traditional role of measurement systems. The sharpest tools are financial measures through which budgets are carefully monitored through variances. Merchant, Kenneth A. 1997. *Modern management control systems: Text and cases.* Upper Saddle River, NJ: Prentice Hall. Stage-gate systems for product development rely to a large extent on this interpretation of measurement systems where action only happens if execution deviates from expectations at the gates. McGrath, Michael E. 1995. *Product strategy for high-technology companies.* New York: Richard Irwin, Inc.

10 The importance of this interaction is highlighted in the concept of *creative abrasion*: Leonard-Barton, Dorothy. 1995. *Wellsprings of knowledge: Building and sustaining the sources of innovation.* Boston: Harvard Business School Press.

11 For more detail, see Simons, Robert. 1995. *Levers of control: How managers use innovative control systems to drive strategic renewal.* Boston, MA: Harvard Business School Press. He uses the term *interactive systems* to describe the learning role.

12 The concept of the Balanced Scorecard was originally formulated and further developed by Robert Kaplan and David Norton. Their bibliography is extensive; an important reference is Kaplan, R. S. and Norton, D. P. 2001. *The strategy-focused organization: How Balanced Scorecard companies thrive in the new business environment.* Boston, MA: Harvard Business School Press.

13 For the relevance of these causal maps, see Kaplan, Robert S. and David P. Norton. 2003. *Strategy maps: Converting intangible assets into tangible outcomes.* Boston, MA: Harvard Business School Press.

14 For a description of this concept, see Epstein, Marc J. and Robert A. Westbrook. 2001. Linking actions to profits in strategic decision-making. *MIT Sloan Management Review*, Spring: 39-49.

15 Rucci, Anthony J., Steven P. Kirn, and Richard T. Quinn. 1998. The employee-costumer-profit chain at Sears, *Harvard Business Review*, 76 (1): 82-98.

16 The Total Quality Management (TQM) philosophy is a widely-used, systematic approach to incremental innovation. The Deming and Baldrige Awards have recognized the TQM efforts of companies such as Boeing or Nippon Telephone and Telegraph (NTT) to put into place systematic approach for incremental innovation.

17 For more detail on measures for human resource-related topics, see Becker, Brian E., Mark A. Huselid, and Dave Ulrich. 2001. *The HR scorecard: Linking people, strategy, and performance.* Boston, MA: Harvard Business School Press.

18 The importance of having a dense network within the company has been highlighted in previous chapters. Also see Chesbrough, Henry. 2003. *Open innovation: The new imperative for creating and profiting from technology.* Boston, MA: Harvard Business School Press.

19 For a broader elaboration of the concept of boundaries, see Simons, Robert. 1995. Control in an age of empowerment. *Harvard Business Review*, 73 (2): 80-89.

20 Portfolios are an important approach to minimizing risk; for recent developments in portfolio management, see Cooper, Robert G. and Scott J. Edgett. 1999. New product portfolio management: Practices and performance. *Journal of Product Innovation Management*, 16 (4): 333-352; Cooper, Robert G., Scott J. Edgett, and Elko J. Kleinschmidt. 2001. Portfolio management for new product development: Results of an industry practices study. *R&D Management*, 31 (4): 361-381; Chen-Fu, Chien. 2002. A portfolio evaluation framework for selecting R&D projects. *R&D Management*, 32 (4): 359-369. For the problems of blindly applying portfolio ranking systems, see Souder, William E. 1987. *Managing new product innovations.* Lexington, KY: Lexington Books. Souder argues for some low-priority projects to be funded in order to establish a beachhead.

21 The information technology age has brought significant power to measurement systems, and nowadays there are numerous software packages that provide this power. See Applegate, Lynda M., Robert D. Austin, and F. Warren McFarlan. 2003. *Corporate information strategy and management: Text and cases,* 6th edition. New York: McGraw-Hill/Irwin.

22 Meyer, Mark H., Peter Tertzakian, and James M. Utterback. 1997. Metrics for managing research and development in the context of the product family. *Management Science*, 43 (1): 88-111.

23   For a very helpful framework to structure leading-lagging measures, see Epstein, Marc J. and Robert A. Westbrook. 2001. Linking actions to profits in strategic decision-making. *MIT Sloan Management Review*, Spring: 39-49.

24   Hauser, John R. Research, development, and engineering metrics. *Management Science*, 44 (12): 1670-1689.

25   For the original formulation of the economic value added, see Stewart, G. Bennett. 1991. *The quest for value*. New York: Harper Business; for additional applications, see Epstein, Marc J. and S. David Young. 1998. Improving corporate environmental performance through economic value added. *Environmental Quality Management*, 7 (4): 1-8; Zimmerman, Jerold L. 1997. EVA and divisional performance: Capturing synergies and other issues. *Bank of America Journal of Applied Corporate Finance*, Summer: 98-108.

26   Smith, Fred. 2002. How I delivered the goods. *Fortune Small Business*, October.

27   For recent ideas on how to improve innovation measurement, see: Meyer, C. 1994. How the right measures help teams excel. *Harvard Business Review*, May-June: 95-103; Meyer, Mark H. and James M. Utterback. 1993. The product family and the dynamics of core capability. *MIT Sloan Management Review*, 34 (3): 29-48; Werner, B.M. and W.E. Souder. 1997. Measuring R&D performance—U.S. and German practices. *Research Technology Management*; Hauser, John R. Research, development, and engineering metrics. *Management Science*, 44 (12): 1670-1689.

28   See for example Davila, Tony. 2000. An empirical study on the drivers of management control systems' design in NPD. *Accounting, Organizations and Society*, 25: 383-409.

29   For a more detailed account of the limitations of subjective evaluation (including theft, compression of ratings, and rent-seeking activities), see Prendergast, Canice. 1999. The provision of incentives in firms. *Journal of Economic Literature*, 37 (1): 7-64.

30   *The New York Times*. 2002. Living on Internet time, in an earlier age. April 4, E7.

31   Navigant Consulting, Inc., and 2001 Arthur D. Little.

Chapter 7

1   There is ample evidence that financial rewards are not the main driver as long as the opportunity costs of engaging in the innovative activity are not high. Busenitz, Lowell W. 1999. Entrepreneurial risk and strategic decision-making: It's a matter of perspective. *Journal of Applied Behavioral Science*, 35 (3): 325-340; Nonaka, Ikujiro and Hirotaka Takeuchi. 1995. *The knowledge-creating company: How Japanese companies create the dynamics of innovation*. New York: Oxford University Press; Shane, Scott and S. Venkataraman. 2000. The promise of entrepreneurship as a field of research. *Academy of Management Review*, 25 (1): 217-226.

2   See for example Judge, William Q., Gerald E. Fryxell, and Robert S. Dooley. 1997. The new task of R&D management: Creating goal-directed communities for innovation. *California Management Review*, 39 (3): 72-85; Krueger, Jr., Norris F. and Deborah V. Brazeal. 1994. Entrepreneurship potential and potential entrepreneurs. *Entrepreneurship Theory and Practice*, 18 (3): 91-104.

3   Accordingly, it has received significant attention at the top management level (Tosi, H.L., and L.R. Gomez-Mejia. 1994. CEO compensation monitoring and firm performance. *Academy of Management Journal* 37 (4): 1002-1016; Ittner, Christopher D., David F. Larcker, and Madhav V. Rajan. 1997. The choice of performance measures in annual bonus

contract. *Accounting Review*, 72: 231-273.) as well as the level of the division (Keating, A.S. 1997. Determinants of divisional performance evaluation practices. *Journal of Accounting and Economics*, 24 (3): 243-273.) and the sales organization (Bartol, K.M. 1999. Reframing salesforce compensation systems: an agency theory-based performance management perspective, *Journal of Personal Selling and Sales Management.* 29 (3): 1-16.).

4 Amabile, Teresa. 1998. How to kill creativity. *Harvard Business Review*, September – October.

5 For the dangers of over-emphasizing incentives, see Amabile, Teresa M. 1997. Motivating creativity in organizations: On doing what you love and loving what you do. *California Management Review*, 40 (1): 39-58; Csikszentmihalyi, Mihaly. 1996. *Creativity: Flow and the psychology of discovery and invention*. New York: Harper Collins.

6 Most books on compensation and rewards provide descriptions of these different rewards. For example, Flannery, Thomas P. 1996. *People, performance, and pay: Dynamics compensation for changing organizations*. New York: Free Press.

7 Work on improved business models for commercial photovoltaics is underway in the California Energy Commission, supported by Navigant Consulting, Inc.

8 Stretch goals should not be used for incentive purposes like regular goals; it breaks their magic. This does not mean that team members should not be rewarded for their effort and for reaching breakthroughs. Rather, the team must be recognized for its efforts and accomplishments.

9 Source: Navigant Consulting, Inc.

10 A survey given to the 1994 PDMA membership.

11 An academic study reports evidence indicating that the evaluation of individual team members and individual reward based on position and status is correlated to a higher satisfaction among team members as opposed to a generic team reward for all members. Survey referenced in Sarin, Shikhar and Vijay Mahajan. 2001. The effect of reward structures on performance of cross-functional product development teams. *Journal of Marketing*, 65: 35-53.

12 Subjective measures can behave as substitutes of objective measures. In particular, their weight in the compensation contract increases with the noisiness of objective measures that receive lower weight (Ittner, Christopher D., David F. Larcker, and Madhav V. Rajan. 1997. The choice of performance measures in annual bonus contracts. *Accounting Review*, 72: 231-255), or when objective measures have congruity limitations (Hayes, Rachel M. and Scott Schaefe. 2000. Implicit contracts and the explanatory power of top executive compensation for future performance. *RAND Journal of Economics*, 31 (3): 273-293). In dynamic settings, subjective measures can behave both as complements and substitutes of objective measures (Baker, G., R. Gibbons, K. J. Murphy. 1994 Subjective performance measures in optimal incentive contracts. *Quarterly Journal of Economics*, 109, 1125-1156).

13 For a more detailed account of the limitations of subjective evaluation (including theft, compression of ratings, and rent-seeking activities), see Prendergast, Candice. 1999. The provision of incentives in firms. *Journal of Economic Literature*, 37 (1): 7-64.

14 See Kohn, Alfred. 1993. Why incentive plans cannot work. *Harvard Business Review*, 71 (5), 54-61.

15   Davila A. 2003. Short-term economic incentives in new product development. *Research Policy*, 32: 1397-1420.

16   A study was done where two groups of people were asked to write a poem; one group received monetary compensation while the other did not. Afterwards, both groups were asked why they wrote the poems; the first group—the one that received monetary compensation—answered that they did it for the money, and the people in the second group replied that love for poetry drove them to write the poems.

17   Amabile, T.M., R. Conti, H. Coon, J. Lazenby, and M. Herron. 1996. Assessing the work environment for creativity. *Academy of Management Journal*. 39: 1154-1184; Deci, E.L., R.M. Ryan. 1985. *Intrinsic motivation and self-determination in human behavior.* New York: Plenum; Skaggs, K.J., A.M. Dickinson, and K.A. O'Connor. 1992. The use of concurrent schedules to evaluate the effects of extrinsic rewards on "intrinsic motivation:" a replication. *Journal of Organizational Behavior Management*, 12: 45-83.

18   See Eisenhardt, K.M., and B.N. Tabrizi. 1995. Accelerating adaptive processes: product innovation in the global computer industry. *Administrative Science Quarterly*, 40: 84-110.

19   Amabile, Teresa M. Motivating creativity in organizations: On doing what you love and loving what you do. *California Management Review*, 40 (1): 39-58.

20   Amabile, T.M., R. Conti, H. Coon, J. Lazenby, and M. Herron. 1996. Assessing the work environment for creativity. *Academy of Management Journal*, 39: 1154-1184.

21   See for example Coughlan, A. T. and C. Narasimhan. 1992. An empirical analysis of sales-force compensation plans. *Journal of Business*, 65 (1): 93-121; Feldman, L. P. 1996. The role of salary and incentives in the new product function. *Journal of Product Innovation Management*, 13 (3): 216-228; Jenkins, G. D., A. Mitra, et al. 1998. Are financial incentives related to performance? A meta-analytic review of empirical research. *Journal of Applied Psychology*, 83 (5): 777-787; John, G. and B. Weitz. 1989. Salesforce compensation: An empirical investigation on factors related to use of salary versus incentive compensation. *Journal of Marketing Research*, 26: 1-14; Kunkel, J. G. 1997. Rewarding product development success. *Research Technology Management* 40 (5): 29-31; Natter, M., A. Mild, et al. 2001. The effect of incentive schemes and organizational arrangements on the new product development process. *Management Science*, 47 (8): 1029-1045; Oliver, R. L. and E. Anderson. 1995. Behavior and outcome-based control systems: Evidence and consequences of pure-form and hybrid governance. *Journal of Personal Selling & Sales Management*, 25 (4): 1-15.

Chapter 8

1   For the importance of fast learning, see Brown, Shona L. and Kathleen M. Eisenhardt. 1997. The art of continuous change: Linking complexity theory and time-paced evolution in relentlessly shifting organizations. *Administrative Science Quarterly*, 42: 1-34; Brown, Shona L. and Kathleen M. Eisenhardt. *Competing on the edge: Strategy as structured chaos.* Boston, MA: Harvard Business School Press. See, for example, Nevis, Edwin C. and Anthony J. DiBella. 1995. Understanding organizations as learning systems. *MIT Sloan Management Review*, 36 (2): 73-86. For the role of learning in the innovation process, see Zahra, Shaker A., R. Duane Ireland, and Michael A. Hitt. 2000. International expansion by new venture firms: International diversity, mode of market entry, technological learning, and performance. *Academy of Management Journal*, 43 (4): 925-950.

2   Leslie, M. 2004. The sales learning curve, always on. http://www.alwayson-network.com. September 9.

3   This is a basic premise of learning processes: Lucifer, Richard, Christopher M.
    McDermott, Gina Colarelli O'Connor, Lois S. Peters, Mark R. Rice, and Robert W.
    Veryzer. 2000. *Radical innovation: How mature companies can outsmart upstarts.*
    Boston, MA: Harvard Business School Press; Gunther McGrath, Rita and Ian C.
    MacMillan. 1995. Discovery driven planning. *Harvard Business Review,* 73: 4-12; Sykes,
    Hollister B. and David Dunham. 1995. Critical assumption planning: A practical tool for
    managing business development risk. *Journal of Business Venturing,* 10 (6): 413-424.

4   The ability of an organization to learn has been studied under the concept of absorptive
    capacity; see Cohen, Wesley M. and Daniel A. Levinthal. 1990. Absorptive capacity: A new
    perspective on learning and innovation. *Administrative Science Quarterly,* 35: 128-152.

5   For the importance of managing uncertainty in product development: Thomke, Stefan
    and Donald Reinertsen. 1998. Agile product development: Managing development flexi-
    bility in uncertain environments. *California Management Review,* 41 (1): 8-31.

6   Burgelman, R. A. 2002. *Strategy is destiny: How strategy-making shapes a company's
    future.* New York: The Free Press.

7   Argyris, Chris. 1977. Double loop learning in organizations. *Harvard Business Review,*
    September-October: 115-124.

8   For the limitations of learning, see Levinthal Daniel A. and James G. March. 1993. The
    myopia of learning. *Strategic Management Journal,* 14: 95-112.

9   See Simons, Robert, Antonio Davila, and Afroze Mohammed. 1996. Becton Dickinson—
    Designing the new strategic, operational, and financial planning process. Harvard
    Business School Case 9-197-014.

10 The second year was briefly outlined in financial and strategic terms. According to the
    CEO, anything beyond year two and even any detail in year two was pure conjecture,
    given the rate of change in the market.

11 A similar concept in the learning literature is the difference between knowledge explo-
    ration and knowledge exploitation: March, James G. 1991. Exploration and exploitation in
    organizational learning. *Organization Science,* 2 (1): 71-88; Kuemmerle, Walter. 1999. The
    drivers of foreign direct investment in research and development: An empirical investiga-
    tion. *Journal of International Business Studies,* 30 (1): 1-25.

12 On the idea of tacit knowledge, see Nonaka, Ikujiro. 1990. Redundant, overlapping
    organization: A Japanese approach to managing the innovation process. *California
    Management Review,* 32 (3): 27-38; Nonaka, Ikujiro. 1994. A dynamic theory of organi-
    zational knowledge creation. *Organization Science,* 5 (1): 14-38.

13 For the importance of learning out of the chaotic nature of innovation, see Cheng, Yu-
    Ting and Andrew H. Van de Ven. 1996. Learning the innovation journey: Order out of
    chaos? *Organization Science,* 7 (6): 593-614.

14 See for example Markides, C. 1997. Strategic innovation. *Sloan Management Review,* 9-23.

15 For more detail on these four systems, see Davila, Tony. 2005. The failure and promise
    of management control systems for innovation and strategic change in *Controlling strat-
    egy: Management, accounting, and performance measurement,* Chris Chapman, editor.
    Oxford: Oxford University Press.

16 For more information on how BP structured its learning processes, see Berzins, Andris,
    Joel Podolny and John Roberts. 1998. British Petroleum (B): Focus on learning. Graduate
    School of Business, Stanford University Case # IB-16B.

17 See Bartlett, Christopher. 1998. McKinsey and Company: Managing knowledge and learning. Harvard Business School Case #9-396-357.

18 See Davila, Tony. 2003. Salesforce.com: The evolution of marketing systems. Graduate School of Business, Stanford University Case # E-145.

19 Wheelwright, Stephen C. and Edward Smith. 1999. The new product development imperative. *Harvard Business Review*, March.

20 Galvin, Robert. 1998. Science roadmaps. *Science*, 280 (5365): 803.

21 Amabile, Teresa. 1998. How to kill creativity. *Harvard Business Review*, September – October: 77-87.

Chapter 9

1 Christensen, Clayton and Kirstin Shu. 1999. What is an organization's culture? Harvard Business School Case 9-399-104, May 20.

2 Fisher, Lawrence M. 2004. How Dell got solutions. 2004. *Strategy & Business*, 36, August: 47-59.

3 Schrage, Michael. 2001. Playing around with brainstorming. *Harvard Business Review*, March: 149-154.

4 Another danger is the size associated with success. Larger organizations need larger opportunities to justify the attention devoted to these opportunities: Bower, Joseph L. and Clayton M. Christensen. 1995. Disruptive technologies: Catching the wave. *Harvard Business Review*, 73 (1): 43-53; Christensen, Clayton M. 1997. *The innovator's dilemma: When new technologies cause great firms to fail*. Boston, MA: Harvard Business School Press; Goold, Michael, Andrew Campbell, and Marcus Alexander. 1994. *Corporate-level strategy: Creating value in the multi-business company*. New York: John Wiley & Sons.

5 Rivlin, Gary and John Markoff. 2004. Can Mr. Chips transform Intel? *The New York Times*, September 12: 3-1, 3-4.

6 The term "cultural entrepreneurship" built through cultural mechanisms such as myths, stories, and reputation can change the innovative culture within a company; see Lounsbury, Michael and Mary Ann Glynn. 2001. Cultural entrepreneurship: Stories, legitimacy, and the acquisition of resources. *Strategic Management Journal*, 22: 545-564.

7 Leonard, Dorothy and Walter Swap. 1999. *When sparks fly: Igniting creativity in groups*. Boston, MA: Harvard Business School Press.

8 Kelley, Tom. 2001. *The art of innovation: Lessons in creativity from IDEO, America's leading design firm*. New York: Currency Books.

9 See, for example, Shane, Scott A., S. Venkataraman, and Ian C. MacMillan. 1995. Cultural differences in innovation championing strategies. 1995. *Journal of Management*, 21 (5): 931-952. For a traditional work on cultural differences, see Hofstede, Geert. 1980. *Culture's consequences: International differences in work-related values*. Beverly Hills, CA: Sage.

10 Sutton, Robert I. 2001. The weird rules of creativity. *Harvard Business Review*, September: 94-103.

11 Ibid.

12 Amabile, Teresa. 1998. How to kill creativity. *Harvard Business Review*, September–October: 77-87.

13 Collins, Jim. 1999. Turning goals into results: The power of catalytic mechanisms. *Harvard Business Review*, July-August: 71-82.

14 *The New York Times*. 2004. Living on Internet time, in an earlier age. April 4, E7.

15 The role of top management is critical: Hambrick, Donald C. The top management team: Key to strategic success. *California Management Review*, 30 (1): 88-108; Hambrick, Donald C., Theresa Seung Cho, and Ming-Jer Chen. 1996. The influence of top management team heterogeneity on firms' competitive moves. *Administrative Science Quarterly*, 41 (4): 659-684.

16 Schrage, Michael. 2001. Playing around with brainstorming. *Harvard Business Review*, March: 149-154.

17 *The Economist's* Third Annual Innovation Awards and Summit, San Francisco, September 14, 2004.

18 Fisher, Lawrence M. 2004. How Dell got solutions. *Strategy & Business*, 36: 47-59.

Chapter 10

1 Mossberg, Walt. 2004. The Rollins effect—More Dell for your money? AlwaysOn Network, October 8.

2 Buckley, Neil. 2002. Revolutionary with a relaxed approach. *The Financial Times*. August 15: 7.

3 *The Economist*. 2004. King of the catwalk. October 2: 61-62.

4 Nakamato, M. 2004. The Japanese art of performance. *Financial Times*, May 18, page 8.

5 Mossberg, W. 2004. The Rollins effect—more Dell for your money? AlwaysOn Network, October 5. www.alwayson-network.com

6 Griffith, Victoria. 2003. How Gillette's media-shy boss led it back to the cutting edge. *The Financial Times*. May 7: 10.

7 Buckley, N. 2004. Search for the right ingredients. *Financial Times*, October 7, page 9.

8 Swisher, Kara. 2004. HP: Invent, innovate, and out-compete. AlwaysOn Network, August 21.

9 Marsh, Peter. 2003. Siemens clocks up top results. *The Financial Times*, August 19: 6.

10 The Economist's Third Annual Innovation Awards and Summit. September 14, 2004. San Francisco.

11 Adapted from Navigant Consulting, Inc.

12 Source: Navigant Consulting, Inc., and Arthur D. Little, Inc.

13 Kleiner, Art. 2004. GE's next workout. *Strategy & Business*, 33: 26-30.

14 Tushman, Michael L. and Charles A. O'Reilly. 1997. Winning through innovation. *Harvard Business Press*.

15 Swisher, K. 2004. HP: Invent, innovate, and out compete. *AlwaysOn*. www.alwayson-network.com. August 21.

BIBLIOGRAPHY

Abell, Derek F. 1993. *Managing with dual strategies*. New York: The Free Press.

Abernathy, William, and James M. Utterback. 1978. Patterns of industrial innovation. *Technology Review*, 80 (7): 40-47.

Abrahamson, Eric. 1991. Managerial fads and fashions: The diffusion and rejection of innovations. *Academy of Management Review*, 16 (3): 586-612.

Adler, Paul S., and Bryan Borys. 1996. Two types of bureaucracy: Enabling and coercive. *Administrative Science Quarterly*, 41 (1): 61-89.

Adner, Ron, and Daniel A. Levinthal. 2002. The emergence of emerging technologies. *California Management Review*, 45 (1): 50-66.

Afuah, Allan. 1998. *Innovation management: Strategies, implementation, and profits*. New York: Oxford University Press.

Ahuja, Gautam, and Riitta Katila. 2001. Technological acquisitions and the innovation performance of acquiring firms: A longitudinal study. *Strategic Management Journal*, 22: 197-220.

Akella, Janaki, James M. Manyika, and Roger P. Roberts. 2003. What high tech can learn from slow-growth industries. *The McKinsey Quarterly 2003*, 3.

Ali, Abdul. 1994. Pioneering versus incremental innovation: Review and research propositions. *Journal of Product Innovation Management*, 11: 56-61.

Alsop, Stewart. 2002. Hollywood's latest flop. *Fortune*, 9 (December): 56.

Amabile, Teresa. 1998. How to kill creativity. *Harvard Business Review*, September–October: 77-87.

Amabile, Teresa M. 1997. Motivating creativity in organizations: On doing what you love and loving what you do. *California Management Review*, 40 (1): 39-58.

Amram, Martha, and Nalin Kulatilaka. 1999. *Real options: Managing strategic investment in an uncertain world*. Boston, MA: Harvard Business School Press.

Anderson, Phillip, and Michael L. Tushman. 1990. Technological discontinuities and dominant designs: A cyclical model of technological change. *Administrative Science Quarterly*, 35 (4): 604-633.

Andrew, James P., and Harold L. Sirkin. 2003. Innovating for cash. *Harvard Business Review*, September: 76-83.

Andrews, Tom, and Keith Yamashita. 2003. Fast-forward to innovation. *Strategy & Innovation*, September-October.

Ante, Spencer E. 2003. Savings tip: Don't do it yourself. *Business Week*, June 23: 78-79.

Ante, Spencer E. 2004. Servers: More bells and whistles, please. *Business Week*, March 22: 88.

Applegate, Lynda M., Robert D. Austin, and F. Warren McFarlan. 2003. *Corporate Information Strategy and Management: Text and Cases*, Sixth edition. New York: McGraw-Hill/Irwin.

Argyris, Chris. 1977. Double loop learning in organizations. *Harvard Business Review*, September-October: 115-124.

Argyris, Chris. 1994. Good communication that blocks learning. *Harvard Business Review*, July-August: 77-85.

Arino, Africa, Jose de la Torre, and Peter Smith Ring. 2001. Relational quality: Managing trust in corporate alliances. *California Management Review*, 44 (1): 109-132.

Arner, Faith, and Arlene Weintraub. 2004. J&J: Toughing out the drought. *Business Week*, January 26: 84-85.

Baldwin, Carliss Y., and Kim B. Clark. 2000. *Design rules: The power of modularity*. Cambridge, MA: MIT Press.

Banbury, Catherine M., and Will Mitchell. 1995. The effect of introducing important incremental innovations on market share and business survival. *Strategic Management Journal*, 16: 161-182.

Bangle, Chris. 2001. The ultimate creativity machine: How BMW turns art into profit. *Harvard Business Review*, January: 47-55.

Banker, Rajiv D. and Srikant M. Datar. 1989. Sensitivity, precision, and linear aggregation of signals for performance evaluation. *Journal of Accounting Research*, 27: 21-39.

Barker III, Vincent L., and George C. Mueller. 2002. CEO characteristics and firm R&D spending. *Management Science*, 48 (6): 787-801.

Barley, Stephen R. 1998. What can we learn from the history of technology? *Journal of Engineering and Technology Management*, 15: 237-255.

Barrett, Amy. 2003. DuPont tries to unclog a pipeline. *Business Week*, January 27: 103-104.

Barrett, Amy, and John Carey. 2002. Merck's new alchemist: Can Peter Kim shake up the giant's R&D operations? *Business Week*, December 16.

Barrett, Amy, John Carey, Michael Arndt, and Arlene Weintraub. 2003. Feeding the pipeline. *Business Week*, May 12: 78-83.

Barringer, Bruce R, and Allen C. Bluedorn. 1999. The relationship between corporate entrepreneurship and strategic management. *Strategic Management Journal*, 20: 421-444.

Baum, Joel A. C., Tony Calabrese, and Brian S. Silverman. 2000. Don't go it alone: Alliance network composition and startups' performance in Canadian biotechnology. *Strategic Management Journal*, 21: 267-294.

Bayus, Barry, Sanjay Jain, and Ambar Rao. 1997. Too little, too early: Introduction timing and new product performance in the personal digital assistant industry. *Journal of Marketing Research*, 34: 50-63.

Becker, Brian E., Mark A. Huselid, and Dave Ulrich. 2001. *The HR scorecard: Linking people, strategy, and performance*. Boston, MA: Harvard Business School Press.

Bellman, Matthias, and Robert H. Schaffer. 2001. Innovation alert: Freeing managers to innovate. *Harvard Business Review*, June: 32-33.

Berggren, Eric, and Thomas Nacher. 2001. Introducing new products can be hazardous to your company: Use the right new-solutions delivery tools. *Academy of Management Executive*, 15 (3): 92-101.

Berner, Robert. 2003. No more scrub-a-dub-dub? *Business Week*, October 6: 14.

Berner, Robert. 2003. P&G: New and improved. *Business Week*, July 7: 52-63.

Berner, Robert. 2002. Why P&G's smile is so bright. *Business Week,* August 12: 58-60.

Berner, Robert, and Gerry Khermouch. 2002. The tide is turning at P&G. *Business Week*, April 8: 44.

Berry, Kate, and Ellen Almer. 2000. How to put Procter on the road again, after a pileup. *The New York Times*, June 18.

Bhide, Amar V. 1999. *The origin and evolution of new businesses*. Oxford: The Oxford University Press.

Biggadike, Ralph. 1979. The risky business of diversification. *Harvard Business Review*, 57 (3): 103-111.

Birkinshaw, Julian. 2003. The paradox of corporate entrepreneurship. *Strategy and Business*, Spring: 46-57.

Birkinshaw, Julian, and Neil Hood. 2001. Unleash innovation in foreign subsidiaries. *Harvard Business Review*, 79 (3): 131-137.

Block, Zenas, and Ian C. MacMillan. 1995. *Corporate venturing: Creating new businesses within the firm*. Boston, MA: Harvard Business School Press.

Boghani, Ashok B., A. Iason Onassis, Ahmed Benabadji, Cees L.A. Bijl, and Steve Bone. 2000. Global R&D: Reaping the benefits. *Arthur D. Little*, First Quarter: 35-49.

Bossidy, Larry, and Ram Charan. 2002. *Execution: The discipline of getting things done*. New York: Crown Business.

Boulton, Richard E.S., Barry D. Libert, and Steve M. Samek. 2000. *Cracking the value code: How successful businesses are creating wealth in the new economy*. New York: Harper Business.

Bower, Joseph L. 1970. *Managing the resource allocation process*. Boston, MA: Harvard Business School Press.

Bower, Joseph L., and Clayton M. Christensen. 1995. Disruptive technologies: Catching the wave. *Harvard Business Review*, 73 (1): 43-53.

Boyle, Matthew. 2003. Dueling diapers. *Fortune*, February 17: 115-116.

Brown, Mark G., and Raynold A. Svenson. 1998. Measuring R&D productivity. *Research Technology Management*, 41 (6): 30-36.

Brown, Shona L., and Kathleen M. Eisenhardt. 1998. *Competing on the edge: Strategy as structured chaos*. Boston, MA: Harvard Business School Press.

Brown, Shona L., and Kathleen M. Eisenhardt. 1997. The art of continuous change: Linking complexity theory and time-paced evolution in relentlessly shifting organizations. *Administrative Science Quarterly*, 42: 1-34.

Brown, Shona L., and Kathleen M. Eisenhardt. 1995. Product development: Past research, present findings, and future directions. *Academy of Management Review*, 20 (2): 343-378.

Buckland, William, Andrew Hatcher, and Julian Birkinshaw. 2003. *Inventuring: Why big companies must think small*. London: McGraw-Hill Business.

Buderi, Robert. 2003. GE finds its inner Edison. *Technology Review*, October: 46-50.

Burgelman, Robert A. 1983. Corporate entrepreneurship and strategic management: Insights from a process study. *Management Science*, 29: 1349-1364.

Burgelman, Robert A. 1984. Designs for corporate entrepreneurship in established firms. *California Management Review*, 26 (3): 154-166.

Burgelman, Robert A. 1985. Managing the new venture division: Research findings and implications for strategic management. *Strategic Management Journal*, 6: 39-54.

Burgelman, Robert A. 2002. *Strategy is destiny: How strategy-making shapes a company's future*. New York: The Free Press.

Burgelman, Robert A., and Andrew S. Grove. 1996. Strategic dissonance. *California Management Review*, 38 (2): 8-28.

Burgelman, Robert A., and Leonard R. Sayles. 1986. *Inside corporate innovation: Strategy, structure, and managerial skills*. New York: The Free Press.

Burgelman, Robert A., and Yves L. Doz. 2001. The power of strategic integration. *Sloan Management Review*, 42 (3): 28-38.

Busenitz, Lowell W. 1999. Entrepreneurial risk and strategic decision-making: It's a matter of perspective. *Journal of Applied Behavioral Science*, 35 (3): 325-340.

Bylinsky, Gene. 2000. Look who's doing R&D. *Fortune,* November 27: 232C-232F.

Byrne, John A. 2000. How a VC does it. *Business Week,* July 24: 97-104.

Byrnes, Nanette, Dean Foust, Stephanie Anderson Forest, William C. Symonds, and Joseph Weber. 2000. Brands in a bind. *Business Week,* August 28: 234-238.

Cameron, Kim S. 1986. Effectiveness as paradox: Consensus and conflict in conceptions of organizational effectiveness. *Management Science*, 32: 539-553.

Chakravorti, Bhaskar. 2003. *The slow pace of fast change: Bringing innovative ideas to market in a connected world*. Boston, MA: Harvard Business School Press.

Chandy, Rajesh, Jaideep Prabhu, and Kersi Anita. 2002. What will the future bring? Dominance, technology expectations, and radical innovation. *MSI Report 02-122*, Summer.

Chandy, Rajesh K., and Gerard J. Tellis. 1998. Organizing for radical product innovation: The overlooked role of willingness to cannibalize. *Journal of Marketing Research*, 35: 474-487.

Chen-Fu, Chien. 2002. A portfolio evaluation framework for selecting R&D projects. *R&D Management*, 32 (4): 359-369.

Cheng, Yu-Ting, and Andrew H. Van de Ven. 1996. Learning the innovation journey: Order out of chaos? *Organization Science*, 7 (6): 593-614.

Chesbrough, Henry. 2002. Designing corporate ventures in the shadow of private venture capital. *California Management Review*, 42 (3): 31-49.

Chesbrough, Henry. 2002. Making sense of corporate venture capital. *Harvard Business Review*, 80 (3): 90-100.

Chesbrough, Henry. 2003. Managing your false negatives. *Harvard Management Update*. August: 3-4.

Chesbrough, Henry. 2003. *Open innovation: The new imperative for creating and profiting from technology*. Boston, MA: Harvard Business School Press.

Chesbrough, Henry. 2003. The new business logic of open innovation. *Strategy & Innovation*, August.

Chesbrough, Henry. 2003. The new rules of R&D. *Harvard Management Update*, May: 3-4.

Chesbrough, Henry W. 2003. A better way to innovate. *Harvard Business Review*, July: 12-13.

Chesbrough, Henry W. 2003. The era of open innovation. *MIT Sloan Management Review*, Spring: 35-41.

Christensen, Clayton. 1998. Disruptive technologies: Catching the wave—Teaching notes. *Harvard Business School Press*, December 18.

Christensen, Clayton, and Kirstin Shu. 1999. What is an organization's culture? Harvard Business School Case 9-399-104, May 20.

Christensen, Clayton M. 2003. Beyond "The Innovator's Dilemma." *Strategy & Innovation*, March-April: 3-5.

Christensen, Clayton M. 1999. *Innovation and General Manager*. Boston, MA: Irwin McGraw-Hill.

Christensen, Clayton M. 1997. *The innovator's dilemma: When new technologies cause great firms to fail*. Boston, MA: Harvard Business School Press.

Christensen, Clayton M., and Michael E. Raynor. 2003. *The innovator's solution: Creating and sustaining successful growth*. Boston, MA: Harvard Business School Press.

Christensen, Clayton M., Michael Raynor, and Matthew Verlinden. 2001. Skate to where the money will be. *Harvard Business Review*, November: 72-81.

Christensen, Clayton M., and Michael Overdorf. 2000. Meeting the challenge of disruptive change. *Harvard Business Review*, March-April: 57-76.

Christensen, Clayton M., and Richard S. Rosenbloom. 1995. Explaining the attacker's advantage: Technological paradigms, organizational dynamics and the value network. *Research Policy*, 24: 233-257.

Christiansen, James A. 2000. *Competitive innovation management: Techniques to improve innovation performance*. New York: St. Martin's Press.

Clifford, Lee. 2000. Pfizer vs. Merck: Tyrannosaurus Rx. *Fortune*, October 30: 140-151.

Cohen, Michael D., Roger Burkhart, Giovanni Dosi, Massimo Egidi, Luigi Marengo, Massimo Warglien, and Sid G. Winter. 1996. Routines and other recurring action patterns of organizations: Contemporary research issues. *Industrial and Corporate Change*, 5: 653-698.

Cohen, Wesley M., and Daniel A. Levinthal. 1990. Absorptive capacity: A new perspective on learning and innovation. *Administrative Science Quarterly*, 35: 128-152.

Cole, Robert E. 1998. Learning from the Quality Movement: What did and didn't happen and why? *California Management Review*, 41 (1): 43-74.

Collins, Jim. 1999. Turning goals into results: The power of catalytic mechanisms. *Harvard Business Review*, July-August: 71-82.

Cooper, Arnold, and Clayton Smith. 1992. How established firms respond to threatening technologies. *Academy of Management Executive*, 6 (2): 55-70.

Cooper, Robert. 1998. Benchmarking new product performance: Results of the best practices study. *European Management Journal*, 16 (1): 1-17.

Cooper, Robert G. 2000. *Product leadership: Creating and launching superior new products*. Reading, MA: Perseus Books.

Cooper, Robert G. 1990. Stage-gate systems: A new tool for managing new products. *Business Horizons*, May-June: 44-54.

Cooper, Robert G. 1993. *Winning at new products: Accelerating the process from idea to launch*. Second edition. Reading, MA: Perseus Books.

Cooper, Robert G., and Elko J. Kleinschmidt. 1994. Determinants of timeliness in product development. *Journal of Product Innovation Management*, 11: 381-396.

Cooper, Robert G., and Elko J. Kleinschmidt. 1987. New products: What separates winners from losers? *Journal of Product Innovation Management*, 4: 169-184.

Cooper, Robert G., and Scott J. Edgett. 1999. New product portfolio management: Practices and performance. *Journal of Product Innovation Management*, 16 (4): 333-352.

Cooper, Robert G., and Scott J. Edgett. 1999. *Product development for the service sector: Lessons from market leaders*. Cambridge, MA: Perseus Books.

Cooper, Robert G., Scott J. Edgett, and Elko J. Kleinschmidt. 2001. Portfolio management for new product development: Results of an industry practices study. *R&D Management*, 31 (4): 361-381.

Courtney, Hugh, Jane Kirkland, and Patrick Viguerie. 1997. Strategy under uncertainty. *Harvard Business Review*, 75: 66-79.

Coy, Peter. 2000. Research labs get real. It's about time. *Business Week,* November 6: 51.

Csikszentmihalyi, Mihaly. 1996. *Creativity: Flow and the psychology of discovery and invention.* New York: Harper Collins.

Curtis, Carey C. 1997. Agile companies need a balanced scorecard to track best practices in research and development. *Agility & Global Competition,* 2 (1): 1-7.

Curtis, Carey C. 1994. Nonfinancial performance measures in new product development. *Journal of Cost Management,* Fall: 18-26.

Curtis, Carey C., and Lynn W. Ellis. 1997. Balanced scorecards for new product development. *Journal of Cost Management,* May-June: 12-18.

Curtis, Carey C., and Lynn W. Ellis. 1998. Satisfy customers while speeding R&D *and* staying profitable. *Industrial Research Institute,* September-October: 23-27.

Damanpour, Fariborz. 1996. Organizational complexity and innovation: Developing and testing contingency models. *Management Science,* 42 (5): 693-701.

Damanpour, Fariborz. 1991. Organizational innovation: A meta-analysis of effects of determinants and moderators. *Academy of Management Journal,* 34 (3): 555-590.

Dann, Jeremy B. 2003. Beware the 'Aztek Effect.' *Strategy & Innovation,* August.

Dann, Jeremy B. 2003. Can khakis really be disruptive? *Strategy & Innovation.* Harvard Business School, article S0309E.

Dann, Jeremy B. 2003. Imaging innovation. *Strategy & Innovation,* March-April.

Danneels, Erwin. 2002. The dynamics of product innovation and firm competences. *Strategic Management Journal,* 23: 1095-1121.

Datar, Srikant, Susan Cohen Kulp, and Richard A. Lambert. 2001. Balancing performance measures. *Journal of Accounting Research,* 39 (1): 75-92.

D'Aveni, Richard A. 1994. *Hypercompetition: Managing the dynamics of strategic maneuvering.* New York: Free Press.

Davenport, Thomas H., Laurence Prusak, and H. James Wilson. 2003. *What's the big idea? Creating and capitalizing on the best management thinking.* Boston, MA: Harvard Business School Press.

Davila, Tony. 2000. An empirical study on the drivers of management control systems' design in NPD. *Accounting, Organizations and Society,* 25: 383-409.

Davis, Julie L., and Suzanne S. Harrison. 2001. *Edison in the boardroom: How leading companies realize value from their intellectual assets.* New York: John Wiley & Sons.

Day, Diana L. 1994. Raising radicals: Different processes for championing innovative corporate ventures. *Organizational Science,* 5: 148-172.

Day, George S., and Paul J. H. Shoemaker. 2000. Avoiding the pitfalls of emerging technologies. *California Management Review,* 42 (2): 8-33.

Davenport, Thomas H., Laurence Prusak, and H. James Wilson. 2003. *What's the big idea? Creating and capitalizing on the best management thinking.* Boston, MA: Harvard Business School Press.

De Bono, Edward. 1985. *Six thinking hats.* Boston, MA: Little, Brown, & Co.

Dell, Michael. 2000. Inspiring innovation. *Harvard Business Review,* 80 (8): 39.

Denison, Daniel R., Jane E. Dutton, Joel A. Kahn, and Stuart L. Hart. 1996. Organizational context and the interpretation of strategic issues: A note on CEO's interpretation of foreign investment. *Journal of Management Studies,* 33 (4): 453-474.

Dereck, R. L. and C. L. Donna. 1995. Measuring R&D performance. *Research Technology Management,* May-June: 47-52.

Dewar, Robert D., and Jane E. Dutton. 1986. The adoption of radical and incremental innovations: An empirical analysis. *Management Science*, 32 (11): 1422-1433.

Dimancescu, Dan, and Kemp Dwenger. 1996. *World-class new product development: Benchmarking best practices of agile manufacturers.* New York: AMACOM.

Dixit, Avinash K., and Robert S. Pindyck. 1994. *Investment under uncertainty.* Princeton, NJ: Princeton University Press.

Dixit, Avinash, and Robert Pindyck. 1995. The options approach to capital investment. *Harvard Business Review*, May-June: 105-115.

Donnelly, George. 2000. A P&L for R&D. *CFO*, February: 44-50.

Dosi, Giovanni. 1982. Technological paradigms and technological trajectories. *Research Policy*, 11: 147-162.

Dougherty, Deborah, and Cynthia Hardy. 1996. Sustained product innovation in large, mature organizations: Overcoming innovation-to-organization problems. *Academy of Management Journal*, 39: 1120-1153.

Dougherty, Deborah, and T. Heller. 1994. The illegitimacy of successful product innovation in established firms. *Organizational Science*, 5: 200-218.

Dresselhaus, Bill. 2000. *ROI: Return on innovation.* Irvine, CA: Dresselhaus Design Group.

Dressler, Ronald, Robert S. Wood, and Vincent Alvarez. 1999. Evaluating R&D using the cost savings metric. *Industrial Research Institute*, 42 (2): 13-14.

Drucker, Peter F. 1985. *Innovation and entrepreneurship.* New York: Harper & Row.

Drucker, Peter F. 1988. The discipline of innovation. *Harvard Business Review*, 80 (8): 95-102.

Duh, Rong-Ruey, and Ming-Huang Chiang. 2000. Research and development strategy and performance measures: An empirical test of the balanced scorecard concepts. *Journal of Management*, 563-589.

Dundon, Elaine. 2002. *The seeds of innovation: Cultivating the synergy that fosters new ideas.* New York: Amacom.

Duvall, Mel. 2003. How companies prove IT. *CIO Insight*, January 17.

Ehrenberg, Ellinor. 1995. On the definition and measurement of technological discontinuities. *Technovation*, 15: 437-452.

Eisenhardt, Kathleen M., and Behnam N. Tabrizi. 1995. Accelerating adaptive processes: Product innovation in the global computer industry. *Administrative Science Quarterly*, 40: 84-110.

Eisenhardt, Kathleen M., and Charles Galunic. 2000. Co-evolving: At last a way to make synergies work. *Harvard Business Review*, January-February: 91-101.

Eisenhardt, Kathleen M. and Jeffrey A. Martin. 2000. Dynamic capabilities: What are they? *Strategic Management Journal*, 21:1105-1121.

Eisenhardt, Kathleen M., Jean L. Kahwajy, and L.J. Bourgeois III. 1997. How management teams can have a good fight. *Harvard Business Review*, 74 (4): 77-85.

Ellis, Lynn W., and Carey C. Curtis. 1995. Speedy R&D: How beneficial? *Research and Technology Management*, July-August: 42-51.

Ellsworth, Richard R. 2002. *Leading with purpose: The new corporate realities.* Stanford, CA: Stanford University Press.

Elton, Jeffrey J., Baiju R. Shah, and John N. Voyzey. 2002. Intellectual property: Partnering for profit. *The McKinsey Quarterly*, 4.

Eppinger, Steven D. 2001. Innovation at the speed of information. *Harvard Business Review*, January: 149-158.

Epstein, Marc J. 2000. Organizing your business for the Internet revolution. *Strategic Finance*, 82 (1): 56-61.

Epstein, Marc J., and Jean-François Manzoni. 1998. Implementing corporate strategy: From tableaux de bord to balanced scorecards. *European Management Journal*, 16 (2): 190-204.

Epstein, Marc J., and Marie-Josée Roy. 2001. Sustainability in action: Identifying and measuring the key performance drivers. *Long Range Planning*, 34: 585-604.

Epstein, Marc J., and Robert A. Westbrook. 2001. Linking actions to profits in strategic decision-making. *MIT Sloan Management Review*, Spring: 39-49.

Epstein, Marc J., and S. David Young. 1998. Improving corporate environmental performance through economic value added. *Environmental Quality Management*, 7 (4): 1-8.

Ettlie, John E., William P. Bridges, and Robert D. O'Keefe. 1984. Organizational strategy and structural differences for radical versus incremental innovation. *Management Science*, 30: 682-695.

Feder, Barnaby J. 2001. Eureka! Labs with profits: IBM masters the way to make research pay off now. *The New York Times*, September 9.

Feltham, Gerald A., and Jim Xie. 1994. Performance measure congruity and diversity in multi-task principal/agent relations. *Accounting Review*, 69: 429-453.

Flaherty, Julie. 2003. In handling innovation, patience is a virtue. *The New York Times*, September 29.

Foster, Richard N. 1986. *Innovation: The attacker's advantage*. New York: Summit Books.

Foster, Richard N., and Sarah Kaplan. 2001. *Creative destruction: Why companies that are built to last underperform the market—and how to successfully transform them*. New York: Currency Books.

Frigo, Mark L. 2002. Strategy, business execution, and performance measures. *Strategic Finance*, May: 6-8.

Garud, Raghu, and Andrew H. Van de Ven. 1992. An empirical evaluation of the internal corporate venturing process. *Strategic Management Journal*, 19: 1193-1201.

Gatignon, Hubert, Michael L. Tushman, Wendy Smith, and Phillip Anderson. 2002. A structural approach to assessing innovation: Construct development of innovation locus, type, and characteristics. *Management Science*, 48 (9): 1103-1122.

Gawer, Annabelle, and Michael A. Cusumano. 2002. *Platform leadership: How Intel, Microsoft, and Cisco drive industry innovation*. Boston, MA: Harvard Business School Press.

George, Catherine, and J. Michael Pearson. 2002. Riding the pharma roller coaster. *The McKinsey Quarterly*, 4.

Geroski, P.A. 2003. *The evolution of new markets*. Oxford: Oxford University Press.

Gersick, Connie J.G. 1994. Pacing strategic change: The case of a new venture. *Academy of Management Journal*, 37: 9-45.

Gilbert, Clark. 2003. Pursuing new-market disruption. *Strategy & Innovation*. Harvard Business School, article S0307C: July-August.

Gilbert, Clark. 2003. The disruption opportunity. *MIT Sloan Management Review*, Summer: 27-32.

Goldenberg, Jacob, and David Mazursky. 2002. *Creativity in product innovation*. Cambridge: Cambridge University Press.

Goldenberg, Jacob, Roni Horowitz, Amnon Levav, and David Mazursky. 2003. Finding your innovation sweet spot. *Harvard Business Review*, March: 120-129.

Gompers, Paul A., and Josh Lerner. 1999. *The venture capital cycle*. Cambridge, MA: MIT Press.

Goold, Michael, Andrew Campbell, and Marcus Alexander. 1994. *Corporate-level strategy: Creating value in the multibusiness company*. New York: John Wiley & Sons.

Gorman, Michael, and William A. Sahlman. 1989. What do venture capitalists do? *Journal of Business Venturing*, 4: 231-248.

Green, Stephen, Mark Gavin, and Lynda Aiman-Smith. 1995. Assessing a multidimensional measure of radical innovation. *IEEE Transactions Engineering Management*, 42 (3): 203-214.

Greene, Jay, John Carey, Michael Arndt, and Otis Port. 2003. Reinventing corporate R&D. *Business Week*, September 22: 74-76.

Griffin, Abbie, and Albert L. Page. 1996. PDMA success measurement project: Recommended measures for product development success and failure. *The Journal of Product Innovation Management*, 13: 478-496.

Grossman, Gene M., and Elhanan Helpman. 1994. Endogenous innovation in the theory of growth. *Journal of Economic Perspectives*, 8 (1): 23-45.

Grove, Andy. 2003. Churning things up. *Fortune*, August 11: 115-118.

Gupta, Ashok K., and David L. Wilemon. 1990. Accelerating the development of technology-based new products. *California Management Review*, Winter: 24-44.

Guyon, Janet. 2000. Mr. Gent takes a whack at the web. *Fortune*, October 30: 154-166.

Hall, Doug. 1996. *Jump start your business brain: Win more, lose less, and make more money with your new products, services, sales and advertising*. Cincinnati, OH: Brain Brew Books.

Hall, Stephen S. 2003. Revitalizing drug discovery. *Technology Review*, October: 38-45.

Hambrick, Donald C. 1987. The top management team: Key to strategic success. *California Management Review*, 30 (1): 88-108.

Hambrick, Donald C., David A. Nadler, and Michael L. Tushman. 1998. *Navigating change: How CEOs, top teams, and boards steer transformation*. Boston, MA: Harvard Business School Press.

Hambrick, Donald C., Theresa Seung Cho, and Ming-Jer Chen. 1996. The influence of top management team heterogeneity on firms' competitive moves. *Administrative Science Quarterly*, 414: 659-684.

Hamel, Gary. 2001. 10 rules for designing a culture that inspires innovation. *Fortune*, April 30: 134-138.

Hamel, Gary. 1999. Bringing Silicon Valley inside. *Harvard Business Review*, September-October: 71-84.

Hamel, Gary. 2001. Edison's curse. *Fortune*, March 5: 175-182.

Hamel, Gary. 2001. Innovation's new math. *Fortune*, July 9: 130-132.

Hamel, Gary. 2001. Is this all you can build with the Net? Think bigger. *Fortune*, April 30: 134-138.

Hamel, Gary. 2000. *Leading the revolution*. Boston, MA: Harvard Business School Press.

Hamel, Gary. 2000. Reinvent your company. *Fortune*, June 12: 98-118.

Hamel, Gary. 2001. Revolution vs. evolution: You need both. *Harvard Business Review*, 150-153.

Hamel, Gary. 2001. Smart mover, dumb mover. *Fortune*, September 3: 191-193.

Hamel, Gary. 2000. Waking up IBM: How a gang of unlikely rebels transformed Big Blue. *Harvard Business Review*, July-August: 137-146.

Hamel, Gary, and C.K. Prahalad. 1994. *Competing for the future*. Boston, MA: Harvard Business School Press.

Hamel, Gary, and Peter Skarzynski. 2001. Innovation: The new route to wealth. *Journal of Accountancy*, November: 65-68.

Hamel, Gary, and Yves L. Doz. 1998. *Alliance advantage: The art of creating value through partnership*. Boston, MA: Harvard Business School Press.

Handfield, Robert B., Gary L. Ragatz, Kenneth J. Petersen, and Robert M. Monczka. 1999. Involving suppliers in new product development. *California Management Review*, 42 (1): 59-82.

Hansen, Morten T., Henry W. Chesbrough, Nitin Nohria, and Donald N. Sull. 2000. Networked incubators: Hothouses of the new economy. *Harvard Business Review*, September-October: 74-84.

Haour, Georges. 2004. *Resolving the innovation paradox: Enhancing growth in technology companies.* New York: Palgrave Macmillan.

Hargadon, Andrew. 2003. *How breakthroughs happen: The surprising truth about how companies innovate.* Boston, MA: Harvard Business School Press.

Hargadon, Andrew, and Richard I. Sutton. 2000. Building an innovation factory. *Harvard Business Review,* May-June: 157-166.

Harrington, Ann. 2003. Who's afraid of a new product? *Fortune*, November 10: 189-192.

Harris, Chris. 2002. *Hyperinnovation: Multidimensional enterprise in the connected economy.* New York: Palgrave Macmillan.

Harris, Gardiner. 2001. Cost of developing drugs found to rise. *The Wall Street Journal,* December 3, B14.

Harris, Gardiner. 2003. Where are all the new drugs? *The New York Times*, October 5.

Hauser, John R. 2000. Metrics thermostat. *Journal of Product Innovation Management,* 18: 134-153.

Hauser, John R. 1998. Research, development and engineering metrics. *Management Science,* 44 (12): 1670-1689.

Hauser, John R., and Florian Zettelmeyer. 1997. Metrics to evaluate R, D, & E. *Research Technology Management,* 40 (4): 32-38.

Hauser, John R., and Gerald M. Katz. 1998. Metrics: You are what you measure! *European Management Journal,* 16 (5): 517-528.

Hayes, Rachel M., and Scott Schaefer. 2000. Implicit contracts and the explanatory power of top executive compensation for future performance. *RAND Journal of Economics*, 31 (3): 273-293.

Hays, Constance L. 2001. Flavor wafers pack a bang. *The New York Times*, December 3.

Henderson, Rebecca M., and Kim B. Clark. 1990. Architectural innovation: The reconfiguration of existing product technologies and the failure of established firms. *Administrative Science Quarterly*, 35 (1): 9-30.

Hertenstein, Julie H. 1997. Techniques for improving design management results. *Design Management Journal*, 8: 10-19.

Hertenstein, Julie H., and Marjorie B. Platt. 2000. Performance measures and management control in new product development. *Accounting Horizons*, 14 (3): 303-323.

Hesselbein, Frances, Marshall Goldsmith, and Iaian Somerville. 2002. *Leading for innovation and organizing for results*. San Francisco: Jossey-Bass.

Hill, Charles W. L., and Frank T. Rothaermel. 2003. The performance of incumbent firms in the face of radical technological innovation. *Academy of Management Review*, 28 (2): 257-274.

Hisrich, Robert D., and Michael P. Peters. 1986. Establishing a new business unit within a firm. *Journal of Business Venturing*, 1: 307-322.

Hofstede, Geert. 1980. *Culture's consequences: International differences in work-related values.* Beverly Hills, CA: Sage.

Hollenbeck, John R., Berry Gerhart, Patrick M. Wright, and Raymond Andrew Noe. *Human Resource Management: Gaining a Competitive Advantage*. New York: McGraw-Hill/Irwin, 2000.

Holmes, Stanley. 2003. GE: Little engines that could. *Business Week,* January 20, 62-63.

Holmstrom, Bengt. 1979. Moral hazard and observability. *Bell Journal of Economics*, 10, no. 1: 74-91.

Holstein, William J. 2001. Going global? Forget borders. *The New York Times*, December 23.

Holstein, William J. 2002. The fringe is full of ideas. *The New York Times*, August 25.

Horibe, Frances. 2001. *Creating the innovation culture: Leveraging visionaries, dissenters and other useful troublemakers in your organization*. Toronto: John Wiley & Sons.

Hornsby, Jeffrey S., Douglas W. Naffziger, Donald F. Kuratko, and Ray V. Montagno. 1993. An interactive model of the corporate entrepreneurship process. *Entrepreneurship Theory and Practice*, 17 (2): 29-37.

Iansiti, Marco, F. Warren McFarlane, and George Westerman. 2003. Leveraging the incumbent's advantage. *MIT Sloan Management Review*, Summer: 58-64.

Ittner, Christopher D., David F. Larcker, and Madhav V. Rajan. 1997. The choice of performance measures in annual bonus contracts. *Accounting Review*, 72: 231-255.

Jarillo, J. Carlos. 1989. Entrepreneurship and growth: The strategic use of external resources. *Journal of Business Venturing*, 4: 133-147.

Jassawalla, Avan R., and Hemant C. Sashittal. 2000. Strategies of effective new product team leaders. *California Management Review*, 42 (2): 34-51.

Johnson, Lauren Keller. 2003. Promotions and the bottom line. *MIT Sloan Management Review*, Summer: 6-7.

Jolly, Vijay K. 1997. *Commercializing new technologies: Getting from mind to market*. Boston, MA: Harvard Business School Press.

Jonash, Ronald S., and Tom Sommerlatte. 1999. *The innovation premium: How next generation companies are achieving peak performance and profitability*. Reading, MA: Perseus Books.

Judge, William Q., Gerald E. Fryxell, and Robert S. Dooley. 1997. The new task of R&D management: Creating goal-directed communities for innovation. *California Management Review*, 39 (3): 72-85.

Juran, J.M. 1992. *Juran on Quality by Design: The new steps for planning quality into goods and services*. New York: The Free Press.

Kambil, Ajit. 2002. *Good ideas are not enough: Adding execution muscle to innovation engines*. Cambridge, MA: Accenture Institute for Strategic Change.

Kanter, Rosabeth Moss. 1989. Swimming in new streams: Mastering innovation dilemmas. *California Management Review*, 31 (4): 45-69.

Kanter, Rosabeth Moss. 1982. The middle manager as innovator. *Harvard Business Review*, 60 (4): 95-105.

Kaplan, Robert S., and David P. Norton. 2003. *Strategy maps: Converting intangible assets into tangible outcomes*. Boston, MA: Harvard Business School Press.

Kaplan, Robert S., and David P. Norton. 2001. *The strategy-focused organization: How balanced scorecard companies thrive in the new business environment*. Boston, MA: Harvard Business School Press.

Kaplan, Robert S. and David P. Norton. 2001. Transforming the balanced scorecard from performance measurement to strategic management: Part II. *Accounting Horizons*, 15 (2): 147-160.

Kaplan, Robert S., and David P. Norton. 1996. Using the balanced scorecard as a strategic management system. *Harvard Business Review*, 74 (1): 75-86.

Kaplan, Steve Neil, and Per Johan Stromberg. 2004. Characteristics, contracts, and actions. Evidence from venture capitalist analyses. *Journal of Finance*, 59 (5): 2177-2211.

Keller, Robert T. 2001. Cross-functional project groups in research and new product development: Diversity, communications, job stress, and outcomes. *Academy of Management Journal*, 44 (3): 547-555.

Kelley, Tom, and Jonathan Littman. 2001. *The art of innovation: Lessons from IDEO, America's leading design firm*. New York: Currency Books.

Kennedy, Carol. 1997. From competing to value innovation. *MBA*, December: 61-63.

Kerr, Steven. 1975. On the folly of rewarding A, while hoping for B. *Academy of Management Journal*, 18 (4): 769-784.

Kessler, Eric H., Paul E. Bierly, III, and Shanthi Gopalakrishnan. 2001. *Vasa* syndrome: insights from a 17th-century new-product disaster. *Academy of Management Executive*, 15 (3): 80-91.

Kim, W. Chan, and Reneé Mauborgne. 1998. A corporate future built with new blocks. *The New York Times*, March 29.

Kim, W. Chan, and Reneé Mauborgne. 1997. Fair process: Managing in the knowledge economy. *Harvard Business Review*, July-August: 65-75.

Kim, W. Chan, and Reneé Mauborgne. 1997. How to leapfrog the competition. *The Wall Street Journal Europe*, March 6.

Kim, W. Chan, and Reneé Mauborgne. 1997. On the inside track. *The Financial Times*, April 7.

Kim, W. Chan, and Reneé Mauborgne. 1997. Opportunity beckons. *Financial Times*, August 18, 8.

Kim, W. Chan, and Reneé Mauborgne. 1997. Value innovation: The strategic logic of high growth. *Harvard Business Review*, January-February: 103-112.

Kim, W. Chan, and Reneé Mauborgne. 1998. Value knowledge or pay the price. *The Wall Street Journal Europe*, January 29, 6.

Kim, W. Chan, and Reneé Mauborgne. 1997. When "competitive advantage" is neither. *The Wall Street Journal*, April 21, A22.

Kinni, Theodore. 2003. Four secrets of successful idea practitioners. *Harvard Management Update*, May.

Kirkpatrick, David. 2001. From Davos, talk of death. *Fortune,* March 5.

Kirkpatrick, David. 2003. How to erase the middleman in one easy lesson. *Fortune*, March 17, 122.

Klein, Katherine J., and JoAnn Speer Sorra. 1996. The challenge of innovation implementation. *Academy of Management Review*, 21: 1055-1080.

Kline, David. 2003. Sharing the corporate crown jewels. *MIT Sloan Management Review*, Spring: 89-93.

Krishnan, V., and Karl T. Ulrich. 2001. Product development decisions: A review of the literature. *Management Science*, 47 (1): 1-21.

Krueger, Norris F., Jr., and Deborah V. Brazeal. 1994. Entrepreneurship potential and potential entrepreneurs. *Entrepreneurship Theory and Practice*, 18 (3): 91-104.

Kuemmerle, Walter. 1998. Optimal scale for research and development in foreign environments: An investigation into size and performance of research and development laboratories abroad. *Research Policy*, 27: 111-126.

Kuemmerle, Walter. 1999. The drivers of foreign direct investment in research and development: An empirical investigation. *Journal of International Business Studies*, 30 (1): 1-25.

Kuratko, Donald F., Ray V. Montagno, and Jeffrey S. Hornsby. 1990. Developing an intrapreneurial assessment instrument for an effective corporate entrepreneurial environment. *Strategic Management Journal*, 11: 147-179.

LaDuke, Patty, Tom Andrews, and Keith Yamashita. 2003. Igniting a passion for innovation. *Strategy & Innovation*, July-August.

Latimer, Michael F. 2001. Linking strategy-based costing and innovation-based budgeting. *Strategic Finance*, March: 39-42.

Leaf, Clifton. 2004. Why we're losing the war on cancer, and how to win it. *Fortune,* March 22: 76-97.

Lee, M. 1994. Determinants of technical success in product development when innovation radicalness is considered. *Journal of Product Innovation Management*, 11: 62-68.

Lee, Peggy M., and Hugh M. O'Neill. 2003. Ownership structures and R&D investments of U.S. and Japanese firms: Agency and stewardship perspectives. *Academy of Management Journal*, 46 (2): 212-225.

Leifer, Richard, Christopher M. McDermott, Gina Colarelli O'Connor, Lois S. Peters, Mark R. Rice, and Robert W. Veryzer. 2000. *Radical innovation: How mature companies can outsmart upstarts*. Boston, MA: Harvard Business School Press.

Leifer, Richard, Gina Colarelli O'Connor, and Mark Rice. 2001. Implementing radical innovation in mature firms: The role of hubs. *Academy of Management Executive*, 15 (3): 102-113.

Leonard, Dorothy, and Jeffrey F. Rayport. 1997. Spark innovation through empathic design. *Harvard Business Review*, November-December: 102-113.

Leonard, Dorothy, and Susaan Straus. 1997. Putting your company's whole brain to work. *Harvard Business Review*, July-August: 111-121.

Leonard, Dorothy, and Walter Swap. 2000. Gurus in the garage. *Harvard Business Review*, November-December: 5-12.

Leonard, Dorothy, and Walter Swap. 1999. *When sparks fly: Igniting creativity in groups*. Boston, MA: Harvard Business School Press.

Leonard-Barton, Dorothy. 1992. Core capabilities and core rigidities: A paradox in managing new product development. *Strategic Management Journal*, 13: 111-125.

Leonard-Barton, Dorothy. 1995. *Wellsprings of knowledge: Building and sustaining the sources of innovation*. Boston, MA: Harvard Business School Press.

Lerer, Leonard, and Mike Piper. 2003. *Digital strategies in the pharmaceutical industry*. New York: Palgrave Macmillan.

Lev, Baruch. 2001. *Intangibles: Management, measurement, and reporting*. Washington, D.C.: Brookings Institute Press.

Levinthal, Daniel A., and James G. March. 1993. The myopia of learning. *Strategic Management Journal*, 14: 95-112.

Levitt, Barbara, and James G. March. 1988. Organizational learning. *Annual Review of Sociology*, 14: 319-340.

Linder, Jane C., Sirkka L. Jarvenpaa, and Thomas H. Davenport. 2003. *Innovation sourcing really matters*. Cambridge, MA: Accenture Institute for Strategic Change, March.

Linder, Jane C., Sirkka L. Jarvenpaa, and Thomas H. Davenport. 2003. Toward an innovation sourcing strategy. *MIT Sloan Management Review*, Summer: 43-49.

Linder, Jane C., and Susan Cantrell. 2000. *So what is a business model anyway?* Cambridge, MA: Accenture Institute for Strategic Change, March 2.

Loch, Christoph. 2000. Tailoring product development to strategy: Case of a European technology manufacturer. *European Management Journal*, 18 (3): 246-258.

Loch, Christoph, Lothar Stein, and Christian Terwiesch. 1996. Measuring development performance in the electronics industry. *Journal of Product Innovation Management*, 3: 3-20.

Loch, Christoph H., and U.A. Staffan Tapper. 2002. R&D performance measures that are linked to strategy. *Journal of Product Innovation Management*, 19: 185-198.

London, Simon. 2003. Why disruption can be good for business. *The New York Times*, October 2.

Lorange, Peter, and Johan Roos. 1992. *Strategic alliances: Formation, implementation, and evolution*. Cambridge, MA: Blackwell Publishers.

Lounsbury, Michael, and Mary Ann Glynn. 2001. Cultural entrepreneurship: Stories, legitimacy, and the acquisition of resources. *Strategic Management Journal*, 22: 545-564.

Lynn, Gary S. 1998. New product team learning. *California Management Review*, 40 (4): 74-93.

Lynn, Gary S., Joseph G. Morone, and Albert S. Paulson. 1996. Marketing and discontinuous innovation: The probe and learn process. *California Management Review*, 38 (3): 8-37.

March, James G. 1991. Exploration and exploitation in organizational learning. *Organization Science*, 2 (1): 71-88.

Markides, Constantinos. 1997. Strategic innovation. *MIT Sloan Management Review*, 38 (3): 9-23.

Markides, Constantinos C. 2000. *All the right moves: A guide to crafting breakthrough strategy*. Boston, MA: Harvard Business School Press.

Markides, Constantinos. 1998. Strategic innovation in established companies. *MIT Sloan Management Review*, 39 (3): 31-42.

Maritan, Catherine A. 2001. Capital investment as investing in organizational capabilities: An empirically grounded process model. *Academy of Management Journal*, 44: 513-531.

Mass, Nathaniel J., and Brad Berkson. 1995. Going slow to go fast. *The McKinsey Quarterly*, 4: 19-29.

Mathews, Ryan, and Watts Wacker. 2002. *The deviant's advantage: How fringe ideas create mass markets*. New York: Crown Publishing Group.

Mauzy, Jeff, and Richard Harriman. 2003. *Creativity, Inc.: Building an inventive organization*. Boston, MA: Harvard Business School Press.

McGrath, James, Fritz Kroeger, Michael Traem, and Joerg Rockenhaeuser. 2001. *The value growers: Achieving competitive advantage through long-term growth and profits*. New York: McGraw Hill.

McGrath, Michael E. 1995. *Product strategy for high-technology companies*. New York: Richard Irwin, Inc.

McGrath, Rita Gunther. 2001. Exploratory learning, innovative capacity, and managerial oversight. *Academy of Management Journal*, 44 (1): 118-131.

McGrath, Rita Gunther, and Ian C. MacMillan. 1995. Discovery driven planning. *Harvard Business Review*, 73: 4-12.

McGrath, Rita Gunther, and Ian McMillan. 2000. *The entrepreneurial mindset: Strategies for continuously creating opportunity in an age of uncertainty*. Boston, MA: Harvard Business School Press.

Merchant, Kenneth A. 1997. *Modern management control systems: Text and cases*. Upper Saddle River, NJ: Prentice Hall.

Meyer, Christopher. 1994. How the right measures help teams excel. *Harvard Business Review*, May-June: 95-103.

Meyer, Mark H., and Edward B. Roberts. 1986. New product strategy in small technology-based firms: A pilot study. *Management Science*, 32 (7): 806-822.

Meyer, Mark H., and James M. Utterback. 1993. The product family and the dynamics of core capability. *MIT Sloan Management Review*, 34 (3): 29-48.

Meyer, Mark H., Peter Tertzakian, and James M. Utterback. 1997. Metrics for managing research and development in the context of the product family. *Management Science*, 43 (1): 88-111.

Miller, Danny. 1990. *The Icarus paradox: How exceptional companies bring about their own downfall*. New York: Harper Business.

Miller, Danny, and Jamal Shamsie. 2001. Learning across the life cycle: Experimentation and performance among the Hollywood studio heads. *Strategic Management Journal*, 22: 725-745.

Mintzberg, Henry. 1987. Crafting strategy. *Harvard Business Review*, 65 (4): 66-76.

Mintzberg, Henry. 1994. The fall and rise of strategic planning. *Harvard Business Review*, 74 (3): 75-84.

Mintzberg, Henry. 1987. The five Ps for strategy. *California Management Review*, 30 (1): 11-24.

Mone, Mark A., William McKinley, and Vincent L. Barker. 1998. Organizational decline and innovation: A contingency framework. *Academy of Management Review*, 23: 115-132.

Moore, Geoffrey A. 1991. *Crossing the chasm: Marketing and selling technology products to mainstream consumers*. New York: Harper Business.

Moser, Martin R. 1985. Measuring performance in R&D settings. *Research Management*, September/October: 31-33.

Mullaney, Timothy J., and Jay Greene. 2003. At last, the Web hits 100 MPH. *Business Week*, June 23, 80-81.

Nalebuff, Barry, and Ian Ayres. 2003. *Why not? How to use everyday ingenuity to solve problems big and small*. Boston, MA: Harvard Business School Press.

Neely, David, and Kevin Dehoff. 2004. Innovation's new performance standard. *Strategy + Business*, March.

Nelson, Beebe. 2001. Review essay: From the learning organization to the learning society. *Journal of Product Innovation Management*, November.

Nelson, Beebe. 1998. The discipline of portfolio management: An implementable process. *International Association for Product Development Newsletter*, February.

Nelson, Beebe. 2004. What comes after stage-gate: The need for a new framework for innovation. Working paper, March.

Nelson, Richard R., and Sidney G. Winter. 1982. *An evolutionary theory of economic change*. Boston, MA: Harvard University Press.

Nemeth, Charlan J. 1997. Managing innovation: When less is more. *California Management Review*, 40 (1): 59-74.

Nevis, Edwin C., and Anthony J. DiBella. 1995. Understanding organizations as learning systems. *MIT Sloan Management Review*, 36 (2): 73-86.

New York Times. 2001. Phillips to sell factories, outsource mature output. August 17.

Noda, Tomo, and Joseph L. Bower. 1996. Strategy making as iterated processes of resource allocation. *Strategic Management Journal*, 17: 159-192.

Nohria, Nitin, and Ranjay Gulati. 1996. Is slack good or bad for innovation? *Academy of Management Journal*, 39: 1245-1264.

Nonaka, Ikujiro. 1994. A dynamic theory of organizational knowledge creation. *Organization Science*, 5 (1): 14-38.

Nonaka, Ikujiro. 1990. Redundant, overlapping organization: A Japanese approach to managing the innovation process. *California Management Review*, 32 (3): 27-38.

Nonaka, Ikujiro, and Hirotaka Takeuchi. 1995. *The knowledge-creating company: How Japanese companies create the dynamics of innovation*. New York: Oxford University Press.

O'Brien, Jonathan P. 2003. The capital structure implications of pursuing a strategy of innovation. *Strategic Management Journal*, 24: 415-431.

O'Connor, Gina Colarelli, and Mark P. Rice. 2001. Opportunity recognition and breakthrough innovation in large established firms. *California Management Review*, 43 (2): 95-116.

O'Connor, Kevin, and Paul B. Brown. 2003. *The map of innovation: Creating something out of nothing*. New York: Crown Business.

O'Hara-Devereaux, Mary, and Robert Johansen. 1994. *Global work: Bridging distance, culture and time*. San Francisco: Jossey-Bass.

Oliver, Richard L., and Erin Anderson. 1995. Behavior- and outcome-based sales control systems: Evidence and consequences of pure-form and hybrid governance. *Journal of Personal Selling and Sales Management*, Fall: 1-15.

Oxman, Jeffrey A., and Brian D. Smith. 2003. The limits of structural change. *MIT Sloan Management Review*, Fall: 77-82.

Palmeri, Christopher. 2002. Mattel's new toy story. *Business Week*, November 18, 72-74.

Palmeri, Christopher. 2003. To really be a player, Mattel needs hotter toys. *Business Week*, July 28, 64.

Pappas, Richard A., and Donald S. Remer. 1985. Measuring R&D productivity. *Research Management*, 28 (3): 15-22.

Patterson, Marvin L. 1998. From experience: Linking product innovation to business growth. *Journal of Product Innovation Management*, 15: 390-402.

Patterson, Marvin L. and Sam Lightman. 1993. *Accelerating innovation: Improving the process of product development*. New York: Van Nostrand Reinhold.

Penrose, Edith T. 1959. *The theory of the growth of the firm*. New York: Wiley.

Pinchot, Gifford, and Ron Pellman. 1999. *Intrapreneuring in action: A handbook for business innovation*. San Francisco: Berrett-Koehler.

Pisano, Gary P. 1997. *The development factory: Unlocking the potential of process innovation*. Boston, MA: Harvard Business School Press.

Polley, Douglas, and Andrew H. Van de Ven. 1996. Learning by discovery during innovation development. *International Journal of Technology Management*, 11: 871-882.

Porter, Michael E. 1980. *Competitive strategy: Techniques for analyzing industries and competitors*. New York: Free Press.

Porter, Michael E. 1996. What is strategy? *Harvard Business Review*, November-December: 61-78.

Porter, Michael E., and Scott Stern. 2001. Innovation: Location matters. *MIT Sloan Management Review*, Summer: 28-36.

Postrel, Virginia. 2003. Specialization is the rage. *The New York Times*, June 19.

Powell, Walter W. 1998. Learning from collaboration: Knowledge and networks in the biotechnology and pharmaceutical industries. *California Management Review*, 40 (3): 228-240.

Prahalad, C.K., and Gary Hamel. 1990. The core competence of the corporation. *Harvard Business Review*, 68: 79-91.

Prahalad, C.K., and Venkatram Ramaswamy. 2003. The new frontier of experience innovation. *MIT Sloan Management Review*, Summer: 12-18.

Prendergast, Canice. 1999. The provision of incentives in firms. *Journal of Economic Literature*, 37 (1): 7-64.

Quinn, James Brian. 2000. Outsourcing innovation: The new engine of growth. *MIT Sloan Management Review*, 41 (4): 13-28.

Quinn, James Brian. 1980. *Strategies for change: Logical incrementalism*. Homewood, IL: Irwin.

Raynor, Michael E., and Joseph L. Bower. 2001. Lead from the center: How to manage divisions dramatically. *Harvard Business Review*, 79 (5): 92-100.

Repenning, Nelson P., Paulo Gonçalves, and Laura J. Black. 2001. Past the tipping point: The persistence of firefighting in product development. *California Management Review*, 43 (4): 44-63.

Roberts, Edward B. Editor. 2002. *Innovation driving product, process, and market change*. San Francisco: Jossey-Bass.

Robertson, Thomas, and Hubert Gatignon. 1998. Technology development mode: A transaction cost conceptualization. *Strategic Management Journal*, 6: 515-531.

Robinson, Alan, and Sam Stern. 1997. *Corporate creativity: How innovation and improvement happen*. San Francisco: Berrett-Koehler Publishers.

Rogers, Paul, Thomas P. Holland, and Dan Haas. 2002. Value acceleration: Lessons from private-equity masters. *Harvard Business Review*, 80 (6): 94-101.

Rovit, Sam, and Catherine Lemire. 2003. Your best M&A strategy: Smart deal makers acquire methodically through good times and bad. *Harvard Business Review*, March: 16-17.

Royer, Isabelle. 2003. Why bad projects are so hard to kill. *Harvard Business Review*, February: 5-12.

Rucci, Anthony J., Steven P. Kirn, and Richard T. Quinn. 1988. The employee-customer-profit chain at Sears. *Harvard Business Review*, 76 (1): 82-98.

Sahlman, William A. 1990. The structure and governance of venture-capital organizations. *Business Economics*, 29: 35-37.

Sarasvathy, D., Herbert Simon, and Lester Lave. 1998. Perceiving and managing business risks: Differences between entrepreneurs and bankers. *Journal of Economic Behavior and Organization*, 33 (2): 207-225.

Sarin, Shikhar, and Vijay Mahajan. 2001. The effect of reward structures on performance of cross-functional product development teams. *Journal of Marketing*, 65: 35-53.

Sathe, Vijay. 2003. *Corporate entrepreneurship: Top managers and new business creation.* Cambridge: Cambridge University Press.

Sawhney, Mohanbir, and Emanuela Prandelli. 2000. Communities of creation: Managing distributed innovation in turbulent markets. *California Management Review*, 42 (4): 25-54.

Schein, Edgar H. 1985. *Organizational culture and leadership.* San Francisco: Jossey-Bass.

Schilling, Melissa A., and Charles W.L. Hill. 1998. Managing the new product development process: Strategic imperatives. *Academy of Management Executive*, 12 (3): 67-81.

Schlender, Brent. 2004. The new soul of a wealth machine. *Fortune*, April 5: 102-110.

Schmidt, Jeffrey B., and Roger J. Calantone. 1998. Are really new product development projects harder to shut down? *Journal of Product Innovation Management*, 15: 111-123.

Schmitt, Ronald W. 1991. The strategic measure of R&D. *Research Technology Management*, 34 (6): 13-16.

Schneiderman, Arthur M. 1998. Measurement, the bridge between the hard and soft sides. *Journal of Strategic Performance Measurement*, April-May: 14-21.

Schneiderman, Arthur M. 1996. Metrics for the order fulfillment process (Part 1). *Journal of Cost Management*, Summer: 30-42.

Schneiderman, Arthur M. 1996. Metrics for the order fulfillment process (Part 2). *Journal of Cost Management*, Fall: 6-17.

Schoonhoven, Claudia Bird, and Elaine Romanelli. Editors. 2001. *The entrepreneurship dynamic: Origins of entrepreneurship and the evolution of industries.* Stanford, CA: Stanford University Press.

Schrage, Michael. 2000. Getting beyond the innovation fetish. *Fortune*, November 13: 225-232.

Schrage, Michael. 2001. Playing around with brainstorming. *Harvard Business Review*, March: 149-154.

Schrage, Michael. 2000. *Serious play: How the world's best companies simulate to innovate.* Boston, MA: Harvard Business School Press.

Schumpeter, Joseph A. 1934. *The theory of economic development.* Cambridge, MA: Harvard University Press.

Scott-Morgan, Peter, Erik Hoving, Henk Smit, and Arnoud Van Der Slot. 2001. *The end of change: How your company can sustain growth and innovation while avoiding change fatigue.* New York: McGraw-Hill.

Shane, Scott A. 1994. Are champions different from non-champions? *Journal of Business Venturing*, 9: 397-421.

Shane, Scott, and S. Venkataraman. 2000. The promise of entrepreneurship as a field of research. *Academy of Management Review*, 25 (1): 217-226.

Shane, Scott A., S. Venkataraman, and Ian C. MacMillan. 1995. Cultural differences in innovation championing strategies. *Journal of Management*, 21 (5): 931-952.

Shapiro, Stephen M. 2002. *24/7 innovation: A blueprint for surviving and thriving in an age of change*. New York: McGraw-Hill.

Sharma, Anurag. 1999. Central dilemmas of managing innovation in large firms. *California Management Review*, 41 (3): 146-164.

Shephard, Charles and Pervaiz K. Ahmed. 2000. NPD frameworks: A holistic examination. *European Journal of Innovation Management*, 3 (3): 160-173.

Siekman, Philip. 2003. A long way from tiny time pills. *Fortune*, July 21: 126C-126H.

Simons, John. 2003. Taking on Viagra. *Fortune*, July 9: 102-112.

Simons, John. 2003. The $10 billion pill. *Fortune*, January 20: 58-68.

Simons, John. 2002. Will R&D make Merck hot again? *Fortune*, July 8: 89-94.

Simons, Robert. 1995. Control in an age of empowerment. *Harvard Business Review*, 73 (2): 80-89.

Simons, Robert. 1995. *Levers of control: How managers use innovative control systems to drive strategic renewal*. Boston, MA: Harvard Business School Press.

Simons, Robert, and Antonio Davila. 1998. How high is your return on management? *Harvard Business Review*, 76 (1): 70-81.

Smircich, Linda. 1983. Concepts of culture and organizational analysis. *Administrative Science Quarterly*, 28: 339-358.

Souder, William E. 1987. *Managing new product innovations*. Lexington: Lexington Books.

Stepanek, Marcia. 2000. You have nothing to lose but your cubicle. *Business Week*, October 16, 26.

Stevenson, Howard H, and Jeffrey L. Cruickshank. 1998. *Do lunch or be lunch: The power of predictability in creating your future*. Boston, MA: Harvard Business School Press.

Stewart, G. Bennett. 1991. *The quest for value*. New York: Harper Business.

Stewart, Thomas A. 2001. Want innovation? Oil the machine and water the garden. *Fortune*, March 5: 224.

Stipp, David. 2003. How Genentech got it. *Fortune*, June 9, 81-88.

Stopford, John M., and Charles W.F. Baden-Fuller. 1994. Creating corporate entrepreneurship. *Strategic Management Journal*, 15: 521-536.

Strategic Finance. 2004. The Datex-Ohmeda strategy map. March: 32.

Stringer, Robert. 2000. How to manage radical innovation. *California Management Review*, 42 (4): 70-88.

Sull, Donald N. 1999. Why good companies go bad. *Harvard Business Review*, July-August: 42-52.

Sutton, Robert I. 2001. The weird rules of creativity. *Harvard Business Review*, September: 94-103.

Sutton, Robert I. 2000. Weird ideas that spark innovation. *MIT Sloan Management Review*, Winter: 83-87.

Sutton, Robert I. 2002. *Weird ideas that work: 11 1/2 practices for promoting, managing, and sustaining innovation*. New York: The Free Press.

Sykes, Hollister B., and David Dunham. 1995. Critical assumption planning: A practical tool for managing business development risk. *Journal of Business Venturing*, 10 (6): 413-424.

Sykes, Hollister B., and Zenas Block. 1989. Corporate venturing obstacles: Sources and solutions. *Journal of Business Venturing*, 4: 159-167.

Tanz, Jason. 2003. From drab to fab. *Fortune*, December 8, 178-184.

Taylor III, Alex. 2003. Just another sexy sports car? Sure. But it's also a whole new way of business at Chrysler. *Fortune*, March 17, 76-80.

Teece, David J., Gary Pisano, and Amy Shuen. 1997. Dynamic capabilities and strategic management. *Strategic Management Journal*, 18: 509-534.

Tellis, Gerard J., and Peter N. Golder. 2002. *Will and vision: How latecomers grow to dominate markets.* New York: McGraw-Hill.

Thomke, Stefan. 2001. Enlightened experimentation: The new imperative for innovation. *Harvard Business Review*, 79 (2): 67-75.

Thomke, Stefan. 2003. *Experimentation matters: Unlocking the potential of new technologies for innovation.* Boston, MA: Harvard Business School Press.

Thomke, Stefan. 2003. R&D comes to services: Bank of America's pathbreaking experiments. *Harvard Business Review*, April: 71-79.

Thomke, Stefan, and Donald Reinertsen. 1998. Agile product development: Managing development flexibility in uncertain environments. *California Management Review*, 41 (1): 8-31.

Thomke, Stefan, and Eric von Hippel. 2002. Customers as innovators: A new way to create value. *Harvard Business Review*, April: 5-11.

Thornhill, Stewart. 2001. A dynamic perspective of internal fit in corporate venturing. *Journal of Business Venturing*, 16 (1): 25.

Tichy, Noel M. 2000. No ordinary boot camp. *Harvard Business Review*, April: 5-11.

Tripsas, Mary. 1997. Unraveling the process of creative destruction: Complementary assets and incumbent survival in the typesetter industry. *Strategic Management Journal*, 18: 119-142.

Trompenaars, Fons, and Charles Hampden-Turner. 1998. *Riding the waves of culture: Understanding diversity in global business.* 2nd edition. New York: McGraw-Hill.

Tushman, Michael L., and Phillip Anderson. 1986. Technological discontinuities and organizational environment. *Administrative Science Quarterly*, 31: 439-465.

Tushman, Michael L, and Johann P. Murmann. 1998. Dominant designs, technology cycles, and organizational outcomes. *Research in Organizational Behavior*, 20: 231-266.

Tushman, Michael L., and Charles A. O'Reilly. 1997. *Winning through innovation: A practical guide to leading organizational change and renewal.* Boston, MA: Harvard Business School Press.

Ulrich, Karl T., and Steven D. Eppinger. 1995. *Product design and development.* New York: McGraw-Hill.

Ulwick, Anthony W. 2003. Do you really know what your customers are trying to get done? *Strategy & Innovation*, March-April.

Ulwick, Anthony W. 2002. Turn customer input into innovation. *Harvard Business Review*, January: 91-97.

Useem, Jerry. 2002. 3M + GE = ? *Fortune*, August 12, 127-132.

Utterback, James M. 1996. *Mastering the dynamics of innovation.* Boston, MA: Harvard Business School Press.

Van de Ven, Andrew H. 1986. Central problems in the management of innovation. *Management Science*, 32 (5): 590-607.

Van de Ven, Andrew H., S. Venkataraman, Douglas Polley, and Raghu Garud. 1989. Processes of new business creation in different organizational settings. Andrew H. Van de Ven, Harold L. Angle, and Marshall Scott Poole. Editors. *Research on the Management of Innovation*, 221-297. New York: Ballinger Press.

Von Hippel, Eric. 2001. Innovation by user communities: Learning from open-source software. *MIT Sloan Management Review*, 42 (4): 82-87.

Von Hippel, Eric. 1988. *The Sources of Innovation*. New York: Oxford University Press.

Von Hippel, Eric, Stefan Thomke, and Mary Sonnack. 1999. Creating breakthroughs at 3M. *Harvard Business Review*, 77 (8): 47-57.

Von Krogh, Georg. 2003. Open-source software development: An overview of new research on innovators' incentives and the innovation process. *MIT Sloan Management Review*, Spring: 14-18.

Ward, Scott, Larry Light, and Jonathan Goldstine. 1999. What high-tech managers need to know about brands. *Harvard Business Review*, July-August: 85-95.

Wiesul, Kimberly. 2002. A CEO never forgets his roots. *Business Week*, October 14, 16.

Welch, David, and Kathleen Kerwin. 2004. Detroit tries it the Japanese way. *Business Week*, January 26, 76-77.

Werner, Bjorn M., and William E. Souder. 1997. Measuring R&D performance—U.S. and German practices. *Research Technology Management*, 40 (3): 28-32.

Wernerfelt, Birger. 1984. A resource-based view of the firm. *Strategic Management Journal*, 5: 171-181.

Wetlaufer, Suzy. 1997. What's stifling creativity at CoolBurst? *Harvard Business Review*, September-October: 2-10.

Wheelwright, Stephen C., and Edward Smith. 1999. The new product development imperative. *Harvard Business Review*, March.

White, Shira P., and G. Patton Wright. 2002. *New ideas about new ideas: Insights on creativity from the world's leading innovators*. Cambridge, MA: Perseus Books.

Whitely, Roger, Trueman Parish, Ronald Dressler, and Geoffrey Nicholson. 1998. Evaluating R&D performance using the new sales ratio. *Research and Technology Metrics*, September-October: 20-22.

Woo, Carolyn Y., Urs Daellenbach, and Charlene Nicholls-Nixon. 1994. Theory building in the presence of 'randomness': The case of venture creation and performance. *Journal of Management Studies*, 31: 507-523.

Zahra, Shaker A. 1993. Environment, corporate entrepreneurship, and financial performance: A taxonomic approach. *Journal of Business Venturing*, 8 (4): 319-340.

Zahra, Shaker A. 1991. Predictors and financial outcomes of corporate entrepreneurship: An exploratory study. *Journal of Business Venturing*, 6 (4): 259-285.

Zahra, Shaker A., and Jeffrey G. Covin. 1995. Contextual influence on the corporate entrepreneurship-performance relationship: A longitudinal analysis. *Journal of Business Venturing*, 10: 43-58.

Zahra, Shaker A., R. Duane Ireland, and Michael A. Hitt. 2000. International expansion by new venture firms: International diversity, mode of market entry, technological learning, and performance. *Academy of Management Journal*, 43 (4): 925-950.

Zaltman, Gerald. 2003. *How customers think: Essential insights into the mind of the market*. Boston, MA: Harvard Business School Press.

Zimmerman, Jerold L. 1997. EVA and divisional performance: Capturing synergies and other issues. *Bank of America Journal of Applied Corporate Finance*, Summer: 98-108.

Zirger, Billie Jo, and Modesto A. Maidique. 1990. A model of new product development: An empirical test. *Management Science*, 36 (7): 867-884.

Zook, Chris, and James Allen. 2002. *Profit from the core: Growth strategy in an era of turbulence*. Boston, MA: Harvard Business School Press.

INDEX

"Great schools have... endeavored to do more than keep up to the respectable standard of a recent past; they have labored to supply the needs of an advancing and exacting world..."

— **Joseph Wharton,** *Entrepreneur and Founder of the Wharton School*

The Wharton School is recognized around the world for its innovative leadership and broad academic strengths across every major discipline and at every level of business education. It is one of four undergraduate and 12 graduate and professional schools of the University of Pennsylvania. Founded in 1881 as the nation's first collegiate business school, Wharton is dedicated to creating the highest value and impact on the practice of business and management worldwide through intellectual leadership and innovation in teaching, research, publishing and service.

Wharton's tradition of innovation includes many firsts—the first business textbooks, the first research center, the MBA in health care management—and continues to innovate with new programs, new learning approaches, and new initiatives. Today Wharton is an interconnected community of students, faculty, and alumni who are shaping global business education, practice, and policy.

Wharton is located in the center of the University of Pennsylvania (Penn) in Philadelphia, the fifth-largest city in the United States. Students and faculty enjoy some of the world's most technologically advanced academic facilities. In the midst of Penn's tree-lined, 269-acre urban campus, Wharton students have access to the full resources of an Ivy League university, including libraries, museums, galleries, athletic facilities, and performance halls. In recent years, Wharton has expanded access to its management education with the addition of Wharton West, a San Francisco academic center, and The Alliance with INSEAD in France, creating a global network.

Wharton

UNIVERSITY *of* PENNSYLVANIA

Academic Programs:

Wharton continues to pioneer innovations in education across its leading undergraduate, MBA, executive MBA, doctoral, and executive education programs.

More information about Wharton's academic programs can be found at:
http://www.wharton.upenn.edu/academics

Executive Education:

Wharton Executive Education is committed to offering programs that equip executives with the tools and skills to compete, and meet the challenges inherent in today's corporate environment. With a mix of more than 200 programs, including both open enrollment and custom offerings, a world-class faculty, and educational facilities second to none, Wharton offers leading-edge solutions to close to 10,000 executives annually, worldwide.

For more information and a complete program listing:
execed@wharton.upenn.edu (sub 4033)
215.898.1776 or 800.255.3932 ext. 4033
http://execed.wharton.upenn.edu

Research and Analysis:

Knowledge@Wharton is a unique, free resource that offers the best of business—the latest trends; the latest research on a vast range of business issues; original insights of Wharton faculty; studies, paper and analyses of hundreds of topics and industries. *Knowledge@Wharton* has over 400,000 users from more than 189 countries.

For a free subscription:
http://knowledge.wharton.upenn.edu

For licensing and content information, please contact:
Jamie Hammond,
Associate Marketing Director,
hammondj@wharton.upenn.edu • 215.898.2388

Wharton School Publishing:

Wharton School Publishing is an innovative new player in global publishing, dedicated to providing thoughtful business readers access to practical knowledge and actionable ideas that add impact and value to their professional lives. All titles are approved by a Wharton senior faculty review board to ensure they are relevant, timely, important, empirically based and/or conceptually sound, and implementable.

For author inquiries or information about corporate education and affinity programs, please contact:
Barbara Gydé, Managing Director,
gydeb@wharton.upenn.edu • 215.898.4764

The Wharton School: http://www.wharton.upenn.edu
Executive Education: http://execed.wharton.upenn.edu
Wharton School Publishing: http://whartonsp.com
Knowledge@Wharton: http://knowledge.wharton.upenn.edu

The Power of Impossible Thinking
Transform the Business of Your Life and the Life of Your Business
BY JERRY WIND, COLIN CROOK, AND ROBERT GUNTHER

How often have we heard: "You can do anything once you set your mind to it," or "It's all in the way you look at it." This book helps readers unleash the straitjacket of your current thinking and unleash your potential with powerful new mental models so you can do the seemingly impossible! Jerry Wind and Colin Crook explain how your mental models stand between you and reality, distorting all your perceptions...and how they create both limits and opportunities. Wind and Crook tell why it's so hard to change mental models, and offer practical strategies for dismantling the "hardened missile silos" that are your old and obsolete models. With profiles on Howard Schultz, Oprah Winfrey, and Andy Grove, the authors provide real examples of their ideas in action. Simply put, this is the first "hands-on" guide to enhancing your mental models: the key to breakthrough success in business—and in life.

ISBN 0131425021, © 2005, 336 pp., $24.95

Built for Growth
Expanding Your Business Around the Corner or Across the Globe
BY ARTHUR RUBINFELD AND COLLINS HEMINGWAY

If there's one thing that's consistent in today's business world, it's rapid change. So how do you not only stay steady but actually grow—and quickly enough to stay safely ahead of your competitors? *Built for Growth* delivers specific solutions to create a brand and presence that generates true customer passion, as you lay a solid foundation for long-term success. Author Arthur Rubinfeld was a major driver in Starbucks' unprecedented retail expansion from 100 stores to more than 4,000—and its transformation into one of the world's most recognized brands. Here he draws on his singular expertise to present a proven, holistic approach to conceiving, designing, and executing your business plan: creating exciting concepts, growing them to fruition in local markets, expanding rapidly, and keeping your brand fresh and relevant as it matures. His revolutionary approach to business strategy embodies strong personal values, promotes exceptional creativity, leverages scientific methodology in finance and market analysis, and brings it all together with "old-time" customer service. Each lesson is clearly distilled with detailed examples from one of the best business writers, Collins Hemingway, co-author with Bill Gates of the #1 bestseller *Business at the Speed of Thought*. So whether you're seeking to reignite growth or planning your first store, *Built for Growth* will be utterly indispensable. Foreword by Jeff Brotman, co-founder and chairman of Costco, the world's #1 warehouse club.

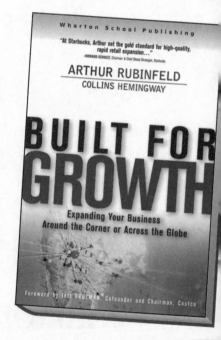

ISBN 0131465740, © 2005, 368 pp., $25.95

An Invitation from the Editors:
Join the
Wharton School Publishing Membership Program

Dear Thoughtful Executive,

We hope that you've discovered valuable ideas in this book, which will help you affect real change in your professional life. Each of our titles is evaluated by the Wharton School Publishing editorial board and earns the Wharton Seal of Approval — ensuring that books are timely, important, conceptually sound and/or empirically based and — key for you — implementable.

We encourage you to join the Wharton School Publishing Membership Program. Registration is simple and free, and you will receive these and other valuable benefits:

- **Access to valuable content** — receive access to additional content, including audio summaries, articles, case studies, chapters of forthcoming books, updates, and appendices.
- **Online savings** — save up to 30% on books purchased everyday at Whartonsp.com by joining the site.
- **Exclusive discounts** — receive a special discount on the Financial Times and FT.com when you join today.
- **Up to the minute information** — subscribe to select Wharton School Publishing newsletters to be the first to learn about new releases, special promotions, author appearances, and events.

Becoming a member is easy; please visit Whartonsp.com and click "Join WSP" today.

Wharton School Publishing welcomes your comments and feedback. Please let us know what interests you, so that we can refer you to an appropriate resource or develop future learning in that area. Your suggestions will help us serve you better.

Sincerely,

Jerry Wind
windj@wharton.upenn.edu

Tim Moore
tim_moore@prenhall.com

Become a member today at Whartonsp.com

Wharton School Publishing
www.whartonsp.com

PEARSON
Education

Wharton
UNIVERSITY *of* PENNSYLVANIA